Nicholas Hagger is a poet, man of letters, cultural historian and philosopher. He has lectured in English at the University of Baghdad in Iraq and the University of Libya, and was a Professor of English Literature at Tokyo University and Keio University in Japan. He has studied Islamic and Oriental philosophy, and led a group of Universalist philosophers. Following his recent work in setting up a World State, which his two epic poems heralded, he was awarded the Gusi Peace Prize 2016 for Literature.

He is the author of more than 40 books. These include a substantial literary output of over 2,000 poems (including over 300 classical odes), two poetic epics, five verse plays and 1,200 short stories; travelogues; and innovatory works in literature, history and philosophy. His catalogued archive of papers and manuscripts is held on permanent deposit as a Special Collection in the Albert Sloman Library at the University of Essex.

By the same author:

The Fire and the Stones
Selected Poems
The Universe and the Light
A White Radiance
A Mystic Way
Awakening to the Light
A Spade Fresh with Mud
The Warlords
Overlord
A Smell of Leaves and Summer
The Tragedy of Prince Tudor
The One and the Many
Wheeling Bats and a Harvest Moon
The Warm Glow of the Monastery Courtyard
The Syndicate
The Secret History of the West
The Light of Civilization
Classical Odes
Overlord (one-volume edition)
Collected Poems 1958–2005
Collected Verse Plays
Collected Stories
The Secret Founding of America
The Last Tourist in Iran
The Rise and Fall of Civilizations
The New Philosophy of Universalism
The Libyan Revolution
Armageddon
The World Government
The Secret American Dream
A New Philosophy of Literature
A View of Epping Forest
My Double Life 1: This Dark Wood
My Double Life 2: A Rainbow over the Hills
Selected Stories: Follies and Vices of the Modern Elizabethan Age
Selected Poems: Quest for the One
The Dream of Europa
Life Cycle and Other New Poems
The First Dazzling Chill of Winter

THE SECRET AMERICAN DESTINY

THE HIDDEN ORDER OF THE UNIVERSE AND THE SEVEN DISCIPLINES OF WORLD CULTURE

UNIVERSALISM AND THE ROAD TO WORLD UNITY

NICHOLAS HAGGER

This edition first published in the UK and USA 2016 by
Watkins, an imprint of Watkins Media Limited
19 Cecil Court
London WC2N 4EZ

enquiries@watkinspublishing.com

1 3 5 7 9 10 8 6 4 2

Designed and typeset by Clare Thorpe

Printed and bound in Finland

A CIP record for this book is available from the British Library

ISBN: 978-1-78028-910-6

www.watkinspublishing.com

To the incoming American President in November 2016, who has the power to urge the UN General Assembly to establish a democratic, bicameral world government, a partly federal World State with limited supranational authority to enforce peace and disarmament.

AUTHOR'S NOTE
ACKNOWLEDGEMENTS

This work is a reflection on the fragmentation and underlying unity of world culture. It draws on all my works, which (as occasional references to their researched findings make clear) can all be seen to have contributed to my present view of world culture,[1] and in particular on *The World Government* (2010), which begins in philosophy and ends with a blueprint for a World State: the secret American destiny. It harnesses the vision of T S Eliot, whose *Notes towards the Definition of Culture* saw religion as crucial to world culture, and of Tennyson, who glimpsed a world federation:

> For I dipt into the future, far as human eye could see,
> Saw the Vision of the world, and all the wonder that
> would be; …
>
> Till the war-drum throbbed no longer, and the battle-flags
> were furled
> In the Parliament of man, the Federation of the world.
>
> There the common sense of most shall hold a fretful realm
> in awe,
> And the kindly earth shall slumber, lapt in universal law.
>
> 'Locksley Hall', 1842

My thinking is dialectical as it ponders global culture from opposite sides (thesis and antithesis) and arrives at a new Universalist perspective (synthesis). It is also contemplative as it combines rational thinking with intuitive thinking that perceives unity and the hidden order in the universe. As in all reflective work, my text sometimes refers back (or forward) to a related passage, and in such cases cross-referencing intended to be helpful takes the reader to the correct page.

This is the third book of my American trilogy about Liberty. I am indebted to Michael Mann, who commissioned the previous two books and immediately grasped the connection between uniting world culture and founding a World State. I began this work on 25 April 2015 (the day after a visit to the historian Lord Asa Briggs, author of *Secret Days*, then 93) and completed it on 21 October 2015, six months later. I am also indebted to my efficient PA Ingrid Kirk who kept up with my blistering pace.

The front cover shows the Statue of Liberty alongside the Chrysler Building in New York, c1928–1930, with an Art Deco crown of seven terraced arches that suggest the seven disciplines of world culture.

'Human society can be saved only by Universalism.'

Emery Reves
The Anatomy of Peace, 1945

'There is no salvation for civilization, or even the human race, other than the creation of a world government.'

Albert Einstein, 1945

'History is now choosing the founders of the World Federation. Any person who can be among that number and fails to do so has lost the noblest opportunity of a lifetime.'

Carl van Doren

'Unless we establish some form of world government, it will not be possible for us to avert a World War III in the future.'

Winston Churchill
Prime Minister of Great Britain, 1945

'The emergency committee of atomic scientists, having explored for two years all means other than world government for making responsible the control of atomic energy [meaning nuclear weapons, really, and by implication, all weapons of mass destruction], has become convinced that no other method than world government can be expected to prove effective, and that the attainment of world government is therefore the most urgent problem now facing mankind.'

1948 UN Resolution

'There is an increasing awareness of the need for some form of global government.'

Mikhail Gorbachev

'Our times demand a new definition of leadership – global leadership. They demand a new constellation of international cooperation – governments, civil society and the private sector, working together for a collective global good.'

UN Secretary-General Ban Ki-moon,
speech at World Economic Forum, Davos, Switzerland,
29 January 2009

CONTENTS

PROLOGUE

THE UNIVERSALIST VISION

This book is the third of my American trilogy. It follows *The Secret Founding of America*, which dwelt on the founding of the North American civilization in 1607 and the consequences of the advent of Freemasonry in the next decade; and *The Secret American Dream*, which dealt with America's ambition to export the American Dream of prosperity to all humankind in the form of a democratic World State.

In those two books I looked at America's materialistic achievement: Liberty's awesome technology, which in my lifetime has enabled man to reach the moon, send spacecraft to explore our solar system and produce images of our galaxy. American satellites send instant pictures to our television screens and American computers send messages round the globe. American drones operated from the Nevada desert take out targets in the Middle East thousands of miles away, and precision bombing and use of co-ordinates have taken warfare to a new level of accuracy, minimalizing civilian casualties. In commerce American multi-national corporations and globalization have transformed the world.

In *The Secret American Dream* I set out the seven paths America has taken during the last 400 years, and covered the growth and expansion of America up to Barack Obama's first two years. I set out an eighth path the North American civilization has begun to take under Obama 'as the benevolent bringer of political and spiritual unity to all the peoples of the world'.[1] Liberty, who welcomed the 'poor' and 'homeless', has the ambition to protect the 'huddled masses yearning to breathe free'[2] throughout the world and raise their material standard of living.

AMERICA'S DESTINY AND WORLD CULTURE

The Secret American Destiny carries the story forward. It takes up the Epilogue of *The Secret American Dream*, 'Liberty's Universalist Destiny', and focuses on the spiritual worldview behind the American global achievement. A World State will seek to unite the religious and non-religious world citizens. According to a Pew Research Center survey in 2010 there were 5.8 billion religiously affiliated (Christians, Muslims, Hindus, Buddhists and followers of other faiths): 84 per cent out of a total world population then of 6.9 billion.[3] (See p 3 for more recent surveys.) America's spiritual vision must accommodate all world citizens regardless of their religious or secular outlook.

Film from space has made us aware of the oneness of the tiny Earth and of the potential unity of its nation-states and world culture. From space it seems only natural that America should attempt to create a political structure that reflects the unity of humankind. The Earth is widely perceived as a disunited complexity racked by local wars. Through American technology Liberty perceives its underlying unity and Universalist destiny – and the unity of the universe which has been mapped by American science.

A new philosophy of Universalism lurks behind America's globalization. The new outlook has several layers. In its narrow theological meaning a 'universalist' 'holds that all mankind will eventually be saved' (*Concise Oxford Dictionary*). A Christian universalist sees all mankind as potentially being saved, including non-Christians. From this narrow meaning 'Universalism' has come to have a wider sense: a focus on the role of all humankind on Earth and in the universe.

'Universalism' incorporates the words 'universe', 'universal' and 'universality'. It focuses on the universe, universal science and the universal principle of order whose effects are found in every aspect of Nature and its organisms. It examines humankind as a whole in its seven disciplines, and the place of humans on Earth and in the universe. It draws attention to the universal being, the deeper self below the rational, social ego which is open to universal cosmic energies that convey the principle of order and structure the growth of plants and organisms.

Universalism is the study of the whole of humankind's activities: the whole of history, international relations, philosophy and the sciences, religion and culture. It incorporates seven disciplines: mysticism, literature, philosophy, history, politics, religion and culture. And so we can speak of seven separate Universalisms – mystical Universalism, literary Universalism, philosophical Universalism, historical Universalism, political Universalism, religious Universalism and cultural Universalism. But ultimately they all belong to one Universalism. I have presented these seven disciplines as seven bands within a rainbow.[4] The bands are separate but they all belong to one rainbow.

Universalism's perspective unifies the seven disciplines of world culture and focuses on the rainbow rather than on its separate bands. It presents a fundamental understanding of the universe by unveiling a whole view that includes all disciplines, which at present appear to be divided. Individual disciplines are separated in university syllabuses, and their approaches are to fragments of a greater whole. Universalism seeks to restore the view of the whole by combining and reconciling divisions in seven partial disciplines of world culture, and in the fragmented disciplines themselves.

In this study I am not concerned with everyday popular culture – what people do in their leisure time: going to shopping malls and restaurants and bars, taking vacations, watching sporting fixtures and talent shows on television, listening to music, news of the Presidential or Royal families, and the like. I am sifting the way 7 billion live by (for example) probing a more fundamental culture that includes how many take part in religious worship and how many do not, and what they understand by the universe. I approach world culture from the seven disciplines and therefore the seven Universalisms. To me, the fundamental world culture is a rainbow with seven bands that overarches the globe and affects everybody.

In 1959 C P Snow delivered a Rede lecture, 'The Two Cultures',[5] in which he drew attention to the gulf between the literary and scientific cultures, which, he argued, should be bridged. Universalism provides that bridge, and the literary and scientific are different bands of the same cultural rainbow.

This book argues that in each of the seven disciplines of world culture there is a conflict between a traditional metaphysical approach and a more modern secular, social approach. These conflicting approaches make for a disunited world culture and a climate of opinion not conducive to a united World State. I argue that they can be reconciled within Universalism and that the reconciled conflicts make a contribution towards reunifying world culture and thereby preparing the ground for a coming World State. In this book I approach each of these seven disciplines from four different perspectives: the metaphysical (ch 1); the social (ch 4); the Universalist reconciliation (ch 5); and the the contribution of the metaphysical and social perspectives to a one-world movement within world culture and therefore to the climate of order a coming World State would need (ch 6).

A study of the whole reveals the order in the universe. 'Order' is 'the condition in which every part or unit is in its right place, tidiness' (*Concise Oxford Dictionary*). This definition of order suggests that insects, fish, birds, mammals and humans have a 'right' place within Nature's system, that the behaviour of each creature reflects the underlying order of Nature and the universe. This order is hidden when the universe is seen partially, but is revealed when the universe is perceived as a whole. 'Order' is also 'a state of peaceful harmony under a constitutional authority' (*Concise Oxford Dictionary*). This definition of 'order' draws attention to the fundamental organization within Nature and the universe, which is behind this harmony. Again, Nature has to be seen as a whole through Universalism's perspective for this apparently hidden order to be revealed. All things are then seen to have their place within the organized and orderly system of the universe.

America's destiny is to restore this sense of order and reunify world culture, and so make possible a new conception of civilization: a World State that can abolish war, famine, disease and poverty. An image for this destiny is: the statue of Liberty beneath a rainbow showing all seven cultural bands.

AMERICAN DESTINY AND WORLD STATE

This book examines the Universalist perspective on world culture that makes possible this American destiny to bring the world together into a World State. It carries forward a section in the Epilogue of *The Secret American Dream* regarding America's political and religious Universalism. My study of 25 civilizations shows that Universalism is already a feature of the North American civilization's present stage,[6] and will feature in a coming – indeed, imminent – stage. The North American civilization is at present in the same stage of its development as the Roman Empire was in its early days, after the two Punic Wars, and the Roman Empire's Universalism brought unity to the culture of the known world during Roman times.

CIVILIZATIONS' RISE-AND-FALL PATTERN

In my study *The Fire and the Stones*, updated as *The Light of Civilization* and *The Rise and Fall of Civilizations*, which I began in Japan, I see 25 civilizations passing through 61 stages. Each civilization is shaped in a parabola like a rainbow: it rises through a metaphysical vision which passes into its religion, and declines when it turns secular and loses some of the *élan* which carried it upward in its early stages. (See appendix 2.) The North American civilization is the youngest of my 25 civilizations, having been founded in 1607, and has reached stage 15, the stage the Roman Empire was in at the beginning of its expansionist phase. This North American stage began c1913. The vision through which the civilization rose was then expressed in American ecumenical Protestantism. Europe's comparable expansion was between c951 and 1244 and included the Crusades (as can be seen in the table on pp 227–8).

Stage 15 is soon followed by the creation of a Light-based heretical sect, after which a 'new people' graft the heresy onto the civilization's main religion and central idea. In Europe's case the new 'heresy' was the early Protestantism of the Reformation and the 'new people' were the Renaissance Humanists. The equivalent North American heresy is a coming Universalism[7] which will draw on the Freemasonic Deistic Illuminatists I wrote about in chapters 4 and 5 of *The Secret Founding of America*, and on the more recent New Age. The 'new people' in the North American civilization will be new Universalists who affirm a universal God drawn from all religions and perceived or experienced as Light.

If my vision of coming history is right, America's expansionist phase (which began in its stage 15) will create a democratic World State with a Universalist outlook that will include a universal God perceived as Light or Fire. This will be grafted on to Christian ecumenical Protestantism and will absorb it and offer a global religion. Just as Renaissance Humanists grafted Protestantism on to the Catholic Light, so new Universalists will graft Universalism on to the American Protestant Light.

THE UNIVERSALIST LIGHT

I have written about my encounter with the ordering Light in *My Double Life 1: This Dark Wood*. It was this experience that took me into the seven disciplines of world culture. I had had external, pantheistic experiences of the oneness of the universe in 1946, 1954,

1959 and 1963. While working in Japan – I was Visiting Professor at three universities from 1963 to 1967 and taught Emperor Hirohito's younger son world history – I visited Zen meditation centres and temples in 1964 and began writing poetry seriously. In 1965 I visited the Zen Ryoanji stone garden in Kyoto twice, and recognized its message: stones raked by the monks into different swirling patterns with large rocks among them presented an image of the universe. This could be seen as stones and rocks, or sea and rocks, or earth and hills, or clouds and mountains, but however it was seen, existence was composed of only one substance – in the stone garden represented as stone – and was a unity. The swirls made the unity appear diverse, but all existence was one. In September 1965 I underwent a centre-shift from the rational, social ego to universal being.

My understanding of oneness deepened soon afterwards when in October 1965 I drank *saké* with Junzaburo Nishiwaki, a poet who was attached to one of my universities, Japan's T S Eliot, and asked him his view of the wisdom of the East. He wrote out on a business reply card he took from my copy of *Encounter* which I happened to have on the table: '+A + –A = 0'. Above the 0 he wrote 'great nothing'. I immediately saw what the algebraic formula meant. Life was pairs of opposites or contradictions: day and night, life and death, time and eternity – and they were all reconciled in the unity of zero, the great nothing. Nishiwaki told me: 'The Absolute is where there is no difference.'

Soon after this, one morning my mind was filled with an inner sun, a 'light' I could 'see' within, and I knew this was significant. My opening to oneness found its way into my long poem 'The Silence'.

My first full encounter with the metaphysical Light took place in London on 10 September 1971.[8] For an hour and a half I saw behind my closed eyes 'white light' flowing up, and then many visions, and a centre of Light shining down from a great height, a white flower. (In the current book 'Light' is spiritual, 'light' physical.)

This was my equivalent of what Pascal experienced in 1654. After his death in 1662 the following lines were found sewn into the lining of his doublet:

> The year of grace 1654,
> Monday, 23 November …
> From about half past ten in the evening until about half past twelve
> FIRE.[9]

The experience was so important to him that he *wore* a reminder of what had happened for the last eight years of his life, which he spent in a Jansenist convent. I was at first inclined to think that I had had the fundamental poetic experience – and I still believe that this is what many of the great poets have written about, particularly the 17th-century Metaphysical poets – but I quickly grasped that my experience was metaphysical, and to date I have had a total of 93 experiences of the Light, all of which are covered and listed in appendices in *My Double Life 1* and *2*.

I was recently asked, 'Do you visualize behind closed eyes?' I replied, 'No, I'm like a puddle reflecting the sun. The puddle doesn't visualize, it just reflects the reality of the sun.' I now see this Light as the One, as Reality. It is the zero or great nothing of '+A + –A = 0'. In the East, Nothingness, the Void, is also a plentitude, a fullness.

So having found myself as a poet in Japan, I had now found myself as a mystic who trod the traditional Mystic Way from awakening to purgation, illumination and eventually the unitive life. The centre-shift from the rational social ego which perceives differences and makes distinctions to the universal being which perceives unity – a shift all mystics experience – opens the way to Universalism's unitive perspective.

Increasingly I wanted to understand the experience that had

happened to me, and while still writing my poems I collected all the recorded experiences of the Light or Fire from all the world's countries – from world culture – during the last 5,000 years in my first full-length work, *The Fire and the Stones*. I then realized that the experience was crucial to many religions: Christ the Light of the World, the first words of the *Koran* seen as written in Fire, the Buddha's enlightenment, Hindu *samadhi* and the Chinese *Tao* all attempted to describe this experience. I saw that civilizations grow after an experience of the Light or Fire has found its way into their religion. Energy is transmitted back to the civilization and pushes it to grow.

I passed from comparative religion to history and unveiled my Grand Unified Theory of world history and religion which presents 61 parallel stages of 25 civilizations. (See appendix 2.) I showed all the world history of the last 5,000 years as being parallel patterns of Light-inspired civilizations.

I then turned to philosophy and realized that there was a tradition of the Light which some philosophers followed, but not others. I wrote *The Universe and the Light*, *The One and the Many* and eventually *The New Philosophy of Universalism* about the order in the universe ignored by linguistic and analytical philosophy.

I was led to world culture. I gave a lecture in Aldeburgh, Suffolk, 'Revolution in Thought and Culture', which found its way into *The One and the Many*. I had been involved in international relations and statecraft (see *My Double Life 1* and *2*), and I dealt with the political implications of Universalism in *The World Government*.

THE METAPHYSICAL TRADITION

In the course of my previous 43 books I have come to see that the fundamental experience of the Light needs to be restored to world culture so that there can be a balance between the metaphysical tradition (which has inspired the world's higher religions) and the secular, social outlook. While continuing my literary work I was able to cover mystical, literary, philosophical, historical, political, religious and cultural Universalism and develop the idea of Universalism as unifying seven disciplines. I have trodden the way of the Renaissance polymaths who were at home in many disciplines, and I have been able to do this because all the disciplines are interconnected and united within one Universalism.

I was inspired to write this book at a gaudy (college reunion) at Worcester College, Oxford, on 6 September 2014. I had talked again with the new Provost, the Shakespearean scholar and author Jonathan Bate, and dined in hall at a long table among those of my contemporaries who were still alive. An academic at Bristol University, a physicist, leaned across the table and asked, 'What are you saying in your books?' I tried to explain what I had to say regarding the fundamental unity of the universe, and described my way of looking at all the disciplines of Western civilization – the North American and European civilizations – in terms of pairs of opposites (+A + –A = 0). I mentioned physics and metaphysics, the finite and the infinite, in relation to the Greek philosophers. He was a secular sceptic. 'The Greeks' beliefs were wrong,' he said, 'so they're irrelevant. We don't need to hear them.' His line was that only contemporary Materialism is true, because it looks at scientific evidence. 'I won't accept any theory such as multiverses being down a black hole,' he said. I agreed with him about multiverses – I stick with the universe I know, and mathematics that posit parallel universes offer unproven theories – but I countered and put the other side, the side he wanted to ignore, in each of seven disciplines.

I said, 'There are two ways the mind works. Analysis drops this glass of water and smashes it into pieces. Synthesis discovers broken potsherds and pieces them together. You're advocating the first but not admitting the second. You're saying everything must be analysed and tested. I'm saying synthesis is a valuable way of arriving at truth:

piecing fragments together and returning to the whole.' He said, 'I am not competent to pronounce beyond the evidence. Seeing the whole is very ambitious.' I said, 'But necessary. It has to be done. The whole has to be seen. All the opposites have to be reconciled within the origin and evolution of the universe and man's place in it.'

The conversation continued after dinner in the Buttery and a group gathered round us, listening. I wished I had a book that summarized my thinking over the past few decades which I could send him. This book about the secret American destiny to bring a Universalist vision and outlook to all humankind in the seven disciplines of world culture *is* that book.

PART ONE

CONFLICT IN WORLD CULTURE

CHAPTER 1

CONFLICTING APPROACHES IN SEVEN DISCIPLINES

Ever since the first English settlers left England, crossed stormy seas in fragile wooden ships, probed the shores of the River James and founded the Jamestown Settlement in 1607, migrants have crossed the Atlantic to the New World. Refugees from religious persecution and wretched living conditions in Europe have settled on America's East Coast. Towards the end of the 19th century the first sight of America that refugees had from their ship was the Statue of Liberty. To them, America was a land of promise where migrants could fulfil their dreams of a prosperous life for their families and themselves.

During the 20th century Liberty began looking outwards. The new dream was to export prosperity to the peoples of the world, the poor and huddled yearning to breathe free. During the oppressive time of Communism, Fascism and the Cold War America rolled back tyranny. And after the fall of the Soviet Union there were dreams of a new order that would transcend nation-states and bring a new era of peace to the Earth. There was a yearning for all humankind to be united under a World State, a dream rudely interrupted by regional wars in Iraq, Afghanistan, Libya and Syria. But the dream did not fade and still remains to be turned into reality.

AMERICA'S VISION OF SPIRITUAL UNITY

My study of history shows that it is America's destiny to establish a political supranational World State with a democratic structure that can export the American Dream to all humankind.[1] To bring such a benevolent political unity to the peoples of the world, America must proclaim and disseminate a vision of the spiritual unity of humankind and world culture that will welcome and nourish political unity. In a world population rising each second, and standing at 7.33 billion in July 2015 according to an April 2015 survey by WIN (World Independent Network) Gallup International, 63 per cent regard themselves as religious, 26 per cent as non-religious and 11 per cent as atheists.[2]

At present world culture is too disunited to welcome and sustain such a spiritual vision. It is important to examine the disunity in the seven disciplines of world culture and consider what needs to change for such a vision of spiritual unity to be widely welcomed and accepted by (according to a 2012 survey by Adherents.com) the 2.2 billion Christians, 1.6 billion Muslims, 1 billion Hindus, 0.376 billion Buddhists and the 1.1 billion secular, non-religious, agnostic and atheist world citizens who comprised 15.35 per cent of the then world population of 7.167 billion.[3] (The unaffiliated non-religious were put at 16.3 per cent rather than 15.35 per cent in another survey by Pew Research Center in December 2012.)[4] It is America's destiny to change and reunify world culture with a world outlook that will have the moral authority to bring about world unity and create the new World State, which will be widely endorsed throughout world culture.

CIVILIZATIONS' METAPHYSICAL RISE AND SECULAR FALL

As we saw in the Prologue (p xvii), my study of history shows that for 5,000 years 25 civilizations have undergone a rise-and-fall pattern. They rise following experiences of the One (Reality, the metaphysical Light or Fire that is beyond the world of physics), which pass into their religion;[5] and they fall when the metaphysical vision ceases to be strong and turns secular. Civilizations have the structure of a curved rainbow which rises and falls as the metaphysical vision turns secular and social. (See appendix 2.)

Within each of the 25 civilizations there is a pair of opposites, a thesis and antithesis, a '+A + –A': the metaphysical and the social. The +A, the civilization's metaphysical central idea, is strong during its growth; the –A, a focus on the secular and social at the expense of the civilization's original metaphysical vision, is strong during its decline and decay. When a civilization has run its course it passes into another civilization, as did the Egyptian civilization and its god Ra – Egypt passed into the new Arab civilization and worshipped Allah from 642.

All civilizations from their outset are a tension between the '+A + –A' of their metaphysical/religious vision and their secular/social approach. Although during their growth the metaphysical vision is in the ascendancy and during their decline the secular mindset predominates, in every decade and century of a civilization's life there is an underlying tension between the two, which is reflected in the seven disciplines.

THE EUROPEAN CIVILIZATION'S STAGE 43 AND UNIVERSALISM

In the early growing period of a civilization, the metaphysical outlook exercises a unifying control of the civilization's culture. A unified culture is like a tree with sap in its branches that are all nourished by its trunk.[6] An image of the European civilization is: a tree with all the European nation-states as branches.

The European civilization had a unified culture during its growth. In the Middle Ages, the time of the Crusades, all the seven branch-like disciplines of the European culture – including European art, literature and music – were nourished by its central interconnecting metaphysical idea, the trunk of its Christian religion, and there was unity of culture and 'unity of being' (W B Yeats's phrase).[7] European art, sculpture, music, literature and philosophy all expressed the Christian vision of the illumined soul, or halo. The expressions of European culture reflected the examined life, progress to sainthood and contemplation of the divine in serene and ordered Gregorian chants and stone angels. The inspiration that imbued the disciplines was 'metaphysical' (in the sense of a 'Reality beyond the world of physics and Nature' and 'beyond the senses') and involved energy manifesting into the universe from beyond itself.

Despite the Reformation, unity of European culture persisted during the Elizabethan age and the time of the 17th-century Metaphysical poets. However, since the 18th century the metaphysical idea expressed through Christianity has dwindled and European culture has turned secular.

The European civilization has now reached stage 43, as can be seen in the table on pp 239–40. As *The Rise and Fall of Civilizations* shows,[8] a post-imperial colonial conflict in stage 41 led to decolonization, and there is now a loss of national sovereignty to an inheriting secular conglomerate – the European Union. The conglomerate has brought in stage 44, when syncretism and universalism are prevalent as religious sects draw together with Light as a common source. Universalism earlier surfaced in stages 15, 29 and 34.[9] There is a revival of cultural purity in stage 45, which in Europe's case is likely to be a revival of the Classical/Baroque vision of stage 28.[10] (The Arab civilization's stage 45 has been heralded by IS or ISIL, the terrorist group better known in the Arab world as Daesh.) In stage 46 there will be a further attempt at counter-thrust under a foreign federalist influence as the European Union gives way to a looser, federal arrangement (just as the USSR gave way to the Russian Federation in its stage 46), and it is possible that there will be a 50-state United States of Europe ahead.[11]

THE NORTH AMERICAN CIVILIZATION'S STAGE 15 AND UNIVERSALISM

My study of history shows that the North American civilization is still in stage 15, a stage all the world's civilizations have been through (as can be seen in the table on pp227–8): the expansion into empire and Light-led renewal of growth, the stage the Roman Empire was in at its height, the ideal stage in which to create a World State. We have just seen that Europe had a unified culture in its stage 15, and we would expect the American culture to be unified, its branches energized by sap from its trunk, ecumenical Protestantism. American church attendance in 2013 was 37/39 per cent[12] (a relatively high figure typical of stage 15) against 6 per cent in Britain (a relatively low figure typical of stage 43). European church attendance is hard to measure but in 2010 49 per cent of the population in the EU states did not believe in God (again, a relatively high figure typical of stage 43).[13] America has been largely populated by migrants from Europe, beginning in a time when there was still a unified European culture and continuing today when the European culture is disunited, and although (judging from the above percentages) the metaphysical central idea of the North American civilization is clearly stronger than its European equivalent, both a metaphysical vision and a secular/ social approach co-exist in contemporary America.

I have written elsewhere that America's recent stage 15 path was expansionist and led to superpowerdom or hyperpowerdom, and that interventionist expansion (abandoned by Obama)[14] was inspired by a Universalist Light-led renewal of growth under radical American ecumenical Protestantism that funded the World Council of Churches. African churches have been supported by donations from the church-attending 37–39 per cent of America's population.[15] In due course this ecumenical, internationalist Protestant vision can be expected to blend with the Universalist New Age vision of the metaphysical Light.[16]

The 400-year-old North American civilization (founded in 1607 and now in stage 15) and the 1,600-year-old European civilization (founded in the 5th century CE after the fall of Rome and now in stage 43), which, though separate civilizations, together make up Western civilization, are at different stages in their 61-stage cycles. Other living civilizations, such as the Indian, Byzantine-Russian,

Chinese, Japanese and Arab civilizations, have lived through their own stages 15 and 43 and have therefore known Universalism. There are pockets of Universalist outlook in different parts of the world, having surfaced within all the world's civilizations in those two stages. American Universalism is at present a blend of Christian and New Age, themselves a '+A + –A' or pair of opposites, and the younger American Universalism has undoubtedly influenced the drawing together of sects in older Europe. Universalism is known on both sides of the Atlantic in different historical contexts.

METAPHYSICAL AND SOCIAL APPROACHES IN SEVEN DISCIPLINES

The growing North American civilization's metaphysical outlook is signalled by the confident 'In God we trust', which the US currency proclaims. Although the North American civilization is younger and more metaphysical than the more secular European civilization, in both civilizations both the metaphysical vision and social approach co-exist within the seven disciplines of world culture, as we have just seen.

We can now see that in each of the seven disciplines the original metaphysical approach has been challenged by, and now co-exists with, a secular, social approach. In each of the seven disciplines there is a '+A + –A' or pair of opposites that make for disunity in world culture.

As we look at each of the seven disciplines, our focus is on the last 4,500–5,000 years and each discipline has a strong European contribution. America has inherited each discipline and added to it during the last century or more, often with distinguished and impressive results.

MYSTICISM

For 5,000 years (from before the time of the Great Pyramid) mysticism has been dominated by two conflicting approaches: one inner, the other outer.

The dictionary definitions of 'mysticism' convey the traditional, inner approach. A 'mystic' is defined as 'a person who seeks by contemplation and self-surrender to obtain unity or identity with or absorption into the Deity or the ultimate reality, or who believes in the spiritual apprehension of truths that are beyond the understanding' (*Concise Oxford Dictionary*). 'Mysticism' is 'belief in the possibility of union with the Divine nature by means of ecstatic contemplation; reliance on spiritual intuition as the means of acquiring knowledge of mysteries inaccessible to understanding' (*Shorter Oxford English Dictionary*).

Evelyn Underhill set out the inner tradition of mysticism in *Mysticism* (1911). She defined the mystic union as a practical spiritual activity involving love and a psychological experience that is never self-seeking.[17] The mystic experiences unity – union with the Absolute – by contemplation and self-surrender, whereas the mystical philosopher reflects on the data and may not be a mystic.

The practical Mystic Way, which Underhill charts, begins with the awakening of the self to consciousness of Reality, and proceeds to purgation (which purifies the self) and detachment from the senses (which leads to illumination and visions). The self is enabled ('now it looks upon the sun')[18] and is then plunged into a Dark Night in which the sun of Reality is absent. After recollection, quiet, contemplation, ecstasy and rapture, the self achieves union with the Light and experiences unitive life as a permanent condition.

Underhill's Mystic Way is a Christian way which includes the experiences of mystics within other religions, since the experience of the Light is common to all religions. The Christian mystic aims for union with God. A Universalist mystic is open to the experiences of all religions and may not want to label the experience in terms of any one religion, and may refer to 'union with Reality'. Labelling aside, the traditional mystic has a profound inner experience of Light – as I had on 10 September 1971[19] – in which the soul mirrors the sun.

I set out the inner, 'introvertive' tradition of the Light or Fire in *The Fire and the Stones* (1991), the first part of which was updated as *The Light of Civilization*, in Part Two of which I collect all the mystic experiences of the world's mystics civilization by civilization. I state the Light within each of my 25 civilizations[20] and present the traditions of: the Indo-European Kurgan Light; the Mesopotamian Light; the Egyptian Light; the Aegean-Greek Light; the Roman Light; the Anatolian Light; the Syrian Light; the Israelite Light; the Celtic Light; the Iranian Light; the European Light; the North American Light; the Byzantine-Russian Light; the Germanic-Scandinavian Light; the Andean Light; the Meso-American Light; the Arab Light; the African Light; the Indian Light; the Southeast Asian Light; the Japanese Light; the Oceanian Light; the Chinese Light; the Tibetan Light; and the Central Asian Light.

The section on the European Light is very long[21] but we can form a bird's-eye view of it by drawing on the headings which cover the experiences of individual European mystics and their sources:

> The *New Testament* Jesus: Transfiguration and Parables of Light; Jesus as the Gnostic Light of the World, God as Light; Paul's Blinding Light: the Gentilized Light in the 'Epistles'; the Light of the Christian-Gnostic Alexandrian School: Clement's Gnosis of Light, the Logos of Light; the New Roman Light in the Early Middle Ages; the Christian Neoplatonist Light: St Augustine's Unchangeable Light, Dionysius's Darkness beyond Light; the Benedictines: Pope Gregory's Unencompassed Light; the West Roman Empire's Christian Light; the Cistercian Light: St Bernard's Consuming Fire; the Living Light of Hildegarde and Flowing Fire of Mechthild; the Late Medieval Brightness; the Italian Franciscans' Light Supreme of St Bonaventura; the Energizing Fire, Infinitesimal Point of Light and Light

> of Glory of Dante; the German Dominican Light of Wisdom and Spark of the Soul of Meister Eckhart; the Flemish Eternal Brightness or Light; the English and Late Italian Fire of Love of Rolle and St Catherine of Siena; the Renaissance Dimming; the Reformation Light; the Light of the Jesuits and Carmelite Counter-Reformation: St John of the Cross's Supernatural, Burning Light and St Teresa of Avila; the Protestant Lutheran Light of Boehme; the Church of England Light of the Metaphysical Poets Donne, Herbert, Vaughan, Traherne; the Puritan or Non-Conformist Light of Marvell, Milton and Bunyan, the Quaker Inner Light of Fox; the Later Counter-Reformation: the Jansenist Fire of Pascal, the Light of Quietism of Mme Guyon; the Light of the Evangelical Revival of John Wesley; the Dimming Christian Light; Secularized Established Church; the Victorian Dimming of the Christian Light in European Literature c1880 after Tennyson, Browning, Arnold and Goethe; Secularization of English Hymns between 1889 and 1951; the Vanishing Light; the Christian Light Today; and the 20th-century Mystic Reawakening and T S Eliot.

The section on the North American Light[22] draws on the following headings:

> Transcendentalism of Emerson and Thoreau; New Thought and Trine; and Protestant Evangelism

After presenting the tradition of the Light, I present as a sub-tradition the heretical Light in Western civilization.[23] Again, we can form a bird's-eye view of this heretical sub-tradition by drawing on the headings of the 11 sections which cover the occult experiences of individual heretical mystics and their sources:

> The Essene Light; the British Druid Light; the Gnostic Light and the Spark; the Hermetic Light and Alchemy; the Manichaeist Light; the Templar Light; the Grail Light; the Kabbalist Light; the Esoteric Light, Including the Freemasonic, Rosicrucian and Romantic Neoplatonist Light; the Theosophical Light and the Spiritual Sun; and the New Age Light.

This sub-tradition is the Western occult tradition which has given rise to another definition of mysticism: 'applied loosely to any religious belief associated with self-delusion and dreamy confusion of thought; sometimes applied to philosophical or scientific theories which assume occult qualities of which no rational account can be given' (*Shorter Oxford English Dictionary*).

Elsewhere[24] I have listed some of those who have known the Light in all cultures:

> Patanjali, Zoroaster, the Buddha, Mahavira, Lao-Tzu, Jesus, St Paul, St Clement of Alexandria, Plotinus, Mani, Cassian, St Augustine, Pope Gregory the Great, Mohammed, Bayazid, Al-Hallaj, Omar Khayyam, Suhrawardi, Hafez, Symeon the New Theologian, Hildegarde of Bingen, Mechthild of Magdeburg, Moses de Léon, Dante, Angela of Foligno, Meister Eckhart, Tauler, Suso, Ruysbroeck, Kempis, Rolle, Hilton, Julian of Norwich, St Catherine of Siena, St Catherine of Genoa, St Gregory Palamas, Padmasambhava, Sankara, Guru Nanak, Hui-neng, Eisai, Dogen, Michelangelo, St Teresa of Avila, St John of the Cross, Boehme, Herbert, Vaughan, Crashaw, Traherne, Norris, Law, Cromwell, Marvell, Milton, Bunyan, Fox, Penn, Naylor, Mme Acarie, Baker, Pascal, St Francis of

> Sales, Mme Guyon, John Wesley, Blake, Swedenborg, Shelley, Emerson, Tennyson, Browning, Arnold, Newman, Mme Blavatsky, Trine, Jung and T S Eliot.

To this list could be added a host of others who enshrine the best of Western and Eastern culture.

The Light is a metaphysical experience.[25] It is 'beyond' or 'behind' ('*meta*') the physical world of the five senses. We can see its 'beyondness' if we look at a couple of examples of experiences mystics on this list have had, starting with St Augustine's 'eyewitness' view of the Light, c400:

> I entered [within myself]. I saw with the eye of my soul,
> above (or beyond) my mind, the Light Unchangeable. ...
> It shone above my mind. ... All who know this Light
> know eternity.[26]

Hildegarde of Bingen (who died in 1179) gives a similar 'eyewitness' account:

> From my infancy up to the present time, I now being more than seventy years of age, I have always seen this light, in my spirit [or soul, Jung's translation] and not with external eyes. ... The light which I see is not located, but yet is more brilliant than the sun. ... I name it 'the cloud of the living light'. ... But sometimes I behold within this light another light which I name 'the living light itself'.[27]

Traditional inner mysticism is the tradition Underhill and I have described of the individual's inner, 'introvertive' quest to experience the metaphysical Reality that orders the universe. Alongside has always been present an alternative outer, 'extrovertive' mysticism that presents an awareness of the unity of the natural, social and outer universe without any inner vision. This is a form of pantheism in which the mystic experience of union is of an outer union with Nature in which stars, a heath, a lake or a pond are seen as part of the One, as I experienced in my four experiences of oneness in 1946, 1954, 1959 and 1963.[28] Wordsworth described the oneness behind his Nature mysticism:

> … A motion and a spirit, that impels
> All thinking things, all objects of all thought,
> And rolls through all things.[29]

This pantheistic mysticism is of the visible rather than the invisible (or seen shining behind closed eyes), of the seen rather than the unseen.

The secular, social view of the universe includes outer glimpses that all is a oneness in a system recognized by scientific Materialism. In this outer mysticism ultimate Reality is only implicitly present. There is no contemplation or spiritual vision, just a sense that Nature is one.

Standard anthologies of mystical experience – such as Dom Cuthbert Butler's *Western Mysticism*, Raymond Van Over's *Eastern Mysticism*, and W T Stace's *The Teachings of the Mystics* – offer mystics' writing about their experiences from the past tradition of inner mystical experience and are largely silent about such inner experience today. Michael Cox in *A Handbook of Christian Mysticism* includes the writings of Teilhard de Chardin and Thomas Merton as contemporary mystics, while F C Happold in *Mysticism* offers the Nature mysticism of Richard Jefferies.

It is clear from the anthologies that what used to be a strong tradition of inner mysticism has given ground to outer Nature mysticism. I do not decry Nature mysticism, having had four experiences of it myself. The point is that the inner experience of the Light now co-exists with the outer experience of the oneness of Nature, which is more widely known today.

LITERATURE

For 4,600 years world literature has displayed two conflicting literary approaches.

In *A New Philosophy of Literature: The Fundamental Theme and Unity of World Literature* I showed that ever since literature appeared in the Mesopotamian civilization c4600 BCE and threw up, over several centuries, successive versions of *The Epic of Gilgamesh*, there has been a tradition describing the hero's quest for metaphysical Reality. The literary Gilgamesh (based on a historical king who ruled Uruk in modern Iraq in the 27th century BCE) wants immortality and the theme of the questing hero in literature originated in works associated with him.

I put forward 12 Universalist characteristics of the metaphysical aspect of the fundamental theme of world literature:[30]

- The infinite (*to apeiron*) that surrounds the universe
- The metaphysical Reality perceived in all cultures as Light (or Fire, which is a universal cosmic energy)
- The universal principle of order in the universe (universal in the sense that its effects are found in all aspects of Nature and its organisms)
- The oneness of known humankind behind its apparent diversity
- The similarities in cultures and civilizations
- The universal being (or self) that opens to the Light behind the rational, social ego
- Universal virtue, a standard by which to measure human follies, vices, blindness, corruption, hypocrisy, self-love and egotism in relation to an implied universal virtue (when human interaction is considered from a secular perspective, separated from its context

of Reality)

- The promise of immortality of the universal being or spirit
- An inner transformation or centre-shift from ego to universal being
- The quest of the purified soul to confront death – in the ancient cultures by journeying to the Underworld – and to receive the secret Light of infinite Reality
- A sensibility that approaches Reality through more than one discipline, the sensibility of a polymath
- A new perspective of unity in key disciplines: seeing world history as a whole; seeing the common essence (the inner experience of the Light) of all world religions; seeing the One that can be revealed by philosophy and science; seeing the World State that can unify international politics; and seeing the unity of world literature

I cover ten historical periods in ten chapters, and at the end of each chapter I have a literary summary which shows how these characteristics of the Universalist metaphysical aspect of the fundamental theme of world literature are reflected in the literature of each of the ten periods: the ancient world; the classical world; the Middle Ages; the Renaissance; the Baroque; the Neoclassical, Romantic, Victorian and Modernist periods; and the 20th-century anarchy. The literary summaries track each characteristic of Universalism through each of these ten periods, and we can form a bird's-eye view of the metaphysical aspect of the fundamental theme of world literature by following eight of these characteristics through the ten periods and noting the religious texts, poets and literary authors in which they are expressed:

- The infinite (*to apeiron*) that surrounds the universe – Heaven/Elysian Fields and Underworld; Iranian light and dark; Fire of Brahman; the *Tao* 'infinite and boundless'; Yahweh; Homer, Anaximander's *to apeiron*, Plato, Virgil; the *Koran*; Grail legends,

Dante; Ficino's letters, Marlowe's *Dr Faustus*; Donne, Milton's *Paradise Lost*, Bunyan's *Pilgrim's Progress* and Dryden; Pope, Johnson and Goethe; Blake's infinite, Coleridge, Wordsworth's One, Shelley's One; Tennyson, Arnold, Emily Brontë and Emerson; Eliot, Yeats and Rilke's 'We are bees of the invisible'; and the Neo-Romantics

- Metaphysical Reality perceived as Light – Utu-Shamash, Ra, Ahura Mazda, Agni-Brahman, T'ien and Yahweh; Pindar, Parmenides's One, Xenophanes's 'one god', Plato's 'universal' light, Socrates's 'pure light', the *New Testament*, the Essene Dead Sea Scrolls, Gnostic, Manichaean and Neoplatonist texts, *The Golden Ass*, St Augustine's *Confessions* and Pope Gregory the Great; Perceval, Dante, *Piers Plowman*, the *Koran*, Sufi, Buddhist, Hindu and Tibetan texts, Neo-Taoist Clear Light and Japanese Zen; Donne, Cervantes, Milton's *Paradise Lost*, Vaughan, Traherne and Bunyan's *Pilgrim's Progress*; Pope and Goethe; Blake, Coleridge, Wordsworth, Shelley and Keats; Tennyson, Emerson and Thoreau; Eliot and Yeats; and Dylan Thomas and David Gascoyne

- The universal principle of order in the universe – gods who ordered the universe: Anu and Utu-Shamash, Ra, Ahura Mazda, *rta* (harmony in Nature), the *Tao* and Yahweh; Zeus and Jupiter in Homer, Greek myths and Sophocles, Plato, Virgil's Fate, Caesar's omens, Horace, Ovid, the *New Testament*, the Essene Dead Sea Scrolls and Gnostic texts; the *Elder Edda*, the *Kalevala*, the *Nibelungenlied*, Dante and Buddhist, Hindu and Neo-Taoist texts; Ficino's letters and Shakespeare's 'Great Chain of Being'; Donne, Milton's *Paradise Lost*, Bunyan and Dryden; Pope and Goethe; the One of Blake, Coleridge, Wordsworth and Shelley, and the Truth of Keats; Tennyson, Emily Brontë, Emerson and Tolstoy; Hulme, Eliot, Pound, Yeats and Hesse; and Iris Murdoch and Solzhenitsyn

- The oneness of known humankind – oneness in *The Epic of Gilgamesh*, the Egyptian *Book of the Dead*, the *Avesta*, the *Rig Veda* and *Upanishads*, the *Tao Te Ching* and the *Old Testament;* the Athenian Empire, Plato, the Roman Empire and the *New Testament*; Augustine's *De Civitate Dei* and Dante's *De Monarchia*; More's *Utopia* and Marlowe's *Tamburlaine the Great*; Donne's 'No man is an island' and Bunyan; Pope's 'stupendous whole'; Blake; Emerson and Whitman; Eliot and Hesse; and Heidegger, Eliot and Churchill

- The universal being (or self) that opens to the Light – the *akh*, Atman and soul; Plato's soul as charioteer, Virgil's Aeneas who 'shone in the bright light', the *New Testament* and Gnostic texts; Dante, St Catherine of Siena and the Neo-Taoist *The Secret of the Golden Flower*; Ficino and Erasmus; Marvell; Pope, Johnson and Goethe; Blake, Coleridge and Wordsworth; Emerson, Dostoevsky and Tolstoy; Eliot, T E Lawrence and Hesse; and Heidegger

- The promise of immortality of the universal being or spirit – the rituals of Dumuzi/Tammuz, the Egyptian *Book of the Dead*, Agni, Gilgamesh, the *Rig Veda*, *Avesta*, Brahmanism, Taoism and the Shekhinah's covenant with the Israelites; Homer's Underworld and Elysian Fields, Pindar, Plato, Virgil's Elysium and the *New Testament*; Beowulf's journey to Valhalla, 'The Dream of the Rood', Dante, Everyman's quest, and Buddhist, Hindu and Neo-Taoist texts; Ficino's letters, More and Erasmus; Donne's *Sermons* and Milton's *Paradise Lost*; Johnson and Goethe; Blake, Wordsworth and Shelley; Tennyson's *In Memoriam* and Tolstoy; Eliot, T E Lawrence and Hesse; and Greene and Waugh

- An inner transformation or centre-shift from ego to universal being – Tammuz's dying and rising, the birth of the *akh* in

'Making the Transformation into a Living Soul' in the Egyptian *Book of the Dead*, 'end to all Duality' in the *Avesta*, the innermost self in the *Upanishads*, the Chinese transformation from sense-perception, the Israelite transformation from the ego to the soul in prayer; the Mycenaean mysteries at Eleusis, Plato, the Roman rites of Vesta, Ovid, the *New Testament*, St Augustine and Pope Gregory the Great; Dante and St Catherine of Siena; Ficino and Erasmus; Marvell; Pope's 'Eloisa to Abelard'; Blake, Coleridge and Wordsworth; Dostoevsky (Victorian Europe); Eliot and Hesse; and Jaspers and Pasternak

- The quest of the purified soul to confront death by journeying to the Underworld, and to receive the secret Light of infinite Reality – Gilgamesh's quest for immortality, the rituals of the Egyptian *Book of the Dead*, the *Avesta*'s 'place of Everlasting Light', the quest of the *rsis* (inspired poets), Arjuna, Buddha and Mahavira, the quest for the *Tao*, the quest for the Light of Yahweh in the Tabernacle; the Greek mysteries, Odysseus's visit to the Underworld, Plato's assertion that earthly life is one episode of a long journey, Aeneas's visit to the Underworld, the rites of Roman religion, and the *New Testament*; *Beowulf*, Sir Galahad's quest for the Grail, Dante and Zen; Ficino, More and Spenser's *The Fairie Queene*; Donne, Milton and Dryden; Goethe; Blake, Coleridge, Wordsworth and Shelley; Tennyson's *Idylls of the King*, Arnold's 'The Scholar-Gipsy'; Joyce's *A Portrait of the Artist as a Young Man* and T S Eliot; and Durrell's *Alexandria Quartet* and Golding

Alongside this traditional, metaphysical aspect of the fundamental theme of world literature from early times co-existed a social aspect: condemnation of social follies and vices in terms of an implied universal virtue. We can form a bird's-eye view of this social aspect of the fundamental theme of world literature by following another of the Universalist characteristics through the ten periods:

- Universal virtue, a standard by which to measure human follies, vices, blindness, corruption, hypocrisy, self-love and egotism in relation to implied universal virtue (when human interaction is considered from a secular perspective, separated from its context of Reality) – the stories of Gilgamesh, Dumuzi/Tammuz, the people in the Egyptian *Book of the Dead*, Mithras, Arjuna, Lao-Tze and the *Old Testament* prophets; Homer's criticism of Achilles, Aeschylus, Sophocles, Euripides and Menander, Plato, Plautus, Terence and Seneca, Horace and the *New Testament*; Dante, *Everyman* and *Sir Gawayne and the Grene Knight*; Donne, Milton, Corneille, Racine, Molière and Restoration comedy; Pope, Swift, Johnson, Jane Austen and Goethe; Blake, Shelley's *Prometheus Unbound* and Byron's *Don Juan*; Pushkin and English, French and Russian novelists; Ibsen, Shaw and Forster; and Greene, Waugh, Orwell and Solzhenitsyn

The two aspects of the fundamental theme are in a dialectic and are present throughout the history of world literature. My study shows that the conflicting metaphysical and social aspects – the quest for Reality and immortality and the condemnation of social vices in relation to an implied virtue – each dominate some of the ten periods. All works of literature draw on one or other of these two aspects of the fundamental theme of world literature, or combine both. When the civilization is growing, the quest for Reality predominates; and when it turns secular, condemnation of follies and vices is to the fore. Literature that describes the quest is mostly found in the literature of the ancient world, the Middle Ages and the Baroque, Romantic and Modernist periods, while literature that condemns social vices is mostly found in the classical world and in the Renaissance, Neoclassical, Victorian and 20th-century periods.

We shall see that Universalism seeks to combine and reconcile these two aspects. I reflect the metaphysical and social aspects of the fundamental theme in my own works. I have described my earliest use of this approach:

> I was asked to write an article on contemporary English literature for the Japanese magazine *The Rising Generation* (*Eigo Seinin*). In the coming weeks I wrote 'The Contemporary Literary Scene in England: The Missing Dimension', which eventually appeared in the July 1964 issue. I distinguished the many writers who had a social and secular vision (such as the Angry Young Men) from the few who had a metaphysical perspective (such as Eliot). From the outset in December 1963 I was aware of the conflict between sceptical and metaphysical writers that I would later reflect in *A New Philosophy of Literature*.[31]

The 'missing dimension' was the metaphysical aspect. In 1991 my *Selected Poems: A Metaphysical's Way of Fire* divided my poems into two Parts:

> I had the idea for splitting the *Selected Poems* into social and metaphysical poems and wrote: 'Does the social/metaphysical split help the Baroque idea or hinder it? The metaphysical and the social, they are together, not in opposition.' I implemented this idea: Part One of my *Selected Poems* had 'Social World' in its title, and Part Two had 'Metaphysical World'. And the contradiction between the social and metaphysical can be found in the theme of *A New Philosophy of Literature*.[32]

In 2015 I presented my poems and stories in relation to these two aspects. In my *Selected Poems: Quest for the One*, Part One is entitled 'Quest for the One' and Part Two 'Follies and Vices' – and 220 vices are listed in the Preface. And in my *Selected Stories: Follies and Vices of the Modern Elizabethan Age*, Part One is entitled 'Follies and Vices' and Part Two 'Quest for the One' – and 150 vices are listed in the Preface.[33] It can be seen that there has been a consistency of outlook in my works stretching from 1963 to 2015.

As with mysticism, the traditional literary quest for the One – for metaphysical Reality, the infinite and the Light – has dwindled, and in the 20th century only a few poets have continued it. One of them was T S Eliot, whose last line of 'Little Gidding' is 'And the fire and the rose are one.' Frank Warnke's *European Metaphysical Poetry* stated the European metaphysical tradition in poetry. In contrast, the alternative condemnation of social follies and vices is relatively widespread and has expressed itself in modern satire. Many practising poets have an exclusively secular, social perspective, and the social aspect of the fundamental theme of world literature currently co-exists with its traditional metaphysical aspect.

PHILOSOPHY AND SCIENCES

For 2,700 years philosophy and the sciences have had two conflicting approaches.

In *The New Philosophy of Universalism: The Infinite and the Law of Order* I showed[34] that ever since the pre-Socratic Greek philosophers of the 6th and 5th century BCE there has been a tradition describing the inner quest for metaphysical Reality. Anaximander of Miletus wrote of 'the eternal, infinite boundless' (*to apeiron*). Xenophanes and Parmenides wrote of space being a plenum, a fullness, and of the One, which Xenophanes called god (or God). Anaximenes wrote of *aither* (ether) and Heraclitus of a moving 'ever-living Fire'. To the Greeks, the *kosmos* was an 'ordered whole', and the universe was ordered and unified.

The early religions spoke of an ordered universe. The Indo-European Kurgan shamanism saw the Underworld, Earth and Sky united in the World Tree, and the early Indian *rta*, or harmony in Nature, reflected metaphysical harmony. The *Upanishads* wrote of supreme good as being One. Zoroastrianism sought to 'gain the reign of the One'. The Chinese *Tao* was like an ocean, a sea of moving energy 'infinite and boundless'.

Plato carried on the metaphysical tradition of a hidden Reality. It was continued in Plotinus's One, Augustine's 'Intelligible Light' and Grosseteste's metaphysical 'Uncreated Light'. In the 15th century Christian philosophers such as Ficino turned to Neoplatonism. Rationalism took over the metaphysical tradition. René Descartes saw philosophy as a tree whose roots were metaphysics, whose trunk was natural philosophy (physics) and whose branches were medicine, mechanics and morals. His physics (trunk) was founded in metaphysics (the roots). He systematically doubted all assumed knowledge and wrote that the only basis for certainty was '*Cogito ergo sum*': 'I think, therefore I am.' He based certainty on reason and argued there were two independent worlds of mind and body, a dualistic position not acceptable to Universalists. Baruch Spinoza, Gottfried Wilhelm Leibniz and Immanuel Kant perpetuated Rationalism, as did the Enlightenment, which proclaimed dedication to reason, belief in intellectual progress, being inspired by Nature and advocating tolerance and freedom. Metaphysical Idealism was advocated by F H Bradley. The Intuitionism of Henri Bergson and Alfred North Whitehead had a metaphysical emphasis, and led to Existentialism's focus on being and Phenomenology's on consciousness.

Alongside this quest for metaphysical Reality co-existed from early times a social, empirical view of reality, a scientific tradition which was begun by Aristotle. His *Metaphysics* was in three parts: ontology (the study of Being and existence), natural theology (the study of the prime mover, his equivalent of God, the existence of the divine) and universal science (the study of first principles and laws). He laid the groundwork for science, 'which studies Being'.[35] His early students spoke of metaphysics as '*ta meta ta phusika*', 'what comes after physics'. Originally metaphysics was on an equal footing with physics and came after it chronologically in Aristotle's works. The Atomism of Democritus and Lucretius developed scientific awareness. Aristotelianism was taken up by Aquinas and triumphed over Platonism in the 13th century. After 1500 Renaissance Humanists saw the universe as pluralistic, mechanistic and ruled by mathematical laws and subject to physical causes, not ruled by God and subject to divine interventions; and philosophy fragmented. Humanism and Empiricism took up the scientific tradition. John Locke, George Berkeley and David Hume turned away from metaphysics (in its sense of 'the study of Being') and led to Utilitarianism and Pragmatism, logical positivism, linguistic analysis and the anti-metaphysical utterances of the Vienna Circle.

In our time the two conflicting approaches have expressed themselves in philosophy as: intuitionism versus logical and linguistic analysis.

The sciences were pursued within the context of the quest for metaphysical Reality until c1500. The growing empiricism and observation of the universe led to Nicolaus Copernicus's view in 1510 that the Earth goes round the sun (which rejected Ptolemy's flawed view that the planets and stars revolved round the Earth), Johannes Kepler's work in optics and telescopes, Galileo Galilei's advanced telescope and Isaac Newton's discoveries of the properties of light, gravity, calculus and mechanics. A growing mechanistic worldview concentrated on the physical laws of the universe, which Newton stated in a form that lasted until Albert Einstein's theory of relativity. The huge technological advances during the 20th century made possible the Hubble telescope and a clearer picture of our galaxy and, through CERN, confirmation of what happened in the first second after the Big Bang took place, and confirmation of the Higgs field.

In 1926 the quest for metaphysical Reality found itself co-existing with holism, a new term coined by the South African statesman Jan Smuts in his work *Holism and Evolution*. Holism saw the universe as an irreducible whole that was materialistic and physicalist, with no metaphysical dimension. Holism weakened the traditional metaphysical approach by offering a materialistic alternative to the scientific tradition.

Scientists' theories have impressively been confirmed by experiments; and (as we shall see on pp 132–3) reductionism, which sees the universe in purely physical and materialistic terms, does not merely co-exist with the tradition of metaphysical Reality, but now claims to have superseded it. Empirical science has risen high and there are claims that it is on the verge of a Materialistic Theory of Everything, although more sober scientists who have worked on the Standard Model that unites forces and particles deny that this is near. Contemporary science is dismissive of the traditional metaphysical outlook, and has led to the views of the British academic I described at the end of the Prologue, who would not look beyond materialist evidence and regarded a whole view of the universe as ambitious.

In our time the two conflicting approaches have expressed themselves in the sciences as holism versus reductionism. The final section of my 1993 book *The Universe and the Light* is entitled 'Reductionism, Holism and Universalism',[36] and distinguishes between physicalist holism and metaphysical Universalism.

HISTORY

For 5,000 years history has had two conflicting approaches.

Attempts to describe and interpret the events of history by philosophical reflection belong to speculative philosophy of history. Speculative philosophy assumed that history is linear, that it has a direction, order or design and is not a random flux without a pattern.

In my work to prepare the ground for my study of civilizations[37] I reviewed the traditional approach of describing world history in terms of metaphysical Reality (as expressed in religions) and the pattern of all civilizations.

In the religious texts of the ancient cultures there was always an attempt to explain the direction of human events and to interpret them. In the classical world the *Bible* interpreted human events in relation to Providence. St Augustine of Hippo saw history as being influenced by Providence in *City of God.* His approach was metaphysical and theological. Thomas Aquinas synthesized Aristotelian philosophy and Christianity, and saw historical events in relation to the eventual significance of history. Jacques-Bénigne Bossuet's *Discours sur l'histoire universelle* (*Discourse on Universal History*, 1681) attributed the rise and fall of empires to Providence. He tried to reconcile the existence of God with the existence of evil, and saw history as having a progressive direction. Leibniz raised the question of why a good God permits evil – he called the attempts to answer this question 'theodicy' in 1710 – and he and Bossuet grappled with the involvement of God in evil historical events, just as I did in my poetic epic *Overlord*, which in book 5 asks why a good God permitted Auschwitz. The involvement of Providence was not considered deterministic as leaders had free choice, which either furthered the Providential purpose or caused a reaction against their own policies – which furthered the Providential purpose.

Alongside this speculative linear tradition was another tradition of history, that it is a study of past events connected with individuals, individual countries, specific empires and social movements. In the classical world Herodotus, Thucydides and Livy narrated historical events and tried to assess their significance in a linear way, but were secular evidence-gatherers, realistic students of human nature who regarded human intelligence and judgement as contributing to cause and effect, rather than the will of the gods. Herodotus investigated events, and the Greek word for 'inquiry' (*historia*) passed into Latin and became our subject of 'history'. He is today considered to have been largely reliable in reporting what he was told, even though that was sometimes fanciful. He narrated the events of the Persian invasion of Greece in the 5th century BCE, while Thucydides told of the events of the Peloponnesian War and Livy the expansion of the Roman Empire. Machiavelli, in his *Discourses on Livy* (c1517), about the expansion of Rome to the end of the Third Samnite War, saw political greatness such as Rome's as a phenomenon that appeared in cycles.

With the Enlightenment came a more secular speculative approach that ignored Providence. The Rationalist Enlightenment Deist philosopher Edward Gibbon, influenced by Hume's scepticism, put the linear direction of history in reverse in *The History of the Decline and Fall of the Roman Empire* (1766–88). The history of the Roman civilization was a retrogression rather than a progress, owing to moral decadence, barbarism and religion (to which Gibbon was hostile). Georg Wilhelm Friedrich Hegel saw history as a dynamic dialectic between spirit and matter – which can be seen as a conflict between the Light and Materialism – and there were traces of the traditional linear Providential view of history in his secular speculative approach. Marxist history saw history as a dialectic between the workers and the ruling class. In *The Decline of the West* (1922) Oswald Spengler saw civilizations as organisms with life cycles from youth to old age and a limited span of life. He asserted that the soul of the West had died and that decline into dictatorship was imminent. It *was* in Germany, but the West is still a positive force and in the wider European perspective he was wrong.

Yeats in *A Vision* (1925), which he wrote while reading Gibbon (bought with money from his 1923 Nobel prize) and influenced by his wife's automatic writing, saw history as cycles of 2,000-year-long ages, which, it has to be said, do not relate to the dates of the rise and fall of empires. His 'rough beast' slouched towards Bethlehem at the end of the Christian 2,000-year-long Age, an arbitrary date; but with IS (or ISIL) attacking Christians, Yeats's lines now seem prophetic. Arnold Toynbee's comparative study of the cycle of civilizations in *A Study of History* (1934, 1939, 1954, 1959, 1961) was inductive and deemed unscientific – he identified 21 different civilizations in 1934, changed the figure to 23 in 1954 and to 30 in 1961[38] – but it continues the more secular speculative approach and again there are traces of the traditional Providential view of history. Toynbee wrote of a civilization's growth and decay and was acutely aware of religions' role in the cycle of civilizations.

Recent histories have continued the secular speculative approach. Paul Kennedy's *The Rise and Fall of the Great Powers* (1987) studied the Great Powers from 1500 to 1980 and their decline through imperial overstretch. Francis Fukuyama's *The End of History and The Last Man* (1992) saw the post-Cold War world becoming a permanent liberal democracy. He asserted that liberal democracy had triumphed and that history had ended in the Hegelian sense: a dialectic had ceased and there was now permanent stability. However, though a World State is desirable and America will build it, wars in Afghanistan and Iraq and Russia's revival of a Cold War policy in the Ukraine meant that the Hegelian end of history did not happen in the aftermath of 1992. Samuel P Huntington's *Clash of Civilizations and the Remaking of World Order* (1993, 1996) argued that post-Cold War conflict is for cultural, not ideological reasons. So Ukraine might split into Catholic-western Ukraine and Orthodox-eastern Ukraine, an event that has nearly happened. With a secular speculative approach he argued that the West should abandon democratic universalism and military interventionism. But the World State will be based on democratic universalism.

Along with the secular speculative approach many historical works present events connected with individuals, asserting that

Napoleon Bonaparte and Winston Churchill were great men who changed the course of history by their strength of will rather than being swept along by linear or cyclic patterns of history whose power they expressed. Pericles, Augustus, Napoleon and Churchill may have believed that they controlled history, but it can be argued that they were in fact the creation of their civilization's stages. In my verse play *The Rise of Oliver Cromwell* I examine Oliver Cromwell's life and see him as the creation of stage 30 of the European civilization (seceders from the 'new people'). Many contemporary works have abandoned traditional attempts to interpret the events of history and merely record the evidential secular and social facts regarding individual countries, empires and social movements.

I have continued both the metaphysical/Providential and secular/speculative traditions in my own study of history, *The Fire and the Stones*, Part Two updated as *The Rise and Fall of Civilizations* (1991, 2008). I taught Gibbon, Spengler and Toynbee to postgraduate students in Japan and to Emperor Hirohito's second son from 1965 to 1967, and saw a fourth way, of seeing world history as a 'whole history', a common historical process in different cultures, which I describe as Universalism. As I have said (p xvii), I see 25 civilizations going through 61 stages. Each civilization then passes into a younger civilization. The growth takes place through the importing of a metaphysical vision, as I have shown[39], and when this vision begins to fail the civilization turns secular and declines. I see history as both linear and cyclical:[40] cyclical because the Light recurs in different rising and falling civilizations, but linear because it spirals in a linear direction like a spiral staircase towards one worldwide civilization, the coming World State. My rise-and-fall patterns are cyclical, but the direction of each civilization's metaphysical vision is linear – progressing towards a World State.

COMPARATIVE RELIGION

For 5,000 years all religions have had two conflicting approaches.

In the traditional ancient religious texts, from the Egyptian *Book of the Dead* to the *Upanishads* and the Neo-Taoist *The Secret of the Golden Flower*, there was an inner quest for metaphysical Reality, the Light. I have shown (in Part One of *The Fire and the Stones*, 'The Tradition of the Fire', and Part Two of *The Light of Civilization*, 'The Tradition of the Light'; and also in *The Universe and the Light* and *The Rise and Fall of Civilizations*[41]) that all the early religions – the religions of the Mesopotamian, Egyptian, Aegean-Greek, Roman, Anatolian, Syrian, Israelite, Celtic, Iranian, Germanic-Scandinavian, Indian, Southeast Asian, Japanese, Chinese and Tibetan civilizations – had a common experience of the Light or Fire, as did (judging from their 'stones', their megalithic ruins and statues) the religions of the Indo-European Kurgan, Oceanian and Central Asian civilizations. (The other seven civilizations I do not regard as 'ancient'.)

I have shown (in *The Universe and the Light*)[42] the influence of religions as the driving force of the history of civilizations. I have described how the Light or Fire enters and takes hold in new civilizations:

> A contemplative mystic has a vision of the Fire which migrates to a new area and forms a new religion. This becomes associated with the State, and increases the power of a priestly class who performs its rites. Peoples are attracted to the Fire and a political unification takes place around it. The Fire inspires the civilization's expansion. Foreign invaders create a revival of a past culture, the religion turns worldly and undergoes a Reformation and a new people adopt a heresy as the new orthodoxy. There is another expansion. Eventually the religion declines. This decline is associated with the decolonization. The Fire is now absent, the civilization enters

> a conglomerate and is increasingly secularized. Eventually after a period of federalism, the civilization is occupied and it ends up passing under its successor's religion.[43]

This vision happened in all 25 civilizations, and the one Light or Fire was seen by a contemplative before it passed into each civilization. The Light or Fire is therefore common to all rising-and-falling civilizations. For how the Fire spread from civilization to civilization, see the chart of 25 civilizations and cultures in appendix 1.

I then described the experience of the Fire, the growth of the religion and the consequent growth and development of the civilization as a result of its driving force, in ten religions: the Egyptian, Islamic, Hindu, Chinese, Japanese, Orthodox, Christian, Buddhist, Tibetan Buddhist and Judaistic religions.

I have set out (in *The Light of Civilization*)[44] 21 civilizations with distinctive religions and four civilizations with related religions (that are early phases or later branches of the 21 distinctive civilizations). It is worth listing the gods of the distinctive religions of all 25 civilizations to make the point that in their worship within these religions and sects contemplatives all see the common Light:

> Dyaeus Pitar/Magna Mater (Sky Father/Earth Mother); Anu/Ogma/Utu, Shamash/Tammuz/Marduk, Shuqamuna/ Ashur; Ra/Amun/Aton, Horus/ Osiris/Apis; Zeus/Apollo, Anat/Athene (or Athena); Jupiter/Apollo, Gnostic God as Light; Mistress of Animals/Storm and Weather god Tarhun or Teshub/Sharruma/Arinna, Cybele/Attis; El/Dagon/Baal/ Mot/ Resheph/Molech (or Moloch), Koshar/Astarte/Anath (or Anat), Adonis, Ashtoreth, Hadad/Rammon/Atargatis; El Shaddai/Yahweh; Du-w ('Yoo-we', cf 'Yahweh')/Lug/Beli (cf Baal)/ Taran/Yesu; Mithras/ Zurvan (of Medes)/Ahura Mazda/Mani, Inshushinak/Kiririshna (cf Indian Krishna)/

> Nahhunte/Huban; God as Light; Wodan/Odin; Smiling god ('El Lanzon', 'the Great Image'), Inti/Quetzlcoatl/Kukulcan (or Kukulan); Kinich Ahau/Itzamna/Huitzilopochtli; Allah; Mwari/Nzambi/Cghene/ Ngai/Leza/Ndjambi Marunga/ Raluvhimba/Olodumare; Agni/Brahman/ Atman/Siva/ Sakti, Visnu/Rama/Krishna/Om Kar, the Buddha; Kami / Amaterasu; Io (Maoris); Shang Ti/T'ien Ti/the *Tao*.

We can get close to the common Light the contemplatives saw during their quest for metaphysical Reality within all these religions and sects by studying the invocations to Ra in the Egyptian *Book of the Dead* and the experiences of the European Christian mystics, including Augustine and Hildegarde (whom we met on p 12).

Alongside comparative religion's emphasis on the inner quest for metaphysical Reality is another approach which focuses on outer observance in the services in their churches, temples and mosques. This approach concentrates on rituals in places of worship and emphasizes social religion. I have shown evidence[45] that this social approach secularized English hymns after 1889: the Light or Fire has more or less vanished from hymns and been replaced by social, humanist subjects.

I have also set out[46] the times in each civilization when the Light weakens during religions' and civilizations' times of decline under foreign threat or rule. In North America the only time of decline was during the period before and after the Civil War, c1854–96. In Europe the most recent time of decline was c1880 to c1991 when the Germans subjected Europe to two world wars and the Russians occupied Eastern Europe until the fall of the Berlin Wall. I believe that the incorporation of Eastern European nation-states into the EU and the ratification of the Lisbon Treaty in the first decade of the 21st century have ended this European time of decline – and weakening of the Light in Europe.

We saw on p 3 that according to a WIN Gallup International poll, 63 per cent of the world's population think of themselves as religious and 11 per cent as atheists. Of a (then) world population of around 7.3 billion, around 4.6 billion regard themselves as religious and 0.8 billion as atheists. And on p xiv we saw that a survey claimed that 5.8 billion of the world's population had a religious affiliation in 2010. Even on the lower WIN Gallup figure adherents to the traditional metaphysical approach outnumber adherents to the secular, social approach by nearly 6 to 1.

INTERNATIONAL POLITICS AND STATECRAFT

For 2,600 years – and probably for 5,000 years – international politics and statecraft ('the art of conducting affairs of state', *Concise Oxford Dictionary*) have been conducted by two conflicting approaches.

In the early stages of the ancient civilizations when the Fire or Light within their religion was managed by a priestly class who performed State rites, the State was dominated by the Fire or Light, and the vision of metaphysical Reality attracted surrounding peoples and led to political unification and expansion. The growing, expanding civilization's diplomacy maintained the metaphysical vision enshrined in its religion, and in ancient Egypt, Mesopotamia, Iran, India, China and the other early civilizations the Pharaoh or priest-King or Supreme Ruler derived his authority from the chief god of the new religion. International politics and statecraft, and diplomacy, maintained the *status quo* of the unifying vision of metaphysical Reality, which saw the oneness of surrounding humankind, and perpetuated its local forms. The Greek Athenian Empire united Greek city-states for a while, and Zeus and other Greek gods blended with some of the Ionian and Egyptian gods. The Roman Empire syncretistically merged Jupiter and Juno with many of the Near Eastern local gods and cults of Asia Minor previously listed (pp 30–1), thus perpetuating the local gods as embodiments of metaphysical Reality and associating them with the grander Roman vision of metaphysical Reality. The same would apply to the British Empire, which ruled a quarter of the world's population (between 470 and 570 million) by 1921 and blended Jesus with (for example) local African gods. In the 25 civilizations there were numerous blendings of gods: Ogma-Herakles; Marduk-Amon (and later Marduk-Zeus); Zeus-Serapis; Dionysus-Serapis; Mithra-Anahita, Zeus-Tarhun; Baal-Marduk; and Thor-Christ.[47]

In the kingdoms of Europe during the Middle Ages the State was dominated by the Church: the Pope or (as in the case of Henry II) his Archbishop. During the time of the Crusades, religion and the vision of metaphysical Reality led diplomacy in Europe. The Renaissance brought a new outward-looking spirit of intellectual inquiry, opened up by the flow of classical texts from the libraries of Constantinople and renewed interest in geography. Cities grew and prospered, leagues of states formed: the Hanseatic League and Habsburg Empire flourished, and little by little politics grew away from religion. England broke with the Pope, and the Reformation loosened the Catholic grip on politics. Revolutions against the monarchy in England and France weakened religion's control over the State. My study of all the revolutions from 1453 to 1920, *The Secret History of the West*, showed that secret societies were behind the growing revolutionary nationalism. Coinciding with advances in map-making, nations emerged, and slowly nations of city-states turned into nation-states in which the State was secular. Following the unifications of Germany and of Italy, the State was secular in much of Europe.

Alongside the tradition of international politics and statecraft being controlled by religion's vision of metaphysical Reality, affirming a vision of unified peoples and acknowledging the religion of local groups, there now co-existed a new approach to international politics and statecraft that emphasized the secular and social relationships of sovereign nation-states as they competed with each other in continental wars. From the 19th century on, nationalism was a force, which swiftly expressed itself through rival imperialisms in Africa and elsewhere. In the late 19th and 20th centuries ten colonial empires were born: the British, French, German, Dutch, Belgian, Italian, Spanish, Portuguese, Danish and American Empires. The longer-standing Ottoman and Russian Empires were strong in the 19th century. Conflicting nation-states competed in Africa and Asia to found colonies, as had the ancient Greeks and Romans (whose empires were considered a model for the British Empire and dominated school syllabuses). The diplomats of nation-states were driven by national self-interest and not by Papal or Reformation considerations.

The decolonization of the 20th century – the result of two European civil wars (which is how they appear from the perspective of a unified European civilization) – ended much of the competing national self-interest of European powers in distant continents. Nationalism continued outside Europe especially in the decolonized states and newly revolutionary nation-states such as Libya and Iran. My books on these two countries[48] are ultimately about the limitations of nationalism.

Nationalism was challenged by a plan for a New World Order. Conceived by self-interested élitist families I have described collectively as 'the Syndicate' (most notably the Rothschilds and Rockefellers) who created the Bilderberg Group, they worked to bring in a world government that would loot the Earth's resources. Rockefeller-backed banks acquired Russia's energy in the 1990s at knock-down prices (sold by Yeltsin's Prime Minister, Viktor Chernomyrdin),[49] and the Earth was covered with a network of oil and gas pipelines. In 2008 Rothschild banks were found to control the central banks of 187 of the 192 UN member states – at the time of writing there are 193 member states after the admission of South Sudan in 2011 – and only Iran, Sudan, Cuba, Libya and North Korea were not under their influence.[50] The Syndicate are motivated by their own business profits, increasing their trillions into quadrillions at the expense of the peoples of the Earth, and are not interested in perpetuating a vision of metaphysical Reality that embraces the oneness of humankind. In my work *The Syndicate*, while wanting a world government that will improve the lot of humankind I stood up to the self-interested international politics and statecraft of 'the Syndicate'.

There has long been a yearning for a genuine World State as opposed to one that would enable families of an élite to become quadrillionaires. The idea of a World State is present in Egyptian, Indian, Chinese and Graeco-Roman thought.[51] In *Convivio* (*The Banquet*, 1304) Dante Alighieri proposed one government under one ruler, a universal monarch or Emperor, and in *De Monarchia* (*On Monarchy*, 1317–18) he proposed that Pope and Emperor should co-operate.[52] Both would act to perpetuate the vision of metaphysical Reality that proclaimed the oneness of humankind. Sir Thomas More's *Utopia*, which set out the ideal State, can be viewed as statecraft. Kant in *Perpetual Peace* proposed a federation of free states that would avoid war. As nation-states made war on each other, calls for a World State increased. A federal World State was proposed by Tennyson in 'Locksley Hall' (1837–8, 'the Federation of the world'; see p vi) and by H G Wells in *The Outline of History* (1920, revised 1931: 'A federation of all humanity' appears in a section headed 'Some Possibilities of a Federal World State'). Aldous Huxley wrote of a World State in *Brave New World* (1932). Calls for a World State have been made by President Harry S Truman, Einstein, Churchill, Mahatma Gandhi, Bertrand Russell, Dwight D Eisenhower, John F Kennedy and Mikhail Gorbachev.[53]

In *The World Government* I set out a blueprint for a democratic World State,[54] and we shall return to this in due course. The point now is that there is an honourable tradition of respected thinkers calling for a World State that would recognize the oneness of humankind as perceived in the unifying vision of metaphysical Reality. The World State is an ideal that would abolish war, famine, disease and poverty and see off the greed and self-interest of élites who care more about their family fortunes than the whole of humankind. In the 21st century, international politics and statecraft are as much about regional groups such as the European Union as about diplomacy between nation-states, and in pockets of the world nationalism has already started to be transcended by Universalism.

CULTURE

For 5,000 years culture – 'the arts and other manifestations of human intellectual achievement regarded collectively; the customs, civilization, and achievements of a particular time or people' (*Concise Oxford Dictionary*) – has been dominated by two conflicting approaches.

We have seen (on pp29–30) that the vision of metaphysical Reality entered each civilization and passed into its religion, that all cultures had the Fire or Light in common. I reproduce a chart which shows this process very clearly (see appendix 1).[55] The Fire originated in the Central Asian civilization and passed to the Indo-European Kurgan civilization and after that passed between civilizations as the arrows show, ending in a 'worldwide civilization' which will be the coming World State. The chart is subtitled 'The Fundamental Unity of World Culture' and demonstrates the underlying cultural unity the Fire or Light makes possible.

In the early civilizations, civilization's culture was unified like a tree whose branches are nourished from its religious trunk (as we have seen on p 4). Within all the civilizations, including the European civilization, the arts – the tree's branches – expressed the vision of metaphysical Reality that had passed into its religion. Each civilization's culture was originally a unity, and in the European civilization until the Renaissance its works of art – in philosophy, painting, music and literature – all expressed the civilization's central idea, its vision of metaphysical Reality round which the civilization had grown. This vision can be found in European thought and in the European arts: in the philosophy of Christian Platonism and Aristotelianism which looked back to Heraclitus's 'ever-living' Fire ('Fragment 30'), Plato's Fire or 'universal Light' which causes shadows to flicker on the wall of the cave, and Plotinus's 'authentic Light' which 'comes from the One and is the One'; in paintings such as Jan van Eyck's *Adoration of the Lamb*, Fra Angelico's angels in *Christ Glorified in the Court of Heaven* and Michelangelo's Sistine Chapel ceiling; in the sacred choral music of Palestrina, Thomas Tallis, William Byrd and Claudio Monteverdi and in the Hallelujah Chorus of George Frideric Handel's *Messiah*; and in the literature of Dante, and in particular in Dante's sempiternal rose in his *Paradiso*. All expressed the sublime vision of Paradise. During the Renaissance, Plato-inspired Marsilio Ficino and Sandro Botticelli shared Dante's vision. Unity of culture continued during the Elizabethan time in spite of the Reformation, and during the time of the Metaphysical poets (the stage-30 secession from the Renaissance Humanists by Cromwell's Puritans, who wanted more rather than less metaphysical vision), the time of John Milton's 'God is light, … Celestial light' in *Paradise Lost*, book 3.

Alongside the vision of metaphysical Reality which dominated the rise of each civilization co-existed a secular, social approach whose artists presented a secular, social perspective in works of art. In the European civilization the 18th-century Augustans espoused Enlightenment reason and social virtue, and condemned social vices, and the vision of metaphysical Reality took second place. Since the 18th century the metaphysical idea has weakened. This weakening was captured in works of art within philosophy, painting, music and literature: in the Vienna Circle's verification progress; in the French Impressionists and John Constable and J M W Turner; in programme music that tells a social story and evokes images; and in the 18th-

and 19th-century novel. In the second decade of the 21st century, works of art by Metaphysical poets are outnumbered by works of art with social themes. The rise of film has encouraged this trend: as a medium, film is better able to describe social events than inner visions. We are living in a time when the inner has given way to the outer in many areas of our lives.

I have listed (in *The New Philosophy of Universalism*)[56] 50 'isms' or doctrinal movements that arose after the weakening of Christianity. They represent secular, philosophical and political traditions that indicate fragmentation and loss of contact with the One, and disunity within European civilization:

> humanism; scientific revolution/reductionism; mechanism; Rosicrucianism; Rationalism; Empiricism; scepticism; Atomism/ Materialism; Enlightenment/deism; Idealism; Realism; liberalism; capitalism; individualism; egoism; atheism; radicalism; utilitarianism; determinism; historicism; nationalism; socialism; Marxism; anarchism/syndicalism; Darwinism; accidentalism; nihilism; Communism; conservatism; imperialism; totalitarianism; Nazism; Fascism; Stalinism; pragmatism; progressivism; Phenomenology/ Existentialism; stoicism; vitalism; intuitionism; modernism/ post-modernism; secularism; objectivism; positivism; analytic and linguistic philosophy/logical empiricism; ethical relativism; republicanism; hedonism/Epicureanism; structuralism/post-structuralism; and holism

These 50 'isms' give a bird's-eye view of the fragmentation and disintegration of the once-unified European and (insofar as European civilization impacted on the world as a major part of Western civilization) world culture.

AMERICAN CULTURE

American culture has been influenced by European culture, especially British culture in colonial America, and is also Western. However, it has also been influenced by its Native American, African, Asian, Latin American and Polynesian ethnic groups and roots. Its cultural diversity has been shaped by its history, which has left behind regional cultures: New England has been shaped by Puritan migrants from England's East Anglia from 1629 to 1640; British Cavalier migrants came to Chesapeake Bay between 1640 and 1675 and influenced the growth of the Southern American culture; between 1675 and 1725 European Quakers led by William Penn settled in the Delaware Valley and influenced the General American culture; and between 1717 and 1775 English and Scottish settlers came to Appalachia and influenced the culture of the Upland South.[57] It can be argued that these are all regional cultures, and that there *is* no American culture – just regional cultures such as the Yankee, New Netherland, Midland, Tidewater, Greater Appalachia, Deep South, New France, El Norte, Left Coast, Far West and First Nation cultures.[58]

Nevertheless, the North American civilization with English as its official language is unified by ecumenical Protestantism and is still growing through its stages, and we *can* speak of North American culture. All countries, including the UK, have regional emphases due to historical influences, but these are part and parcel of their civilization's culture. In keeping with their roots in English settlements – Quakers in Pennsylvania, Catholics in Maryland, Puritans in Massachusetts Bay Colony and Separatist Congregationalists in Plymouth – America is one of the most religious developed countries, with more than half claiming that religion plays an important part in their lives and a strong belief that the democratic process is the will of God. America is younger than Europe, but in all its regions the two approaches are plain to see.

My work includes both approaches. I have written poems on inner

Reality and literary works that reflect the social approach. Concerned that the vision was not finding its way into many modern works of art, in 1997 I gave a lecture in Aldeburgh, Suffolk, 'Revolution in Thought and Culture',[59] calling for a rebalancing of our world culture: artists should open to the vision of metaphysical Reality and feature it in contemporary works of art.

Enough has been said to establish that in each of the seven disciplines of world culture the traditional approach now co-exists with a secular, social approach which has brought disunity to world culture.

CHAPTER 2

ORDER AND ACCIDENT IN THE SCIENTIFIC UNIVERSE

Note: For an explanation of numbers in powers of 10 (eg 10^{11}, 10^{-43}), see appendix 3

For thousands of years, mystics have seen humankind as a unity. The religions of the ancient Egyptians, Chinese, Indians and Greeks all saw a humankind united under their gods. In *The City of God* (*De Civitate Dei contra Paganos*) St Augustine saw all Christian souls within a unity, and the medieval vision of God presiding over society was brought to America by the early settlers. The Puritans' God presided over the souls of all settlers. The Christian unity did not include other faiths. Freemasonry introduced (along with rituals and off-putting mumbo jumbo) the all-world perspective and the acknowledgement of a number of gods with equal status. The jumbled letters on the altar of Freemasonry's Holy Royal Arch arrange into 'Je-ho-vah Jah-bul-on', and drawing on four languages (Chaldee, Hebrew, Syriac and Egyptian) 'Jah-bul-on' is an amalgamation of Yahweh, Baal and the Egyptian On, 'Father of All', Osiris-Ra.

Early religious Universalism saw all souls as being saved regardless of what religion they espoused, and this perspective has been followed by the religious Universalism of the American New Age movement. Mystical, philosophical and political Universalism expanded St Augustine's vision into an egalitarian, democratic world union of souls who have spiritual unity, and this perspective is very relevant to the secret American destiny.

AMERICA'S SPIRITUAL VISION AND SCIENCE'S VIEW OF ORDER WITHIN THE UNIVERSE

Liberty knows that America must bring a vision of spiritual unity to world culture if religious and non-religious – metaphysical and secular – humankind is to be united. America pioneered space science during the 20th century, and Liberty knows that science's view of cosmological order is important to the new American vision of spiritual unity.

We have just seen that in each of the seven disciplines of world culture there are two opposite approaches – one traditional and inner, the other outer – which have created a disunited world culture. Inner mystic and religious visions lack objective evidence beyond eyewitness personal experience, and a positive scientific approach seeks to provide objective evidence for the order behind the universe. The approach to metaphysical Reality has its counterpart in science's positive view of the ordered universe (science's +A), and the secular, social approach has its counterpart in science's negative view that the universe is a random accident (science's –A).

It could be said that the view that the universe has order – that everything has a 'right place' within a harmony (see p xvi) – and the view that it is an accident are scientific interpretations of the pair of opposites (+A + –A) we have been examining. On the one hand, the mystic vision of a metaphysical Reality is complemented by a scientifically measurable view that there is order in the universe in which events have a goal and purpose at best, and a meaning or significance at worst. On the other hand, the social perspective is complemented by a scientifically measurable view that there is no vision of Reality, just a secular, social life within a universe that is a random accident in which events are a meaningless flux. An American spiritual vision for world culture includes science's positive perception of the order behind the universe.

What does science say about the origin and structure of the

universe? In *The New Philosophy of Universalism: The Infinite and the Law of Order*[1] I set out the evidence for order in the harmonious system of Nature, and present a bird's-eye view under six headings:

COSMOLOGY AND ASTROPHYSICS

I start with the facts regarding the origin and structure of the universe, the discovery of which is largely an American achievement.[2] 'Cosmology' is 'the study and description of the physical structure, science or theory of the universe', whereas 'astrophysics' is 'a branch of astronomy concerned with the physics and chemistry of celestial bodies' – that is, of the stars of the galaxies (*Concise Oxford Dictionary*). Cosmologists provide a theoretical understanding of the beginning of life and the end of the universe, whereas astrophysicists use the techniques and concepts of physicists to study the stars. Their measurements indicate that galaxies are receding from the Earth. The 1927 cosmological theory of Georges Lemaître advanced the notion of a Big Bang, and the possibility of an expanding universe was allowed in Einstein's equations. In 1929 the American astrophysicist Edwin Hubble confirmed that the universe is expanding at an accelerating rate and that the recession speed of a galaxy (the speed at which a galaxy is receding from the Earth owing to the accelerated expansion of the universe) is proportional to its distance from the Earth. The discovery of cosmic microwave background radiation by the American radio astronomers Arno Penzias and Robert Wilson in 1964 was interpreted as the residual radiation from the hot beginning. By 1970 supporters of the Steady State model of the universe proposed by Hermann Bondi, Thomas Gold and Fred Hoyle were won over by evidence for the Big Bang.

In 1992 the COBE (Cosmic Background Explorer) satellite launched by NASA took measurements and confirmed the uniformity of this radiation throughout the universe, suggesting that the Big Bang had no centre in the universe, for if it had there would be a glow of radiation round the centre and space far removed from the centre would be cold, and that was not the case. Ripples in the radiation showed that 380,000 years after the Big Bang there were already wispy clouds of matter 500 million light years in length, and that 96 per cent of matter is 'missing' – comprising 30 per cent dark matter and 66 per cent dark energy according to the WMAP (Wilkinson Microwave Anisotropy Probe) mapping team of 2003.

Einstein's theory of gravity requires that the universe exploded from a state of infinite density – mathematics cease before infinity – and the general theory of relativity predicts the universe began in a point (before which the theory of relativity breaks down). This hot dense point was a billionth the size of a nuclear particle. Dante wrote of the 'infinitesimal point' in *Paradiso*, canto 28, and it is interesting that a mystic poet should have arrived at Einstein's position regarding the beginning of the universe as early as the 14th century.

This minute point contained all space that would be formed from inflation. In less than a nanosecond a repulsive energy field inflated the point to space's visible size and filled it with subatomic particles, quarks, which clumped into protons and neutrons, the building blocks of atomic nuclei, creating atoms, molecules and clumps of matter starting with hydrogen and helium and then electrons orbiting nuclei from which after 450 million years galaxies and stars would form.

This point became known as a 'singularity'. In 1939 the American theoretical physicists Robert Oppenheimer and Hartland Snyder showed that a massive star could collapse into a space-time singularity and black hole; and in 1965 the British mathematician and physicist Roger Penrose's theorem stated that any body undergoing gravitational collapse must eventually form a singularity. In 1965 Stephen Hawking used Penrose's theorem to establish (by tracing time in reverse) that an expanding universe must have begun in a singularity. In 1970 Penrose and Hawking proved in a theorem that the universe must have a beginning in a Big Bang singularity of infinite density and space-time curvature, which happened everywhere in that one point, and was One; and the universe must have an end. (Penrose disagreed with Hawking's later assertion that the universe had no beginning and no end,[3] but is now toying with the idea that the Big Bang was not the beginning, that there was a previous aeon. He now sees the possibility of a physicalist state before the Big Bang.) The German mathematician Georg Cantor (who died in 1918) had identified three separate types of infinity – the Absolute, physical and mathematical infinities – and the infinity within the singularity was part of the totality of the infinite Absolute, not finite space-time.

Particle physics focused on the first three minutes after the Big Bang and found that the four fundamental forces (the electromagnetic, strong and weak forces and gravity) were unified at the beginning of this stage. The gravitational force separated at 10^{-43} seconds after the Big Bang. (See appendix 3 for numbers in powers of 10.) Mass-energy became the observed universe at 10^{-43} seconds. (One-hundred-trillionth of a second is 10^{-14}, to give an idea of how instant 10^{-43} seconds is.) Three minutes after the Big Bang the temperature was 10^{9}K (Kelvin): 1 billion degrees. The observable universe is 13.798 billion years old (+ or – 0.037 billion years), a figure calculated by NASA's WMAP 2003 mapping project and since refined. Our galaxy, the Milky Way, contains 400 billion stars. The observable universe was thought to contain more than 10^{11} (100 billion) galaxies and 10^{23} (more than 70 sextillion) stars, the same number as the total number of grains of sand on Earth. In 2005, after extensive work on the WMAP mapping project, there were thought to be approximately 170 billion (1.7×10^{11}) galaxies in the observable universe,[4] and in May 2015 the most distant and the earliest galaxy yet observed, EGS-zs8-1, was found to be 13.1 billion light years away.

In 1998 it was discovered that the universe's expansion had been accelerating during the last 5 billion years. It accelerated greatly after the Big Bang, and for 8 billion years decelerated following the initial inflation, but then the acceleration speeded up and has been moving too fast for new galaxies to form. This mysterious speeding-up contradicts the second law of thermodynamics (that a system begins ordered and that its passage through time brings increasing disorder). The speeding-up of expansion can only be explained by the existence of dark energy, an anti-gravity force that opposes gravity.

I discount Hawking's later view that the universe had no beginning and will have no end, and therefore has endless size and goes on forever, and is infinite with galaxies in every direction; and that quantum theory and general relativity are reconciled in a universe that is infinitely old and never had a Big Bang. I am aware that there is increasing support for the view that downgrades the Big Bang, but I stick with Einstein's equations. I also discount the multiverse, the idea that there is an infinite number of other universes (for which there is no evidence). I hold that our universe is finite and shaped like a shuttlecock,[5] and as it is accelerating it must have an edge and be accelerating into something: the infinite. If a surfer could stand on the accelerating edge as on the crest of a surging, advancing wave (see appendix 4), his feet would be in space-time (on the wave) but his chest and head would be breasting the infinite which pre-existed the universe of space-time and from which the singularity emerged. The infinite is metaphysical because it is outside, as well as pervading, finite space-time and our physical universe. The surfer would be experiencing – having practical experience of – the infinite outside our universe.

There are alternatives to the Big Bang model of the universe: Steady State, discredited since the discovery of cosmic microwave background radiation; the unevidential multiverse (that there are several co-existing universes including successive universes), which exists only in mathematics; string theory (that superstrings, not particles, are the elementary ingredients of the universe), for which there is no evidence; and the American multiverse Big Wave model (that our universe began from a black hole caused by the Big Crunch of a previous universe), a variation on the 'multiverse' that came out of Penrose's collaboration with Hawking in the late 1960s when they realized that a bursting-out of the universe was a mirror-image of a collapse into a black hole – for which, again, there is no evidence.

So the Big Bang model is now widely accepted. An infinite state pre-existed the Big Bang. Hawking has claimed that we cannot think of a time before the Big Bang because the Big Bang produced space-time, but that is not good enough, for we *can* think of what is beyond the edge of the accelerating universe, what the surfer encounters. Time began from within the infinite. Inflation began at 10^{-36} seconds and whooshed the universe into existence at 10^{-35} seconds (less than one undecillionth of a second) after the Big Bang, and lasted until between 10^{-33} and 10^{-32} seconds. The universe has been expanding ever since.

A careful scientific view of the origin of the universe takes account of the first singularity as an infinite Absolute not part of space-time, the inflationary whoosh 10^{-35} seconds after the Big Bang, the almost instantaneous separation of the four forces, the creation of particles and elements and of galaxies and stars, the cosmic microwave background radiation with ripples, the deceleration and acceleration of inflation, the surging edge of the finite accelerating universe and the infinite into which it surges. A scientific probing of the origin and structure of the universe, given the above factors, can only come to the conclusion that there was order behind the whoosh that led to so many galaxies and stars, a conclusion we shall reach when we consider biocosmology.

PHYSICS

I also examined the quantum vacuum and the expanding force of light,[6] both of which have been regarded as influencing the order of the universe.

The infinitesimal 'point', the singularity from which the universe inflated, contained the tiny subatomic and vast galactic worlds which were interconnected in the point before inflation. The discovery of radiation in uranium compounds in 1896 produced quantum theory. In 1900 Max Planck saw radiation as multiples of quanta or particles as well as rays. Einstein took up Planck's ideas in 1905 and showed that light behaves as if its energy is quantum packets of energy called photons. Light could be a wave *and* particles, and electromagnetic radiation could behave like waves in some circumstances or like particles in others. Niels Bohr proposed the quantum theory of spectra in 1913, and Louis de Broglie suggested that matter has wave-particle duality, which was later confirmed by experiments. An electron can sometimes act like a particle and occupy one position in space at a time, and can sometimes act like a wave and occupy several places in space *at the same* time.

There was therefore uncertainty in Nature as to whether matter is going to act as particles or waves, as Werner Heisenberg's 'uncertainty principle' pointed out. Nature could only be described by probabilities according to quantum mechanics, which first appeared in 1926 with the matrix theory of Max Born and Heisenberg, the wave mechanics of de Broglie and Erwin Schrödinger and the transformation theory of Paul Dirac and Pascal Jordan, all of which were different aspects of a single body of quantum law. Dirac laid the foundation for quantum electrodynamics (QED), a quantum theory of the interactions of charged particles with the electromagnetic field. This was developed in the 1940s by Richard Feynman together with Julian Schwinger and Sin-Itiro Tomonaga, who held that charged particles interact by emitting and absorbing photons, particles of light that transmit electromagnetic forces. This theory led to knowledge of virtual photons, which can emerge from a quantum vacuum and become real.

Newton's search for order in the universe hinged on light. Newton saw light as associated with ether, which was thought to fill space. Having made discoveries in gravity, light and calculus in 1664–6, from 1669 (when he was 26) Newton spent 30 years researching into alchemy in the hope of finding an expanding force of light that would counteract and balance gravity. It would drive particles apart and, as gravity draws them together, the universe would be kept in balance, static: a Newtonian '+A + –A = 0'. He wrote that every ray of light has four sides. In Query 30 of *Opticks* (the 1718 edition, book III) he wrote of 'Particles of Light', which seemed to anticipate wave-particle duality. He asked: 'Are not gross Bodies and Light convertible into one another, and may not Bodies receive much of their Activity from the Particles of Light which enter their Composition?' In Query 31 he asked: 'Have not the small Particles of Bodies certain Powers, Virtues or Forces by which they act at a distance, not only upon the Rays of Light for reflecting, refracting, and inflecting them, but also upon one another for producing a great part of the Phaenomena of Nature?' In an alchemical manuscript now in the Smithsonian Institution, Washington, DC, he stated: 'Ether is but a vehicle to some more active spirit & the bodies may be concreted of both [ie ether and spirit] together, they may imbibe ether well [sic] as air in generation & in the ether the spirit is entangled. This spirit is the body of light because both have a prodigious active principle.' In other words light, whose body is spirit, combines with ether, and there is a single unified system which includes both spiritual and physiological systems.

Ether, which Newton believed in, had been regarded as a tenuous substance that filled the vacuum and carried light ever since the pre-Socratic Greeks' *aither*. In the 19th century, physicists proposed that the entire universe was permeated by 'luminiferous ether' ('light-bearing ether') and Lord Kelvin, who gave his initial to the temperature measurement K, wrote that ether is 'millions and millions and millions of times less dense than air'. It could vibrate

400 million million times per second yet not resist any body going through it. It was insubstantial, and Theosophy took it up and referred to 'the etheric level'. In 1880 the American physicist Albert Michelson 'disproved' ether by an experiment involving two beams of light, one of which was to be slowed by ether. The two beams arrived at the same time; but perhaps the experiment was faulty.

But what if ether, the Greek *aither*, is a network of dark energy composed of tinier particles than neutrinos – perhaps of photinos? In 2012–13 the existence of the Higgs field and Higgs bosons was confirmed by CERN. Tiny Higgs bosons (scalar and vector bosons) slow particles down, interact with them and attach themselves to objects and give them mass, and had previously gone undetected in atom-smashers. Perhaps *aither*, which has not been found, is a 'vehicle' for spiritual Light as Newton described it, and perhaps light combines with ether as Newton proposed. The Higgs boson is an 'order mechanism', a mechanism of an 'order principle' which orders matter, and ether would be an 'order mechanism', ordering light. We shall see (pp 89–93) that photons have a role in ordering matter, consciousness and the universe, and it may be that an undetected tiny-particle form of light such as Newton pondered exists. It may be that the Higgs field *is* the undiscovered *aither* or ether.

In October 2015 I heard a fascinating defence of the existence of ether by Miles Osmaston, a 90-year-old engineer and author of 143 online scientific papers, who did secret work on Vulcan, the delta-wing strategic bomber, for Avro, the British aircraft manufacturer, for 19 years and (having researched the air more carefully than most) believes in ether, which he sees as a network of electrical charges.

Einstein took up Newton's balancing force – an expanding force of light that balanced the contracting force of gravity – in 1917, when he proposed a 'cosmological constant', an expanding force that repels and balances contracting gravity. Gravity attracts and the expanding force repels and the balance between the two keeps the universe static,

Einstein (like Newton before him) then thought. The constant gave all particles stable interconnectedness, he thought. He abandoned the constant in 1929 when Edwin Hubble established that the universe is expanding and not static, and later described his abandonment as 'the biggest blunder of my life'. The constant has returned in our time as unevidenced dark energy, which repulses gravity within our accelerating universe and which may have been the expanding force Newton was seeking. It is not known if this dark energy is conveyed by light (perhaps mixed with 'ether' and 'spirit' as Newton thought).

Newton believed the expanding force that counterbalances gravity is light, which, he believed, governs human and plant growth. It is possible that light contains a universal principle of order which stimulates chemical composition through DNA and growth through photosynthesis and affects consciousness and human behaviour. It is possible that beyond the gamma rays at the short-wave end of the electromagnetic spectrum is metaphysical Light (Newton's 'ether' and 'spirit') which originated in timeless infinity, manifested into the universe, travelled with the physical light of space-time and arrived among gamma, ultraviolet and radio waves to pervade Nature with order intermixed with physical light. If so, there can be a synthesis of physics, mysticism and metaphysics.

Einstein's last years were devoted to a pursuit of order. In Heisenberg's new quantum mechanics of 1925, randomness is fundamental: identical particles behave with apparent randomness, nuclei decay or do not decay on a random basis. Einstein did not accept the randomness. He was sure the universe was ordered rather than a random accident: 'God does not play dice with the universe.'[7] He proposed a 'hidden variable', which causes some nuclei to decay but not others. He never found a hidden principle of variability and after a difficult meeting with Bohr in 1930 he grudgingly accepted quantum mechanics. He worked on quantum gravity and proposed 'gravitons' (gravity particles which may also act as gravity waves).

Gravitational waves were not detected until 2016. Einstein eventually split with Bohr and spent the last 30 years of his life trying to unite gravity and the strong and weak forces and electromagnetism into a unified field. (Most of this time, from 1933 to his death in 1955, he was living in America.) The elusive hidden variability may be the workings of a universal principle of order. David Bohm, Einstein's protégé, supported hidden variability (as did Penrose, so long as it is non-local), which may come to be explained by the Higgs field.

Bohm, with whom I had a lengthy discussion, saw the quantum vacuum as a reservoir of order. He proposed a hidden order beneath the apparent chaos and lack of continuity of the particles of matter of quantum mechanics. He saw a hidden dimension behind the surface, an 'implicate order'[8] which is the source of all visible 'explicate' matter, and has 'infinite depth' (another way of saying that the implicate is infinity). From the infinity of the implicate order manifests 'explicate' existence. So the apparent randomness of quantum theory has order behind it, according to Bohm. Bohm died in 1992 and dark energy was first postulated in 1998.

The energy of the quantum vacuum has been taken up by the Belgian physicist Edgard Gunzig, who saw the vacuum as 'non-empty' and expelling virtual particles in pairs, one of which lives for a split second and can become a real particle and turn into a photon, according to quantum field theory. Out of such a process came the hot beginning, the Big Bang, he argued, and inflation expanded seeds in the microworld into the galaxies of our universe.

In the 20th century there was incompatibility between classical (that is, pre-quantum) and quantum physics, and our theory of gravity has shortcomings: gravitational force (gravitomagnetism) is exerted by a rotating mass, and allowed gravitational slingshot to propel *Mariner 10* past Venus towards Mercury in 1974. There needs to be a complete theory of gravity that includes quantum mechanics. Attempts to unify the strong and weak forces and electromagnetism in a Grand Unified Theory have been thwarted by the temperature involved, which would presumably have to be the temperature at which they diverged (between 10^{14} and 10^{27} or 10^{28} K), too high to replicate. In an article in *The Daily Telegraph*[9] Hawking claimed that the three forces have been unified, and repeated the claim in a two-part television programme shown later, but that was not the case. The three forces have only been theoretically and potentially unified in mathematics, not actually in an experiment. (I have written about the complexity of this concept elsewhere.)[10]

A reunification of all four forces, including gravity, would create a Theory of Everything, but the temperature required, 10^{32} K, cannot be replicated in existing particle accelerators. A Theory of Everything must include quantum physics (which largely explains much of the particle) and the general theory of relativity (which deals with the universe and gravity). It would put together the very large (relativity) and the very small (quantum mechanics) to explain quantum gravity. It would show an expanding force of light within the first singularity, in which quantum gravity acts as a contracting force – a pair of opposites, light and gravity (+A + –A) present in the first singularity before the Big Bang, within the infinite surrounding it.

The universe is finite and surrounded by infinity, which must therefore pervade the finite and can be experienced in the here and now. The infinite is with us now. Within the Void (or quantum vacuum) were the seeds of the order of the universe. We shall now see that the process is likely to have been orderly rather than random.

BIOCOSMOLOGY: 40 BIOFRIENDLY CONDITIONS FOR LIFE

Biocosmology (the application of cosmology to biological processes or life) advances an orderly view of the universe. One of the main reasons for rejecting the idea of a chance Big Bang and a haphazard, accidental universe condensing, cooling and in a random way creating a layered atmosphere on Earth is that the conditions left by the Big

Bang turned out to be ideal for human life, and any tweaks of these conditions would have made human life impossible.

The anthropic principle was first stated by Alfred Russel Wallace in 1903: the universe is just right for the orderly development culminating in man. Robert H Dicke (1961), Jim Carter (1973) and John Barrow and Frank J Tipler (1986) carried forward anthropic thinking.[11] The point is, the context for life seems orderly rather than fortuitous and random. The context for life is a system too precise to have formed by accident or chance, or to be random, and there seems to be an Order Principle, a principle of order. The obvious order is in the rhythm of days, months and years – the regular rising and setting of the sun, moon and stars, of day following night, the tides and seasons. It seems inconceivable that they could be a random accident.

In *The New Philosophy of Universalism*[12] I set out 40 conditions that are just right for life. I offered a biofriendly model of the universe, the idea that a biofriendly life principle works with the four fundamental forces towards life and intelligence. The 40 conditions are taken from cosmology, physics and astrophysics, quantum mechanics and biochemistry. I present a bird's-eye view of the order of the biofriendly universe, in which all the conditions below are necessary for life:

1 **The Big Bang** The Big Bang gave perfect density (without which the cosmos would have collapsed before inflation), the right amount of ripples and temperature variations (without which there would have been no stars, light or warmth), and perfect symmetry of matter and antimatter (without which no matter would have existed) – all within the first second.

2 **Gravity and rest-mass energy** Gravity held galaxies together as the ratio of gravity to rest-energy (energy equivalent to that of a resting, immobile particle, known as Q, 10^{-5}) was perfect. If Q had been smaller, the universe would have been inert and

structureless, and stars would have formed too slowly. If Q had been larger, gas would not have condensed into structures and the universe would have remained dark.

3 **Dimensions** The three dimensions are perfect for life, they keep planets stable. If there had been two dimensions, planets would have speeded up, there would have been no circulation of blood, and digestive waste would have come out of mouths. If there had been four dimensions, planets would have slowed down and spun into or away from the sun, and electron-orbits would have been unstable. In either case, life would not have existed.

4 **The rate of expansion** The rate of expansion at 10^{-43} seconds after the Big Bang was just right and the speed was H_0, the Hubble constant. The tension between gravity and expansion energy of the material in the universe (galaxies, gas and unevidenced dark matter) was just right so that elements could be cooked in stars. If the rate of expansion had been slower by even one part in a hundred thousand million million when the temperature of the universe was 10^{10} K ten seconds after the Big Bang, galaxies would have fallen towards each other and the universe would have collapsed. If the rate of expansion had been faster, no galaxies could have condensed out of expanding matter. If expansion does not continue forever, in 5 billion years' time the sun will burn up, the Earth will be unwarmed and the Andromeda galaxy will crash into the Milky Way.

5 **Density** The actual density of the universe and the ratio between the actual density and the 'critical density' (the boundary value between universe models that expand forever and those that recollapse, known as Ω) are just right for life. One second after the Big Bang, Ω must have had a value of close to 1, unity. If it

is lower than 1 now, the universe will expand forever. If Ω had been more than 1, the gravitational pull would have defeated the expansion and, unless other forces had intervened, the universe would have collapsed. The kinetic and gravitational energies had to be initially equal to one part in 10^{59}, and the fine balance was achieved in the first 10^{43} seconds. After the universe expanded for 13.798 billion years, + or – 0.037 billion years, to 10^{30} times its original size, taking dark matter into account, the value of Ω is now 0.3 of the density needed to halt expansion – lower than 1 – and so expansion will last forever.

6 **Anti-gravity and acceleration** Anti-gravity, a new force known as λ that balances gravity, was hypothesized in 1988 and is thought to control the expansion of the universe by dominating gravity. λ is near zero. If λ had been five times stronger, it would have destroyed gravity, stopped galaxies and stars from forming, and there would have been no evolution. If λ had been weaker, it would not make much difference. If λ is not zero, expansion will last forever; and today λ is not zero.

7 **Gravitational-electromagnetic ratio and constant** The ratio of gravitational to electromagnetic forces and their fine-structure constants is just right to allow the sun and Earth conditions conducive to evolving life. Gravity is weaker than the electrical forces by a number N, which measures the strength of the electrical forces divided by the gravity between them. N is 10^{36} and the gravitational fine-structure constant is 10^{-40}. If N had been smaller, for example 10^{30}, and if gravity had been stronger, with a constant of, for example, 10^{-30}, the universe would have been miniature, stars would have been close together, and living organisms would have had 10^{20} atoms rather than 10^{28}. If N had been less than 10^{12}, there would have been no human beings.

If N had been larger, stars would have been a billion times less massive and a million times faster in their development. They would only have lived 10,000 years and there would have been no time for evolution: no creature would have been larger than an insect. If N had been larger still, all stars would have been large and our sun would have been too small to exist: there would have been no life on Earth. Newton described the law of gravity as an inverse-square law (in which the force between two objects is proportional to 1 over the square of the difference between them), and if the law of gravity had been an inverse-cube the orbits of the planets would have been unstable: planets would have moved towards or away from the sun forever.

8 **Nuclear binding** Nuclear binding, known as E, controls atomic nuclei, atoms, the power of the sun and how stars transmute hydrogen. The value of E is 0.007 and is just right for life. The hydrogen gas that powers the sun in its core therefore converts 0.007 of its mass into energy. If E had been 0.006, hydrogen would have been less efficient – and would not have fused into deuterium, the first step to forming helium – and in a universe of hydrogen there would have been no life. If E had been 0.008 no hydrogen would have survived the Big Bang: there would have been no hydrogen to fuel the stars and no chance of life in the universe. Only when E is 0.007 can there be a carbon-based biosphere in which humans can exist.

9 **The heat of the universe** The heat of the universe is just right for life. Without temperature variations (confirmed by the WMAP 2003 thermal map of the universe 13.32 million years ago) there would have been no over-dense 'seeds' around which galaxies formed and there would have been no galaxies, stars or planets – or human life.

10 **Mathematical laws** The mathematical laws underpinning atoms, stars, galaxies and people are just right for life. The laws of physics are associated with the principles of symmetry and are biofriendly – without them there would have been no human life.

11 **Flatness** In a flat universe expansion and gravitational pull are balanced as we saw in point 4, so eventually expansion stops without collapsing back, and matter expands at the right speed to allow carbon-based life forms and human life to form. At 10^{-36} seconds after the Big Bang when the universe began expanding, the flatness of the universe was precise to within one part in 10^{60}, which gave all the conditions at the outset for stars, galaxies and human life to form, including carbon.

12 **Carbon** Carbon and heavier elements make human life possible because the ratio of dark matter to baryons (protons and neutrons, 25 per cent of which are hydrogen and helium) is 10:1. Hoyle established that carbon-12 is made inside stars and is 4 per cent above the combined energy of helium-4 and beryllium-8. A reduction of 4 per cent would have depleted the amount of carbon that could be made, reducing the chance of human life happening.

13 **Molecules of life inside stars** The essential molecules of life besides carbon, oxygen, nitrogen and phosphorus were manufactured by thermonuclear processes inside stars after the Big Bang. Gravity, expansion, density and flatness made stars just right for the production of these molecules, which were blown out by exploding supernovae into galactic space, where they helped to develop life forms including evolving human beings.

14 **Temperature** Three minutes after the Big Bang the universe cooled from 10^{32} K to 10^{9} K (1 billion degrees). If the universe

had remained at this temperature or if nuclear reactions had happened faster, all the atoms would have been processed into iron. Nuclear reactions converted 23 per cent of the hydrogen into helium, so they did not become iron. Big Bang theory predicts temperature fluctuations at 10^{-5} seconds to seed galaxy formation, and these were found by the COBE satellite in 1992.

15 **Weak and electromagnetic forces** The unification involving the weak force which controls radioactivity, radioactive decay and neutrinos lasted long enough, until 10^{-4} seconds after the Big Bang, to give the conditions in which galaxies, stars and life later evolved.

16 **The strong nuclear force** The strong nuclear force, the dominant force in the microworld, is of just the right strength to hold the proteins in helium and heavy nuclei together and prolong the sun's warmth. If it had been 1 per cent stronger, it would have burned all carbon into oxygen. If it had been 2 per cent stronger, it would have prevented the formation of protons and given a universe without atoms. If it had been 3 per cent stronger, no known chemical elements could have formed. If it had been 1 per cent weaker, carbon and oxygen atoms would have been unstable, only hydrogen could have existed and there would have been no carbon-based life. If it had been 5 per cent weaker, it would have unbound deuteron and given a universe without stars.

17 **Gravitons** Gravitons (gravity waves, ripples in space-time caused by the violent mergers of black holes) were detected by the Advanced Laser Interferometer Gravitational-Wave Observatory in 2016, a century after Einstein predicted them. They unite gravity and quantum gravity and they played their part in the unification of the four forces until 10^{-43} seconds after the Big

Bang, and provided just the right conditions for the evolution of galaxies, stars and life.

18 **Neutrinos** Neutrinos are formed when a collapsing star explodes violently as a supernova, its burning hydrogen and then helium are exhausted, and it is squeezed inwards causing protons and electrons to merge, forming neutrinos. Neutrinos' weak interaction with baryons (protons and neutrons) blows the star apart, releasing a flood of neutrinos and the heavy elements needed for life. The weak interaction is just right for neutrinos to drive large quantities of gas filled with heavy elements into space, where they could reach the planets and Earth so that human life could take place. If the weak interaction had been weaker, the neutrinos would not have pushed apart the outer layers of the star while bearing heavy elements. If the weak interaction had been stronger, the neutrinos would have been caught up in reactions in the star's core and would not have escaped.

19 **Weak force and helium** The weak force (which is 10^{28} times stronger than gravity) is of just the right weakness to prevent all the original hydrogen from being converted into helium while allowing exploding supernovae that will scatter material. If it had been weaker, all the hydrogen in the universe would have turned to helium, making water impossible, and neutrinos would have been unable to explode stars and scatter material. If it had been slightly stronger, there would have been no helium and all stars would have been made of hydrogen – and life could not have taken place.

20 **The nuclear forces, di-protons and stars** The nuclear force of attraction between two protons creates a di-proton, an atomic nucleus, and is overwhelmed by the stronger electrical force of

repulsion between two protons, which wipes them out unless uncharged neutrons hold them in balance. Stars can gain energy by fusing protons and neutrons into such balanced nuclei. If the nuclear forces had been slightly stronger and able to fuse pairs of protons into di-protons, stars would not have been able to fuse protons and neutrons. If they had been slightly weaker, the universe would have consisted of hydrogen protons and electrons, and there would have been no nuclei for stars to fuse.

21 **Proton-electron ratio** The ratio of the mass of a proton to an electron, 1836.15, could not have been smaller (eg 2) or larger (eg 2 million) because these figures would have produced a physics, chemistry and biology incompatible with life.

22 **Vacuum energy** The energy scale of the vacuum 10^{-38} seconds after the Big Bang during inflation has been calculated as $\omega = 16$, whereas the energy in the universe today is $\omega = -11.5$, three trillion quadrillion times smaller than that of inflation. Scientists assume that dark energy led to inflation, and if so the dark energy today is not the same as during inflation and is just right for life.

23 **The size of the universe** The universe has been found to be 13.798 billion years old (+ or – 0.037 billion years). Because of the connection between distance and the speed of light, our telescopes can look at any region of space, in any direction, 13.798 billion light years (+ or – 0.037 billion light years) away, and light leaving the time of the Big Bang will reach a telescope 13.798 billion light years (+ or – 0.037 billion light years) later – that is, now. From the perspective of the largest telescope the radius of the observable sphere of the universe is 13.798 billion light years (+ or – 0.037 billion light years), for there was no light to travel at 186,000 miles per second before then, and its diameter

is getting on for 28 billion light years. From the perspective of the largest telescope the size of the observable universe, which has 10^{11} (100 billion) galaxies and 10^{23} stars (of which 10 million billion are similar to our sun), is about 13.798 billion light years (+ or – 0.037 billion light years) from the base to the rim of the expanding shuttlecock (assuming inflation is only going in one direction). However, because of the acceleration of inflation and the expansion of the universe, measurements and calculations have established that a spot that was 13.798 billion light years (+ or – 0.037 billion light years) from the Earth at the time of the Big Bang will now be 46.6 billion light years away. The actual (as opposed to observable) universe is now larger than what telescopes can see, and has a radius of 46.6 billion light years, about 33 billion light years of which cannot be seen by any telescope, and a diameter of around 93.2 billion light years. Such a vast size has helped to create the right conditions for life: it takes a few billion years for a galaxy to form and for neutrinos to explode stars to scatter material into space, and more time for new stars to form from the debris for life to evolve. All this had to happen before human life could appear. The size, age and development of the universe have provided just the right conditions for life.

24 **The emptiness of the universe** The empty space between stars has helped evolving life. If the universe had been smaller, stars would have collided, near-misses would have detached planets from orbits round their suns and pulled them into interstellar space, where they would have cooled to hundreds of degrees below zero; and the universe would have been uninhabitable.

25 **Proton-electron charges** The equality of charges of protons and electrons (the + and – in a sum of zero, ie +A + –A = 0) is exactly right for human life. If an electron had had more of a charge than

a proton, objects would have repelled other objects. A 1 per cent difference between the charge of an electron and the charge of a proton would have ripped arms and legs off human and animal bodies. A difference of one part in 100 billion, 10^{14}, would have caused stones and people to fly about. If there had been an imbalance between the charges, every object in the universe would have exploded violently. Our sun has a perfect balance of charges of one part in a trillion, 10^{12}.

26 **Electron-neutron mass ratio** The mass of an electron is 1/1837th of the mass of a neutron. The difference, known as B, guarantees there are large chains of molecules of the right size and makes organisms possible. Any change in the B difference would have changed the size and length of the rings in the DNA double helix, which would then not have been able to replicate itself, making life impossible.

27 **Quantization** The functioning of quanta help to make Nature just right for life. The quantization principle proposed by Bohr in 1913 is essential for the existence and stability of atomic systems and restricts the energy of orbiting electrons to values which are multiples of a universal energy quantum fixed by Planck's constant. If an electron is added to a proton, there is only one orbital radius available to it in quantum theory. If this had not been the case, electrons would have been continuously buffeted by photons and there would have been no stable conditions in which life could evolve.

28 **Freedom of particles** At 10^{-35} seconds after the Big Bang, leptons and quarks were formed. At high energy, elementary particle interactions become asymptotically free. If this had not been the case, strong interaction times would have been too short to obey

gas laws and there would have been no more, nor fewer, than four neutrino species. The universe would have been burned to helium and would now have had no hydrogen, water or life.

29 **A neutron-proton mass differential** The neutron-proton mass differential is just right. The difference in mass between a proton and a neutron is about twice the mass of an electron. If it had been different, all neutrons would have been photons, and vice versa. A neutron outweighs a proton by a tenth of 1 per cent, and so protons are stable and neutrons decay. If a proton had outweighed a neutron, neutrons would have been stable and protons would have decayed, and hydrogen (whose atomic nucleus is a single proton) would not have existed, and so neither would water; and the sun, which is made of hydrogen, would have ceased to exist after 100 years as its protons would have decayed, and no atoms would have formed. No life could have taken place.

30 **Sunlight and chlorophyll** The sun-chlorophyll balance is just right for life. Chlorophyll, the molecule that accomplishes photosynthesis in plants, is programmed to absorb heated brilliant yellow light (photons) and so can absorb sunlight of the right temperature. If the Earth had had no sun nearby, there would have been no plants and therefore no animals. If the Earth had had a hotter star nearby, it would have received dangerous ultraviolet radiation. The sun-chlorophyll balance contributes to the order within Nature.

31 **Bonding elements** In biochemistry the essential elements that make up 1 per cent of all living organisms are oxygen, carbon, nitrogen, hydrogen, phosphorus and sulphur. These form multiple bonds, and nitrogen (which comprises nearly 80 per cent of the Earth's atmosphere) is essential for life as its compounds are the

building blocks of living organisms. Sulphur forms three types of molecules that create three classes of sulphur compounds and one class of phosphorus compounds that together form all known biological high-energy compounds and are just right for life. If phosphorus and sulphur had had stronger bonds, their chemical compounds could not have happened in the right way and the conditions for life would not have been right.

32 **Atmosphere** Earth's atmosphere is just right for life. Its gravity is strong enough to prevent it from evaporating into space as happens on the moon. It has water and a moon that was created from an asteroid's collision and pulls oceans and creates tides that assist evaporation into the atmosphere. It is not too hot like Venus's or too cold, too far from the sun or too near. The Earth is made of iron but volcanic eruptions release carbon dioxide, which regulates the Earth's temperature. The atmosphere is 21 per cent oxygen. If it had been 25 per cent, there would have been lightning-strike fires. Nitrogen gas in the atmosphere is replenished with hydrogen from the sun. The 80 per cent nitrogen in the atmosphere can be converted into ammonia and the building blocks of amino acids for the chemistry of life. The atmosphere's air is just right to allow life to form and survive.

33 **Water and rainfall** The Earth is the correct distance from the sun for liquid water to exist, and has just the right conditions to produce adequate rainfall. Water is lighter in its solid form of ice than in its liquid form: ice floats. If this had not been the case, the oceans would have frozen from the bottom up and the Earth would have been covered with ice. Moisture-laden air is blown to land from oceans, desalinated rain falls on ocean-facing hills and mountains, and as air moves on over the land it receives moisture and evaporation from plants, trees, lakes, rivers, soil, dew and

clouds of water vapour. Water prevents the climate from being too severe and has a role in photosynthesis, and is a source of oxygen in the atmosphere. The Earth has the right conditions to produce adequate rainfall in temperate zones and nurture life in all zones.

34 **Particles-antiparticles** There is a symmetry between the subatomic particles of matter and the subatomic particles of antimatter that was proposed by Dirac in 1928 and has since been confirmed in experiments. There are 10^{78} atoms in the matter of the observable universe and not as many antiatoms. If particles and antiparticles had existed in equal numbers shortly after the Big Bang, all protons and antiprotons would have been annihilated and the universe would have been full of radioactive and dark matter but there would have been no atoms, stars, galaxies or life. Some particles survived as they could not find an antiparticle to be annihilated with, and particles and antiparticles have decayed at different rates. There is a strong symmetry between positrons and electrons (see point 1, on the symmetry of matter and antimatter) and neutrinos and antineutrinos, which suggests an underlying order. The asymmetry allowed protons to survive and therefore the universe and life to form. Without the symmetry and asymmetry of particles and antiparticles the universe would have been atomless.

35 **Bosons** Bosons, virtual subatomic particles considered to carry physical forces, include gravitons (carriers of gravity), gluons, photons (which transmit the electromagnetic force) and vector bosons or weakons (W and Z particles). The Higgs boson transmits mass (see p 50). Bosons unite particles and forces. During the Big Bang there was perfect symmetry and all forces and particles were indistinguishable. When the symmetry between electromagnetic

and weak forces was broken, bosons ceased to be real particles and became virtual particles. Theory claims that each boson has a fermion partner, such as gravitinos, photinos and axions which may be particles of dark matter. Bosons emerge from the quantum vacuum, live a short time with another particle and return to the vacuum. Without the detailed order among the subatomic particles, which suggests the workings of several very small systems, the very large could not have existed.

36 **Cold dark matter** If cold dark matter (which hypothetically forms 23 per cent of the matter in the universe) exists, its ratio to baryons, 10:1 (see point 12), holds the universe together. Cold dark matter explains how galaxies are held together by a gravitational pull of between five and ten times more material than we see, but it only exists in mass and has not yet been detected. It could be present in cold clouds of interstellar dust, MACHOs (massive compact halo objects such as planets and black holes) and neutrino WIMPs (weakly interacting massive particles). It is 'cold', as the particles have speeds lower than the speed of light. A flat universe (in which expansion and gravitational pull are balanced, see point 11) expanded, produced cold dark matter that exceeded protons and neutrons by 10:1, guaranteed the right amount of energy to convert it into mass (in accordance with Einstein's $E = mc^2$, Energy = mass times the square of the velocity of light) and was still flat at the end, allowing life to form.

37 **Dark energy and zero vacuum** If dark energy exists, it creates the accelerated expansion that is a condition of the galaxies, stars and life. Like dark matter, dark energy is a hypothesis to explain powering of the acceleration in the universe's expansion (see point 6). It has been known as anti-gravity or λ, but also has vacuum energy thought to fill 73 per cent of the universe. Empty space is

full of particles – the emptiness is a fullness – but these particles speed expansion up owing to pressure on the vacuum rather than slowing it down. The present acceleration of expansion is 50-odd powers of 10 slower than the acceleration at the start of the universe but pushes with cosmic repulsion (as distinct from pulling with cosmic gravitational attraction) measured at 10^{119} stronger than if it did not exist. If it had been 10^{120}, the universe would have flown apart, no galaxies could have formed and there would have been no life. In classical times there were thought to be four elements – earth, air, fire and water – and the heavens were ruled by a fifth essence or quintessence, whose role this dark energy has assumed.

38 Glacials and climate Long-term cycles have helped to create conditions in which evolving life can take place. There are cycles of Ice Ages and glacials (warmer periods). There is a super-orbit every 413,000 years, and every 100,000 years a new orbiting cycle begins in which the Earth moves closer to and then farther from the sun, causing climate changes. Every 41,000 years the Earth's axis tilts between 21.5 and 24.5 degrees, and the extent of the tilt affects the amount of sunlight the Earth receives. Every 1,470 years there is a cycle linked to solar radiation. Long-term cycles of glacials control the Earth's climate and enable life to grow.

39 The speed of light Light is at the correct speed, 186,000 miles per second, for biological life to take place. At 10^{-43} seconds after the Big Bang the universe expanded by a factor of 10^{54} faster than the speed of light and so the observable universe is more than the 13.798 billion years (+ or – 0.037 billion light years) of its existence, and has a radius of about 46.6 billion light years (see 23). Light travels to the Earth in 8 minutes 20 seconds, and helps to create the warm conditions in which life can grow and survive.

40 **Constants and ratios** I have listed 326 fundamental physical constants and 75 ratios extracted from them.[13] All the laws of Nature have constants associated with them: the gravitational constant, the speed of light, the electrical charge, the mass of the electron, Planck's constant for quantum mechanics, the strong force coupling constant, the electromagnetic coupling constant. These can be grouped under four headings: universal; electromagnetic; atomic and nuclear; and physico-chemical. Eight cosmic densities that have the value of unity or 1 are: the density of the universe, the density of the galaxies, the galactic dark matter density, the density of stars within galaxies, the mean density of the sun, the typical density of planets, the typical density of life-forms and the density of a white dwarf. Outside this range human life would have been impossible. If the constant for gravity had been stronger – 10^{25} times less powerful than the strong nuclear force instead of 10^{38} times weaker – the universe would have been small and swift, stars would only have lived a year and no life would have developed. The entropy (disorder) per baryon in the universe, known as S, is 10^{9}. If S had been more than 10^{11}, galaxies would not have been able to form, planets and life would not have existed. All the constants and ratios are within a correct band that permits galaxies, stars and human life to form. These 326 constants and 75 ratios are evidence that the universe is controlled by the universal principle of order, an 'order principle'.

Each of these 40 conditions – and the 326 constants and 75 ratios – had to happen *in relation to each other* for life to take place. For all these conditions to be present in total is staggering. The probability or likelihood of all being a coincidence we shall consider shortly.

BIOLOGY AND GEOLOGY

If the origin of life and evolution is seen within the context of these 40 biofriendly conditions, life and evolution seem orderly rather than random. Just as the physical universe came out of one point, a singularity, and is fundamentally all one, so all biological species came out of one cell. The Earth began 4.6 or 4.55 billion years ago and the first cell emerged 3.8 billion years ago from what reductionists call a 'warm little pond' (Darwin, 1871) or a 'primordial soup' (Oparin, 1936).[14] Oparin suggested that life began in the sea and that organic molecules were created in an oxygenless atmosphere by sunlight. However, for this to happen amino acids have to become proteins, and one protein requires 10^{130} combinations of amino acids, the building blocks. Alternative hypotheses include Hoyle's extraterrestrial hypothesis, that primitive life formed in space or on a planet such as Mars or the satellites of Jupiter, or in the outer solar systems. Other hypothetical models propose how organic molecules could become photocells in silicate crystals in clay or in deep rocks.

To reductionists, chemical life began when carbon combined with five other atoms – hydrogen, oxygen, nitrogen, sulphur and phosphorus – and life is an electrical gradient or imbalance of charges across a membrane. There is no clear answer as to how, chemically, the first cell was produced. How cell division began is equally problematical. It takes 10^{15} cell divisions to proceed from one cell to a human being, and in each mitosis, when DNA is copied, there is a one-in-a-million (10^{-6}) chance of error. If a cell receives too many instructions it commits suicide. The four building blocks of DNA are A, P, G and C, and if P comes first there is a mutation and the two cells are different, and one cell will grow better than the other.

The first population of living things whose descendants have survived is known as LUCA (the Last Universal Common Ancestor), and can be dated to around 3.8 billion years ago. A huge number of cells have been created during the last 3.8 billion years. There have been somewhere between 90 and 110 billion humans, each of whom has had 10^{15} cells; and mammals, reptiles, birds, fish, insects, plants and bacteria have all had cells during the same period, so the number of cells there approaches infinity. Whereas atoms that came into existence with the Big Bang are still in existence, all cells except those in living humans, creatures and plants have died out. Humans are made of atoms of hydrogen (one-tenth of our weight) which came from the Big Bang and atoms of stardust – atoms of helium from the Big Bang and later stars, iron atoms carrying oxygen from exploding white dwarf stars, oxygen from exploding supernovas and carbon from planetary nebulas.

Reductionism identifies self-replication through DNA, but not a 'mechanism' by which self-replication through DNA leads from cell to organism. What science has missed is the 'mechanism' for a self-organizing, self-ordering principle that can take organic molecules to the first cell and then the first cell to the many species without being driven by blind, random accident.

Having originated, life has evolved despite – or perhaps because of – drifting continents (the result of plate tectonics) and harsh Ice Ages, which have provided extreme environments. Charles Darwin's theory of evolution explains the development of all species as they adapted to changing environments, and our development from unicellar jellies to humans with brains that attempt to understand the universe. An unpaid naturalist on board HMS *Beagle* at a time when the Earth was thought to be only 100 million years old, Darwin studied the *flora* and *fauna* of South America and the Galapagos Islands (the oldest of which is only 4–5 million years old, and the youngest 120,000 years old), where he took specimens. These were analysed back in England, and there were 14 separate species of finch and 4 of mockingbirds. There were 14 subspecies of giant tortoise and different species of lizard.

What Darwin heard set him thinking, and in 1837 he grasped the principle of natural selection (first proposed in Baghdad a thousand years previously by Abu Uthman al-Jahith), which was based on the evidence of adaptive radiation among the birds in the Galapagos Islands: one scion of an ancestor or ancestral group, such as a seed-eating finch, had to survive on a different food, and in adapting to eating insects (warbler finch) or *opuntia* blossoms which are bountiful in the Galapagos Islands (cactus finch), their beaks adapted to gathering these different foods. Having wanted to become close to God by studying His creation, Darwin realized that Creation did not need the idea of God as species evolved in a process that was still continuing. He presented his view of evolution in *The Origin of the Species* (1859). And long before neo-Darwinism restated evolution by natural selection in terms of Mendelian or post-Mendelian genetics and DNA, Darwin came to the conclusion that *Homo sapiens sapiens* had evolved from apes.

I have set out the 22 intermediate extinct species between apes and man (*Homo sapiens sapiens* being the 23rd).[15] The apes go back to 20–10 million years ago, and the intermediates go back to 4.2 million years ago. Our species (*Homo sapiens sapiens*) surfaced between 100,000 and 50,000 years ago in Africa and spread worldwide. There are two competing theories as to how modern humans spread across the globe: a multi-regional view that sees humans appearing from *Homo erectus* (who left Africa 2 million years ago) simultaneously in Africa, Europe and Asia; the other that they appeared from *Homo ergaster* (who lived in Africa between 1.9 and 1.4 million years ago) and spread out into the world from Africa.

Modern humans have 98.4 per cent of genes in common with chimpanzees, and the discovery of DNA, the invisible genetic code, has confirmed that all humankind within *Homo sapiens sapiens* is interrelated. All living humans' female-line ancestry can be traced back to a single female (mitochondrial Eve) living around 140,000–160,000 years ago, and all living male-line ancestry can be traced back to a single male (Y-chromosomal Adam) living around 60,000–70,000 years ago. Human DNA is thought to go back to around 74,000 years ago at the earliest: no human DNA has been discovered before then. We have just seen that *Homo sapiens sapiens* surfaced no earlier than 100,000 years ago, and the lack of evidence of human DNA earlier than 74,000 years ago is broadly consistent with the age of our species. The world's oldest DNA belonged to 419-million-year-old salt-loving bacteria found in the Michigan Basin, USA, in December 2009. A study by Bryan Sykes[16] locates 36 verifiable clans after this time, of which only seven are in Europe, so all Europeans can trace themselves back to seven women. (The Sykes technique traced my maternal line back 10,000 years and my paternal line 40,000 years.)

As all *Homo sapiens sapiens* can be traced back to one clan father and one clan mother, DNA research dramatically reveals the fundamental oneness of the modern *Homo sapiens sapiens* species of humankind. All biological creation is ultimately one and interconnected via measurable DNA, and all species of human and animal came out of one cell. Science's use of DNA reveals the fundamental interconnectedness between every living thing and reinforces Universalism's view of the fundamental oneness of humankind, and of the order of the universe that evolved all creation including all human species out of one cell.

And so doubts have been cast on Darwin's account of the theory of evolution as evolving by random accident. Darwin's theory requires complex structures to work immediately if they are to be preserved – how are such structures built up without being extinguished? Some species of hydra protect themselves with poisonous 'guns' that fire a poisoned hair, and a flatworm occasionally swallows the guns without digesting them and places them on its own body. Such a sense of purpose, intelligence and co-ordinated behaviour even in the lowest forms of life seem contrary to Darwin's theory that chance, random natural selection and instinct account for all creatures' behaviour.

There are ten doubts about Darwinism:[17]

- Species that evolve the least last longest.
- Antibiotic resistance comes from an orderly, organizing 'mechanism' within an organism when evolution and natural selection are supposed to be chance, random, blind.
- Co-operation is important in evolution, contrary to Darwin's survival of the fittest.
- Nature has patterns that exceed chance – for example, marsupial mammals occupy the same or similar niches as eutherian mammals.
- New species appear without a long succession of ancestors, whereas Darwinism requires gradual changes from one species to another.
- Some creatures (such as cockroaches and coelacanths) survive without evolving.
- A bird's lung, a rock lobster's eye and a flagellum of bacteria are too complex to be produced by chance.
- There is little evidence for large changes as a result of natural selection.
- There is not enough time for random evolution as it is continually impeded by natural selection.
- There is no universally accepted descent from apes to humans, and although there are 22 intermediate extinct species, the descent is subject to academic disputes.

Darwinism is an imperfect but unbettered description of a process, but its view that we are alive because of accidental combinations of atoms into a cell is questionable. The perspective of order is missing. Reductionism reduces from the very complex to the very simple, from the whole to the parts. Expansionism expands from the individual cells, structures, organisms and species to seeing humans as products of the whole. It integrates and puts back together what has been broken off. Coleridge wrote of the 'esemplastic power of the imagination'. 'Esemplastic' comes from the Greek *eis en plattein*, 'to make into One'. Universalist thinking restores order and purpose to what seems to be random. When I visited the Darwin Research Station on Santa Cruz on 27 July 2007,[18] I put it to the botanist I spoke to that a 'self-organizing' principle in the genes, which contain 'a plan for growth, a blueprint for a human-to-be, mammal-to-be, reptile-to-be, plant-to-be, organizes adaptations and varieties, and transmutations are conveyed to their successors, even a new species'. To me, the secret of evolution was a self-organizing purposive drive for self-improvement and self-betterment in accordance with an order principle.

ECOLOGY

Ecology is 'the branch of biology dealing with the relations of organisms to one another and to their physical surroundings' (*Concise Oxford Dictionary*). It is the study of interactions among organisms and between organisms and their environment.

Ecology grew out of the work of European and American botanists who studied plant communities from different angles during the 20th century. American biologists came to see the plant and animal communities as a biotic whole, and the unifying concept of ecology has been the ecosystem, which consists of all interacting organisms and all aspects of the environment in a specific area. In an ecosystem, plants and animals are brought together. Ecology has come to describe a vast global ecosystem comprising local sub-ecosystems and featuring biology, botany, entomology, population studies and conservation, but I want to take a narrower view and focus on the order in ecosystems as befits a reflection on world culture, the seven disciplines and the role of order in reunifying world citizens.

Ecology presents Nature's self-running, self-organizing system whose order is evidenced in food chains, food webs, co-operation in symbiosis and co-operation in plants that have properties that heal humans. The vast ecosystem of interactive living, which in the 16th century was thought of as 'the great chain of being', teems with examples of an order principle which seems anything but random or accidental.

There have been several estimates as to how many species exist on Earth. According to one view, there are 2 million species on land. Another view holds that there may be between 2 million and 30 million species of animals and plants. The World Conservation Union estimates that there are between 10 and 100 million species in the sea, and certainly 15 million. Two billion species may have evolved and become extinct during the last 540 million years.[19]

The behaviour patterns and instincts of all species are ordered from the moment of their birth. All species are born with instinctive knowledge of how they should operate. New-born turtles hatched in sand know to wait until dark before emerging to head for the sea so they are not attacked by frigate birds. The inheritance of acquired characteristics advocated by Lamarck c1800 – that giraffes, for example, stretched their necks to eat higher leaves and passed on longer necks to their offspring – was scoffed at: sportsmen cannot pass on their prowess, and Einstein's children did not become geniuses. To a Universalist, the universal principle of order through DNA transmits innate tendencies or instinctive behaviour so they can integrate into their limited ecosystem. So a cactus finch is driven by the principle of order's 'mechanism' within DNA to look for and eat the fruit of the cactus. Robins are born with the instinct to pull worms from the soil in which grass grows. There seems to be a 'mechanism' that thrusts evolution forward to self-improvement and self-betterment.

Many limited ecosystems make up one gigantic, whole ecosystem, within which there is a predisposition to order. We are familiar with conditioned reflexes. The sense of direction of migrating birds, and many creatures' sense of smell and hearing, can be seen as conditioned reflexes or as inherited characteristics, but they can just as easily be seen as the workings of an innate order principle inherited in DNA.

The principle of order can be detected in: the hatching of turtles; the mating rituals of sticklebacks that lead to the laying of eggs in a nest; the innate birdsong of, for example, yellowhammers and cuckoos; the herring-gull's chick's innate pecking at the red spot on the adult's bill; and the return of penguins, seals and salmon to the breeding ground where they were born.

The principle of order can also be found in the food chains which form part of wider food webs. Every creature eats or is eaten in such proportions that by and large the balance of every species' population in relation to other species is preserved in a harmonious way, so there is ample food to go round. Plants convert solar energy to food by photosynthesis. There are four principal ecosystems, featuring ponds, woodlands, lakes and oceans, in each of which there are herbivores (which eat plants), carnivores (which eat animals), insectivores (which eat insects – there are 10^{18} insects on Earth), decomposers (which eat the surface of mud) and detritivores (which eat detritus below the mud). In each there are food chains: plant-fish-bird; tree-insect-bird; algae-fish-bird; and plankton-fish-bird.

I have set out details of food chains and food webs elsewhere.[20] Below, as an example, is the food chain in and around a pond ecosystem:

> Green plants are eaten by fish, which are eaten by herons. Plants are eaten by water snails and water fleas, which are eaten by carnivores such as sticklebacks or omnivores such as caddis-fly larvae that eat both plants and smaller animals. Sticklebacks are eaten by herons. Earthworms, detritivores, feed on dead leaves and the waste matter of animals. Decomposers such as bacteria and fungi eat and accelerate the decay and dispersal of dead organic matter, which is eaten by detritivores such as small fish.

Food chains are linked to form a more complex food web, in which a 'biomass' of organisms is present. This is found at every stage of the food chain. Food webs have a more complex biomass of food because most organisms eat more than one type of plant or animal: they do not eat the same food every meal. Below, as an example, is the more complex food web of ponds and wetlands showing that dragonfly larvae (for example) eat different kinds of food:

> Microscopic plants are eaten by daphnia/water fleas, which are eaten by sticklebacks, dragonfly larvae and great diving beetle larvae, which are eaten by kingfishers, which are eaten by sparrowhawks. Canadian pondweed is eaten by mayfly larvae, which are also eaten by sticklebacks, dragonfly larvae and great diving beetle larvae. Detritus is eaten by common pond snails which are eaten by dragonfly larvae and by lesser water-boatmen, which are eaten by greater water-boatmen, dragonfly larvae and great diving beetle larvae. Also, algae produced through the sun's energy by photosynthesis are eaten by mosquito larvae, which are eaten by dragonfly larvae, which are eaten by perch, which are eaten by man.

The complexity of food webs, of what creatures eat and which creatures are themselves eaten, displays a stunning degree of order. The natural populations are kept stable to preserve an equilibrium. Population densities are controlled by predators and food limitation. In the eating habits which all creatures instinctively know and in their food chains and food webs can be detected a self-running, self-organizing, self-perpetuating system of amazing complexity. This system works in a co-operative way as well as a competitive way. Elsewhere I have set out examples of this co-operative behaviour in all four ecosystems.[21] They maintain the Whole's checks and balances. The place in the ecosystem occupied by organisms feeding on each other and competing for food is called a niche, and below, as an example, is the co-operative behaviour in the ecosystem of woodlands:

> Birds share trees. Nuthatches crawl *down* trees and eat insects in the crevices at the top of segments of bark. Treecreepers crawl *up* trees and eat insects in the crevices at the bottom of segments on bark. They occupy different niches and so there is enough food to go round. The great spotted woodpecker's beak enables it to peck for grubs on the larger parts of trees whereas the lesser spotted woodpecker's beak enables it to peck for grubs on the smaller parts of trees. They occupy different niches (in the UK) and so there is enough food for all. Jackdaws and rooks both feed in ploughed fields, but rooks' beaks enable them to feed well below the surface, whereas jackdaws' beaks enable them to feed close to the surface. They occupy different niches and there is enough food for all.

Organisms assist each other, often against predators, in a form of co-operation called symbiosis. This takes three forms:

First, in mutualism, two organisms live in association that benefits both, and make common cause. I have provided 70 examples.[22] Below are a few:

- Humans feed pet dogs which warn of danger and are also useful for hunting. Benefits: warning/food, companionship.
- Lava lizards perch on Galapagos sea lions and catch and eat flies which are attracted to sea lions' skin. Benefits: food/cleaning.
- Common noddies perch on the heads of brown pelicans after they have dived and surfaced, and pick bits of fish from their bills, thus keeping them clean. Benefits: food/cleaning.
- Butterflies gather nectar from flowers and pollinate them by

transferring pollen from their stamens to their stigma. Benefits: food/pollination.

- Honey bees gather nectar from flowers and turn it into honey, and the flowers are pollinated and fertilized when the stamens, stigma and hair brush the underside of bees. Benefits: food/pollination, fertilization.
- Wrasse clean bass of parasites, which they eat as food. Benefits: food/cleaning.
- Pompeii worms, deep-sea polychaetes, reside in tubes near hydrothermal vents and survive their scalding temperatures by 'wearing' 'fleece-like' thermophilic bacteria on their backs as protection. The bacteria, which thrive at temperatures above 45°C, gain a home and feeding opportunities from the worms' mobility. Benefits: protection/shelter, mobility.
- Glow-worms hold bioluminescent bacteria inside them and provide them with a safe place to live and a source of food. In return they use the light produced by the bacteria for camouflage, as an aid in hunting, to attract food and to attract mates. Benefits: protection, food/shelter, reproduction.

Secondly, parasitism is an association in which an organism lives on or in another organism, its host, for most of its life. I have provided 40 examples.[23] Below are a few:

- Cuckoos invade nests of small nesting birds and lay eggs that mimic the colouring of the host bird's eggs, and cuckoo chicks push all other chicks out of the nest. Benefits: shelter, food.
- Tapeworms living in the bowel of humans (and pigs) attack the lining of their stomachs, eat bacteria and absorb nutrients, causing humans to be thin and ill and scratch the irritation. Benefit: food.
- Mistletoe embeds in the cambium of spruce, poplar trees, apple trees, willows, lindens, hawthorns and oaks, taking nourishment

from them. Benefit: food.

- *Phytophera infestans* mould, potato blight, affects whole crops of potatoes and caused the potato famine in Ireland, which killed over a third of its population. Benefit: food.

Thirdly, commensalism is an association between two species in which one organism derives benefits: the commensal, which is usually the smaller. I have provided 25 examples.[24] Below are a few:

- Scavengers such as hyenas wait for a lion to kill and they eat part of what the lion leaves. Benefit: food.
- Crabs open clams and molluscs for fish to feed on. Benefit: food.
- Bee orchids mimic the shape of a female bee, deceiving male bees into copulating with them and transferring pollen, but receiving no nectar. Benefit: pollination.
- The Saguaro cactus's primary pollinator is the Gila woodpecker. Benefit: pollination.
- Algae attach themselves to turtles whose movement brings them to warm currents and to food. Benefit: food.

Another aspect of the self-running, self-organizing, self-perpetuating system is the way Nature grows cures for ailments, illnesses and diseases. There is a biofriendly connection between humans and plants, and medieval monks knew (and modern homeopaths know) that the universe is biofriendly. I have provided 70 examples.[25] Below is a selection, with the illness in bold followed by the plants that cure it:

- **Arthritis**: angelica, ash, ashwagandha, bay, bean, belladonna, cayenne pepper, feverfew, pine, prickly ash, rhubarb, sassafras, skullcap, turmeric, wormwood, yarrow, yucca
- **Bronchitis**: aconite, adder's tongue, agrimony, baby's breath,

bay, black haw, camphor, castor bean, Chinese cucumber, coffee, coltsfoot, dandelion, elderberry, elecampane, eucalyptus, frankincense, ginger, marjoram, mountain mahogany, osha, pau d'arco, pine, thyme, yellow dock

- **Cancer**: ashwagandha, astragalus, beetroot, birch, bloodroot, chaparral, cinnamon, coffee, comfrey, dill, echinacea, evening primrose, flaxseed, fungus, garlic, magnolia, mountain mahogany, parsley, pau d'arco, pokeroot, poplar, red clover, rhubarb, St John's wort, suma, tea, turmeric, wheat grass, wild Mexican yam, yucca
- **Diabetes**: alfalfa, atractylis, bean, bilberry, cactus, cayenne pepper, dandelion, garlic, goldenseal, guar gum, pine, psyllium, turmeric
- **Headache**: asafoetida, basil, brooklime, bupleurum, cayenne pepper, chamomile, chrysanthemum, cinchona, coca, ginger, lavender, mint, mistletoe, morning glory, sagebrush, spruce, thyme, watercress, wintergreen, wood betony
- **Inflammation**: ashwagandha, beech, bird-of-paradise, borage, box elder, calendula, castor bean, Chinese cucumber, coltsfoot, evening primrose, lobelia, prickly ash, skullcap, snapdragon, tea, turmeric, wild Mexican yam, wormwood, yarrow
- **Obesity**: cayenne pepper, celery, chickweed, citrin, guar gum, kelp, mahuang, psyllium, stinging nettle, wild Mexican yam, yohimbine.
- **Sinusitis**: camphor, eyebright, goldenseal, horehound, horseradish, pine, walnut, watercress, yellow dock
- **Skin ailments**: agrimony, birch, calendula, castor bean, chamomile, club moss, coffee, elderberry, garlic, henna, horseradish, horsetail, jewelweed, marshmallow, mullein oak, pennyroyal, pokeroot, poplar, purslane, roses, rosemary, thyme, turmeric
- **Varicose veins**: bay, bayberry, calendula, gotu kola, oak, pine, zedoary

It is as if every ailment a human 'ex-ape' suffers from is taken care of by a plant. In the past, the remedies were widely known. There was no pharmacy to go to, those unwell went to a meadow and picked their remedy, as I used to find a dock leaf to rub on a stinging nettle rash when I was a boy.

The vast ecosystem which includes all local ecosystems, the eco-whole and its food chains and food webs of which we are a part, its symbiotic relationships (mutualism, parasitism, commensalism) and the interacting between plants and humans who benefit from the healing properties of plants – all provide countless instances of unrandom, seemingly biofriendly order in Nature. If these instances exemplify complex order rather than randomness, could they really have begun in a random way?

PHYSIOLOGY

The order principle in the whole ecosystem of Nature is paralleled in the physiological make-up of each species within it. There is an amazing self-organization and self-regulation in each of the species of the 'great chain of being'. There is no space to consider self-organization and self-regulation in minerals, vegetables, insects, reptiles, birds and mammals. We need to focus on self-organization and self-regulation – and the order principle – in the body, brain and consciousness of humans.

Physiology is 'the science of the functions of living organisms and their parts' (*Concise Oxford Dictionary*), and there are a number of 'mechanisms' (a reductionist word whose mechanistic implications Universalists do not accept, hence the inverted commas) in living organisms that indicate self-organizing systems, a complex degree of order that cannot have been produced by random chance.

The human body's complexity can be judged from the number of its parts: there are 10^{360} possible combinations of DNA strands; 10^{23} bits of information in a human being; 10^{29} particles and 7×10^{27} atoms in the human body; 10^{15} cells in each human body; 10^{12} bacteria on the surface of each human body and 10^{15} bacteria inside it.[26]

The main 'mechanism' that keeps organisms functioning within Nature's ecosystem is *homeostasis* (Greek for 'staying similar'), which implements the body's self-organization and self-regulation. Homeostasis controls seven layers of bodily organization, a system in which each layer controls the layer below it. It combines chemicals into organelles, organelles into cells, cells into tissue, tissue into organs (for example, a heart), organs into systems (for example, a cardiovascular system) and systems into organisms (for example, a human being).[27] Organisms control all the lower layers and interact with the population in the local community, habitat, ecosystem and biosphere.

Homeostasis controls body temperature, blood sugar level, oxygen and carbon dioxide concentrations in blood, water retention and blood pressure. Sweating, urine formation, heart rate and bleeding rate vary but are regulated to maintain the variables at nearly constant. The body's self-regulating system eliminates any deviations from the normal (for example, in body temperature or blood pressure) by negative feedback, which responds to and eliminates any deviation through a skeletal muscle. Elsewhere I have provided 62 examples of homeostasis covering each human organ system.[28] Below are a few examples, one from each of the body's 12 systems:

- In temperature or blood loss, a fall in body temperature stimulates the thermoreceptors in the skin and the hypothalamus. Nerve impulses to the preoptic area of the brain and to the pituitary gland cause nerve impulses to be sent to the blood vessels in the skin and muscles and the release of thyroid-stimulating hormone (TSH). TSH causes the thyroid to release thyroid hormones which increase the metabolic rate, thus creating heat. The skin's blood vessels constrict to save heat, while muscles shiver to generate heat.
- In the embryological system, the human growth hormone stimulates the liver, which then produces more insulin-like growth

to increase cell division in the embryo's growing bones.

- In the pregnancy, birth and post-natal system, release of the hormone relaxin by the placenta stimulates and softens the mother's ligaments, allowing her pelvis to expand during childbirth.
- In the immunological system, a hostile reaction of one of the organism's cells stimulates an immature, developing T cell (an immune-system killer cell). This then undergoes apoptosis, which is programmed self-destruction. Thus, T cells that seek to attack host cells never mature into active killer T cells.
- In the neurological system, the sudden stretching of a muscle stimulates a muscle spindle receptor, which sends a nervous impulse to the spinal cord. This sends a motor impulse to the stretched muscle, which contracts rapidly, preventing damage by overstretching.
- In the haematological system, the release of thromboplastin in response to mechanical cell damage (such as a breach of the skin) stimulates clotting in the blood. Platelet aggregation at the site of the injury creates a platelet plug, or clot, to stem the loss of blood.
- In the cardiovascular system, baroreceptors in the carotid artery in the neck detect reduced blood pressure and stimulate the cardiovascular centre in the brainstem. This sends nerve impulses to increase the heart rate and the force of heart contractions, and to constrict arteries, thereby increasing blood pressure.
- In the respiratory system, chemoreceptors in the brainstem and arteries detect increased carbon dioxide and/or reduced oxygen in the bloodstream due to sudden increase in physical activity. They stimulate the inspiratory centre in the brainstem, which as a result sends nerve impulses to the diaphragm to contract more frequently and more forcibly, thus increasing the breathing rate and the exchange of carbon dioxide for oxygen.
- In the gastro-intestinal system, chemoreceptors in the stomach wall detect an altered Ph (Potential of Hydrogen, a measure of acidity or

alkalinity in a solution) of stomach contents due to food entering the stomach. They stimulate the submucosal nerve plexus in the muscle of the stomach wall, which as a result sends nerve impulses to the parietal cells in the stomach lining to secrete hydrochloric acid to break down the stomach contents for easier absorption.

- In the renal system, stretching of the blood vessels in the kidneys due to increased blood pressure as a result of stress or exertion stimulates the muscle fibres in the kidney blood vessel walls. As a result they contract, reducing the blood flow through kidneys to 'normal', thus maintaining the normal blood filtration rate.
- In the endocrine system, low blood levels of thyroid hormones (which maintain the metabolic rate) stimulate the hypothalamus which as a result releases thyroid-releasing hormone (TRH). This causes the pituitary gland to release thyroid-stimulating hormone (TSH). This in turn causes the thyroid gland to produce more thyroid hormones, which in turn increase the metabolic rate.
- In the reproductive system, the release of oocytes (which produce oestrogen) by ovaries causes a drop in blood-oestrogen, which stimulates the hypothalamus. This releases more gonadotrophin-releasing hormone (GnRH). GnRH causes the pituitary gland to release more follicle-stimulating hormone. This causes follicles in ovaries to develop into oocytes, which in turn produce oestrogen, the level of which then returns to 'normal'.

Each human body has 6 million strands of DNA and 23 pairs of chromosomes. The complex interchange between male and female versions of each chromosome that produce a unique new chromosome during DNA replication has been deemed 'random' in standard textbooks, but when the process is more fully understood it may turn out to be orderly.

Further evidence for an order principle controlling self-regulation can be found in the homeostasis of the brain. The complexity of the brain can be judged from the fact that it has 10^{11} (100 billion) neurons, perhaps even 10^{12} (1 trillion) neurons, and as many non-excitable neuroglial cells. The brain uses 3×10^{14} combinations of cells and can undertake 10^{27} operations per second. There are different levels of brain function, some autonomic or automatic, others more 'conscious' and associated with thought. The lower, more autonomous brain functions involve the brain's self-regulatory homeostasis, whose 'mechanisms' control: the organization of the central nervous system; the brain's self-regulation of its own health; the link between memory and emotion; the brain's control over the immune system; and the effects of cognition and mood on health and disease.

Like the body, the brain controls seven levels of organization: chemicals combine to form organelles; organelles combine to form neurons; neurons combine to form neuron circuits; neuron circuits combine to form structures (such as the hypothalamus); structures combine to form functions (such as memory, emotion, cognition); and functions combine to form the brain, which is head of its own system and interacts with the population of the local community, country, region and humankind.

The brain is a network of multi-functional areas. It regulates its own environment and health; stores information (facts, memories); transfers function from damaged areas to other areas; codes emotion (particularly fear) into some memories; and influences the immune system and our health. The human brain regulates its own homeostasis and environment via the feedback 'mechanism' of 'the blood/brain barrier', which maintains adequate blood flow to the brain and regulates brain temperature. Neural events form in the brain in response to experience owing to its 'plasticity', which helps it adapt to injury. If a brain suffers injury, its multi-functional nature can often bypass the area damaged. Elsewhere I have provided 15 examples of the brain's homeostasis.[29] Below are a few examples, one from each of the brain's seven systems:

- In the blood-brain barrier, the filtration of the blood to form cerebrospinal fluid (CSF) prevents large molecules, including infectious organisms such as bacteria and viruses, from entering the brain. They are too large to pass through the choroid plexi. As brain infections are very often quickly fatal, this 'mechanism' is clearly conducive to the survival of the organism. This is fortunate, as antibiotics are also too large to pass into the brain through the blood/brain barrier.
- In blood flow, the baroreceptors in the carotid arteries in the neck detect reduced blood pressure, which means there is reduced blood flow to the brain, and stimulate the cardiovascular centre in the brainstem. This sends nerve impulses to increase the heart rate and the force of contractions, thereby increasing blood pressure and thus the blood flow to the brain.
- In the brain's temperature system, a rise in blood temperature, possibly due to a fever from infection, stimulates thermoreceptors in the hypothalamus. As a result the sympathetic nervous system (SNS) causes surface blood vessels to expand, thus filling with blood and transferring heat to the skin from where it is lost.
- In the neural circuits, the frequent reactivation of a neural circuit leads to its becoming strengthened and thus more easily 'fired' in future so that we learn that things that happen frequently are 'normal', and thus become able to recognize normal events. This is the basis of learning and experience.
- In memory, a memory of an emotionally charged event is connected through an area of the brain called the amygdala. This creates particularly strong neural pathways, or memories, that cause the original emotion to be experienced when the memory is 'fired' so that an individual feels the emotion associated with the event that imprinted the original memory every time the memory is recalled. This is a survival 'mechanism', as the associations are strongest when fear is the 'imprinting' emotion. (Counsellors

claim this is why, for example, revisiting a location associated with a past trauma can often cause such strong emotional responses, as the emotions imprinted into the memory are so vivid.)

- In brain damage, if an area of the brain that has an important role in a particular function (for example, memory) is damaged (for example, as a result of a stroke or head trauma), an unrelated area takes over some of the lost function, so that the function is not totally lost.
- In stress response, sudden stress or fright stimulates the hypothalamus, which sends a nerve impulse to the adrenal glands on the kidneys. They release stored adrenalin into the bloodstream, which increases the force and rate of heart contractions, releases glucose into muscle cells, raises alertness, diverts blood from the digestive system to the skeletal muscles and dilates the airways, all of which prepare the body for sudden and extreme exertion such as 'fight or flight'.

Photons bombard human retinas and light energy is continuously being converted to chemical energy in the brain and body. Light energy may make homeostasis possible. To put it the other way round, homeostasis may be dependent on the light energy supplied by photons. Photons carry information – and are used to do so in the new science of photonics[30] – and it is possible that light brings information regarding the order principle continuously to our eyes, which the brain absorbs and applies to its self-regulating homeostasis. Each retina has 200 million neurons and 120 million rod photoreceptors (for low-light vision) and 6 million cone photoreceptors. Photoreceptors lie at the back of our eyeballs. The surface layer of the retina contains 20 types of ganglion cells (which are in front of the photoreceptors), impulses from which travel to the brain along 1 million optic nerve fibres. Through the 'mechanism' involving retinas, photons collapse into the retina and are then processed as information. The information transfer from photons to the retinas depends on electrical connections of cells, and human blood is full of biophotons which have been received as photons in the retinas of the eyes.

I submit that the order principle controls the homeostasis of the human brain and body by a persistent flow of photons which pass through the retinas to the human brain and thence to the body's blood as biophotons, which bear instructions that direct the functioning of body and brain: the 62 examples of bodily homeostasis and 15 examples of the homeostasis of the brain. If so, then Newton was right when he saw light as 'convertible' into 'gross bodies' and as combined with spirit and ether (see p49).

Consciousness is 'a state of perceptual awareness' (*Concise Oxford Dictionary*). It is also self-regulating in its lower autonomic and higher, more thoughtful activities. Besides being awareness of the outer world, consciousness is also an awareness of self and of being aware.

The history of the study of consciousness presents a confusing picture. Descartes' dualism, like John Donne's in his poem 'The Exstasie', located consciousness between the eye and the object beheld, outside the body.[31] Materialist, reductionist brain physiologists have seen consciousness as brain function and have looked for it in the brainwaves on an EEG (electroencephalograph). They assert that consciousness can be reduced to physics and chemistry. Francis Crick, who cracked the double-helix genetic code, put consciousness in the claustrum (a thin layer of grey matter in each cerebral hemisphere) in a paper he was correcting on the day he died. The search for the seat of consciousness has been a long one. Although there is a clear link between the higher functions of consciousness and the brain, despite decades of research on EEGs there is still no obvious causal connection between experience and the molecules, neurons and neural circuits of the brain.

There are 12 levels of consciousness if we include unconscious levels, and I set them out in full elsewhere.[32] They are, in ascending order of intensity:

1 **Sleep** – unconsciousness
2 **Dream** – dreaming while asleep
3 **Drowsiness** – being half-awake when ideas can be received from the unconscious immediately after sleep, or being in readiness for sleep, or being in drunken or drugged consciousness
4 **Waking sleep** – the robotic ordinary state of everyday automatic working consciousness, everyday passive social consciousness, reacting to external events (a primarily physical state controlled by the sense experience of the rational, social ego or temporal self)
5 **Awakening consciousness** – more alert everyday consciousness, self-assertion, more considered choices, awareness of the world, noticing every detail of what one observes, alertness (a more psychological state of awareness and observation)
6 **Self-consciousness** – awareness of being aware, awareness of the rational, social ego that is doing the seeing, looking out from a centre that is not the ego (a meditative, reflective state drawing on memory in a 'wise passiveness')
7 **Objective consciousness** – selflessness, losing oneself in concentration, thinking, active working on paper or computer, everyday active social consciousness (an intense soul state)
8 **Higher (or deeper) rational consciousness** – detachment from senses, thinking very deeply, reflecting, discussing issues, debating (a contemplative state)
9 **Higher (or deeper) intuitional and imaginative consciousness** – detachment from senses, feeling very deeply, being immersed in a creative artistic project (an inspirational-imaginative, visionary state)
10 **Superconscious or subconscious monitoring** – an ordering,

organizing functioning that overnight finds and then identifies things left undone (a superconscious or subconscious editing state)

11 **Transpersonal consciousness** – psychic and paranormal consciousness (telepathy, precognition, prophecy, healing), awareness of memories from the womb, past lives or another world seen in the near-death experience, mediumistic contact with departed spirits, rare glimpses seen through the centre known as the spirit which traditions claim has lived before (a spiritual state)

12 **Universal or cosmic (or unity) consciousness** – awareness of oneness with the universe and the infinite when time and space cease to exist, the mystic oneness that is perceived through the centre known as universal being and is often accompanied by a feeling of ecstasy, contemplative experience of the metaphysical Light (a mystical, contemplative state approaching the One Reality, traditionally known as the divine, the highest spiritual state and the highest known state of consciousness)

In the above list numbers 8 and 9 could arguably be reversed, elevating philosophy and science above intuition and imagination. Like the whole organism and brain, the whole consciousness interacts with society: the state, country, region and globe. Those who spend their lives in level 4 will drift passively, and those who spend their lives in levels 5–12 will have drive and purpose.

Science has no answer as to whether consciousness is an effect of the brain like homeostasis, or whether it controls the brain and homeostasis with the aid of photons just as homeostasis controls the body and lower brain and makes the homeostasis possible. Crick never proved his 'astonishing hypothesis' (the title of his book), that mind is merely brain function, and this is still an unproved hypothesis.

So we are left with the order principle in the universe and the order principle in the body, brain and human consciousness, and the possibility that photons bear information and instructions that give order, a 'mechanism' which enables all creatures to be self-organizing and self-regulatory through homeostasis. All bodies, brains and consciousnesses began first in one point, the singularity that began the universe with the Big Bang, and then in the first cell; and ever since they evolved via the ape, human retinas have been open to photons and perhaps to the order they bear; and it seems that while levels 1–4 of consciousness may be autonomic and automatic, higher consciousness at the very least can control the lower brain and body in levels 5–12 – as we have all experienced in moments when we affirm 'mind over matter' – and can live in harmony with the ordered universe.

PROBABILITY OF ORDER

We have been examining what science has to say about order. We have seen from cosmology and astrophysics that the universe came out of a singularity and whooshed into an expansion that has increased its acceleration for the last 5 billion years and obeys orderly rather than haphazard laws. We have seen from physics how the universe emerged from the infinite Void or quantum vacuum and that expanding light can counterbalance gravity in an ordered rather than random way. We have seen from biocosmology that there are 40 conditions which make the existing universe just right for life and that if any one of the 40 had been slightly different, then life would not have happened, suggesting a high degree of order. We have seen from biology and geology that creatures have innate, instinctive behaviour and that evolution may be an ordered drive for self-improvement rather than a random accident. We have seen from ecology that Nature's system is self-running and self-organizing and is orderly in food chains, food webs, symbiosis and healing plants. And we have seen from physiology that a self-regulating homeostasis of body and brain, and the 12 layers of consciousness, all seem orderly rather than random.

We can now return to the 40 biofriendly conditions, 326 constants and 75 ratios, and consider the probability or likelihood that all these are exactly right for life. The 'universal probability bound' (or threshold) below which chance could definitely be precluded or eliminated varies from 10^{94} to 10^{150}, but 10^{120} has been taken as the best indication as this represents the maximum number of bit-operations the universe could have performed in its entire history.[33] It has been calculated that the likelihood of constructing one short protein molecule of 100 amino acids in length is one chance in 10^{130}, and a protein of 150 amino acids in length, 10^{180}.[34]

The probability of all these 40 contextual conditions happening by chance and accident can therefore be taken as 10^{120} (10 with 120 zeros), even though just to construct a protein of 150 amino acids in length is 10^{180} and we are talking about 40 far more complex conditions, 326 constants and 75 ratios all happening together and all the intricate, orderly organization and self-organization we have observed in cosmology and astrophysics, physics, biocosmology, biology and geology, ecology and physiology, in all the sciences, which common sense dictates make the 'probability bound' immeasurably more. Even so, the probability total of 10^{120} is one and a half times the total number of atoms in the observable universe (10^{80}). After considering all the 40 conditions, the 326 constants and 75 ratios and downgrading the probability to less than that of constructing one protein of 150 amino acids in length, it is impossible to believe that the universe is a chance, random accident that happened to explode into all these fine-tuned parameters and ratios in a haphazard way.

At the same time, we must acknowledge that Materialist reductionists who assert the primacy of matter have founded their belief on 4 per cent of the stuff of the universe. For 73 per cent is dark energy and 23 per cent dark matter, and 96 per cent of the matter in the universe is missing, as we have seen. It is better to found a belief about the universe on 100 per cent of the stuff of the universe than on just 4 per cent.

The case for an orderly rather than an accidental universe is, in my view, unanswerable. We have seen that the order principle may transmit instructions to all organisms and creatures through retinas as photons are transmuted into biophotons. Physical light may oversee all creatures' homeostasis, and spiritual Light, which we examined in chapter 1, may also enter all humans' brains and oversee their inner responses.

The social approach we examined in chapter 1 suggests in seven disciplines that the universe is a chance, random accident, that it follows mechanistic laws and lacks purpose and therefore order. We shall return to this view in chapter 4. As I have made clear, Universalism disputes this and holds that the social approach is only half the story.

We have seen that science has much to say about the order in the universe, which can feed into the seven disciplines and world culture and America's vision of spiritual unity which can unite humankind. We now need to see what the metaphysical tradition, as opposed to individual mystical experience, has to say about the order science has confirmed.

PART TWO

TOWARDS A REUNIFICATION: THE HIDDEN ORDER OF THE UNIVERSE AND ITS OPPONENTS, THE TUSSLE BETWEEN THE METAPHYSICAL AND SOCIAL APPROACHES

CHAPTER 3

THE METAPHYSICAL TRADITION, AND ORDER

Persecuted in Europe, the American settlers brought their religion with them, and by the time of the founding of the United States there was a widespread acknowledgement that 'In God We Trust' (which first appeared on American coins in 1864, became the official motto of the United States in 1956 and appeared on paper currency from 1957). Early American religion assumed a universe in which there was a reality beyond the obvious, an assumption that later emerged in the Transcendentalism of Ralph Waldo Emerson and Henry David Thoreau. The universal reality in terms of which settlers attempted to lead their lives had its roots in a long metaphysical tradition that preceded Plato and dominated the Middle Ages. This tradition is behind the spiritual unity that needs to be brought to world culture if the secret American destiny is to include the religious citizens of the world.

I have described Liberty in an earlier book of mine, *The Secret American Dream*. She represents what America stands for and American aspirations, and she protects the Earth's poor and huddled masses yearning to breathe free. Her head is modelled on the Graeco-Roman sun-god Helios and wears Sol's seven-spiked solar crown. She embodies the Light and she knows that the order revealed by the metaphysical tradition in the seven disciplines of world culture is just as important as the role of science's view of order in projecting a spiritual vision that can appeal to the 4.6 billion religious world citizens, and draw them in alongside secular humanists and unify humankind. Indeed, the metaphysical perspective of order lies behind science's view of order.

Science has shown a finite universe manifesting from a singularity or point within a boundless, infinite Void, or One. Any philosophy that is at variance with this view is not fit for purpose. The operation of a universal order principle that has produced the 40 biofriendly conditions, 326 constants and 75 ratios and may transmit information to all creatures through photons via retinas requires us to consult traditional metaphysics, which reflected such a view of the universe. The metaphysical is behind the scientific universe; it precedes it and generates it.

TRADITIONAL METAPHYSICS: RATIONAL AND INTUITIONAL

We saw (on p 23) that metaphysical philosophy has both rational and intuitional strands. The Intuitionists lost faith in the powers of reason and rejected the systems of the Rationalists and brought an Intuitionist metaphysical emphasis to philosophy. Universalists seek to unite the two traditions.

Rational metaphysical philosophy seeks to reveal the structure of 'what is' – of Being and Reality. 'What is' includes the infinite timeless Reality *and* the finite universe. The sum total of everything, both infinite and finite, can be referred to as 'the All' or 'the One', and metaphysics is 'the science of All'.[1] It can also be regarded as Nothingness, which is a Fullness or Plenitude, as Eastern thought has often claimed. In terms of my algebraic, dialectical method that reconciles all contradictions, +A (the infinite) + –A (the finite) = 0 (the All or the One). The One includes all things concrete and abstract, natural and supernatural, known and unknown, probable and improbable, orderly and chaotic, temporal and eternal, material and immaterial, post-Big Bang and pre-Big Bang. It includes every known concept and every possible concept, the manifested and the unmanifest.

Within the One, the infinite has two aspects: all the potentialities of Non-Being (the Void that preceded the Big Bang, which is outside the universe, the Nothingness that contains all potentialities of Being in an unmanifested form) and Being (the void within the finite universe after the Big Bang, the quantum vacuum which appears to be empty but seethes with virtual particles like a sea of energy – and, if we believe in them, Plato's 'virtual' Ideas – and contains all potentialities of everything manifested and all possibilities of Existence). We can therefore say that +A (Non-Being) + –A (Being) = 0 (the infinite).

Within the One, the finite has two aspects: Being (the quantum vacuum which contains the invisible potentialities of Existence) and Existence (the manifestation of Being, the multiplicity within the unity of Being, all atoms, cells, matter and organisms in the universe of space-time). We can say that +A (Being) + –A (Existence) = 0 (the finite).

Manifestation from the metaphysical to the scientific universe proceeds from the infinite to the finite. It originates in Nothingness and becomes Non-Being and then, like a nothingness becoming a virtual particle, becomes an idea in Being whence, like a virtual particle becoming a real particle, it becomes a form in Existence, the world of evolution and organisms. Existence pours out of Being as plenty pours from the cornucopia (horn of plenty). The totality is the All or One. The process of manifestation can be stated clearly in terms of its four tiers:

- **Nothingness/Fullness, or the All or One** – the potentialities of infinite Non-Being, infinite/finite Being and finite Existence
- **Non-Being** – the infinite Void outside the universe that preceded the Big Bang, the potentialities of Being and manifestation of Nothingness
- **Being** – the infinite/finite void which succeeded the Big Bang within the finite universe, the potentialities of Existence and manifestation of Non-Being
- **Existence** – the finite manifestation of Being[2]

The rational approach to metaphysics was well stated by Alfred North Whitehead, who called it 'speculative philosophy'. Metaphysics 'is the endeavour to frame a coherent, logical, necessary system of general ideas in terms of which every element of our experience can be interpreted' (Whitehead's *Process and Reality*). Every element of our experience must include all our experience of the finite world and all our experience (such as it is) of the infinite. It interprets *all* our experience of the universe, including *all* known concepts. My system of ideas – manifestation from the infinite into Nature and biofriendly conditions which helped life to evolve – does include these. A 'system of general ideas' must have one of four metaphysical perspectives: Materialistic monism (that matter gives rise to mind, the Materialist position); dualism (that matter and mind are separate, as Descartes believed); transcendental monism (that mind or consciousness gives rise to matter, the Idealist position); and metaphysical non-duality (that a metaphysical Reality gives rise to both matter and mind, that a unity at the transcendent metaphysical level gives rise to diversity at the immanent physical level). My 'system of general ideas' is a non-duality. It has unity at the infinite level and diversity at the finite level. My system of coherent general ideas explains how unity became diversity by manifestation into matter, light, consciousness and the vegetative world of plants, how the One manifested into many.

Today metaphysics can be said to have four subdivisions, which cover different approaches to Being. In descending order they are:

- **Ontology** (the study of Being), which includes traditional metaphysics
- **Psychology** (what can be experienced of Being), which includes some traditional moral philosophy
- **Epistemology** (what can be known about Being), which includes some ethics

- **Cosmology** (the structure of the universe), which includes traditional natural philosophy[3]

The reason's approach to this scheme differs from the intuition's. Reason sees a universe permeated by the infinite but ruled by reason, which follows mathematical law. The rational study of ontology ('the branch of metaphysics dealing with the nature of Being', *Concise Oxford Dictionary*) is a study of Being manifested into the universe whose structure is rational, and the rational study of cosmology focuses on its compliance with rational, mathematical laws. The rational study of psychology sees the rational, social ego, which uses the reason or higher mind, as *thinking* about infinite Being, and the rational study of epistemology seeks certainty that the infinite exists and seeks social answers to ethical problems.

The four-tier manifestation process, the four subdivisions of modern metaphysics, the 12 levels of consciousness and non-duality are all integrated in the reason's system, as shown in the table below:[4]

MANIFESTATION PROCESS	SUBDIVISIONS OF METAPHYSICS	EXPERIENCES OF 12 LEVELS OF CONSCIOUSNESS	NON-DUALITY
NOTHINGNESS/ FULLNESS			
NON-BEING			
BEING	ONTOLOGY	LEVELS 11–12	UNITY
	PSYCHOLOGY	LEVELS 5–10	
EXISTENCE	EPISTEMOLOGY		DIVERSITY (CONSCIOUSNESS/ MATTER)
	COSMOLOGY	LEVELS 1–4	

As metaphysics includes 'the All' and 'every known concept', the rational metaphysical philosopher accepts that there are rational laws within the universe and admits to the possibility that consciousness survives death and that we have spirits that are immortal – even though he has had no personal experience of this.

Intuitionist metaphysical philosophy adds an 'overlay' to the conclusions of rational metaphysical philosophy. The 'system of general ideas' interprets every element of our *experience*, and the intuitionist metaphysical philosopher experiences Reality rather than thinking about it or approaching it through sense data and the reason.

The intuitionist metaphysical philosopher holds that the Being of ontology (the study of Being) can be *known* within our consciousness when it is its most universal, in level 12 of the multi-levelled self. Intuitional ontology holds that it is possible for humans to *know* Reality when our consciousness is in level 12 by experiencing the 'ever-living Fire' or metaphysical Light in a manifesting form individually and existentially. Whereas the rational metaphysical philosopher establishes Reality rationally through the rational, social ego (level 8), the intuitionist metaphysical philosopher enters the highest, or rather deepest, level of consciousness which is below the rational, social ego and opens existentially to the 'ever-living Fire' or Light of Being as was known in the early religions. Experiencing metaphysical Reality relives the experiences of: Christ, the Light of the World; the Buddha, the Enlightened One; Zen Buddhist *satori*; Mahayana Buddhist *sunyata*; Hindu *samadhi*; and the Taoist 'Void'. Being, the One, pervades the finite universe and organizes it into a self-regulatory equilibrium. The hidden Reality beyond and within Nature is what the mystics have known, as Whitehead knew when he wrote: 'The purpose of philosophy is to rationalize mysticism' (*Modes of Thought*, 1938, from an address given at Harvard in 1935).

Intuitional epistemology (the study of what can be known about Being) is based on the perception of the universal being (level 12 of consciousness) in contrast to rational epistemology, which is based on the rational, social ego (level 8). The universal being is in fact 'the intellect' (Latin *intellectus*, meaning 'perception' and therefore 'understanding', 'comprehension'). Traditionally, 'the intellect' has nothing to do with the reason. It is an intuitional and intuitive faculty – a perceptive faculty lying outside the five senses – that perceives universals and meaning, whereas the reason is a logical faculty that analyses particulars and often sees meaninglessness. The intellect receives wisdom in an area of the brain which is separate from the sensory combinations of neurons, and the infused, revealed knowledge then influences the reason. Today, 'intellect' has been secularized and socialized and is synonymous with 'reason' (the faculty of reasoning in which conclusions are drawn from premises) and an 'intellectual' is regarded as having a highly developed reason.

It seems that the manifesting Light flows into the intellect or universal being from the quantum vacuum and illumines it, and that this manifesting Light is on the electromagnetic spectrum but is so far towards the short-wave end – beyond ultraviolet and gamma rays and manifest in particles or bosons tinier than neutrinos or photinos – that science has not been able to measure it. Receiving the Light may be like receiving healing energy, when molecules of low energy receive photons of high energy channelled by a healer.

In intuitional psychology (which is concerned about what can be experienced of Being and the part of the self where we experience it), the intuition of the intellect or universal being experiences Being, the 'ever-living Fire' or Light. It is instructive to see the intellect or universal being in terms of the seat of consciousness in the 12 levels of the multi-levelled self, which are arranged in descending order below:

- **Universal being or intellect** (*intellectus*) – in universal consciousness, into which illumination shines from the One (level 12)
- **Spirit** (*pneuma*) – in transpersonal consciousness, possibly relating to Non-Being (level 11), more probably relating to Being (level 11)
- **Reason** (*nous*) – higher mind, (levels 7, 8)

- **Soul** (*psyche*) – higher feeling (levels 7, 8, 9)
- **Ego** – rational, social ego (levels 4, 5, 6, 7)
- **Sense** – controlled sense-impressions (level 5)
- **Body** (*soma*) – body consciousness of body-brain system, robotic automaton (level 4)
- **Instinct** – (levels 1–3)[5]

I asked (on p 92) if the mind is brain-function or if it *uses* the brain. What stands out from the 12 levels of the self is that (as I proposed on p 93) mind seems to be brain-function in levels 1–4, and mind seems to use the brain in levels 5–12, where consciousness is not an effect of the brain like homeostasis but rather controls the brain and homeostasis, perhaps through photons as we saw in chapter 2. Consciousness has a two-tier nature and is partly autonomic and partly controlling.

Intuitional psychology sees the self as having levels or seats of consciousness which relate to the four levels of manifestation, as can be seen in this restatement of the table on p 102.[6]

- **Nothingness, the All or One** – infinite metaphysical Light of finest density, too pure to be seen in universal being or intellect (level 12), mystical/'divine'
- **Non-Being** – infinite, denser metaphysical Light but still too fine to be seen in the universal being (level 12) or spirit (level 11), spiritual
- **Being** – infinite/finite, sea of neutrino-like or photino-like particles of metaphysical Light received in universal being or intellect (level 12), and psychic/paranormal energies received in spirit (level 11) as discarnate entities can be expected to be in the sea of Being, spiritual; soul (levels 7, 8, 9), archetypes (including Ideas if they exist), psychological
- **Existence** – natural phenomena and natural light seen by the

physical, rational, social ego (lower mind, levels 5, 6, 7) and bodily instinct known to levels 1–4, physical

The intuitional approach to the four subdivisions of metaphysics is in descending order as follows:[7]

- **Ontology** – studying the infinite or timeless Being through experiences of Reality, 'the ever-living Fire' or metaphysical Light, in the intellect of level 12 (source: All-One/Non-Being/Being)
- **Transpersonal (or spiritual) psychology** – how the spirit of level 11 can know the potentialities of Existence in Being, particularly how it can know psychic or paranormal phenomena and what seem to be far memories of distant lives (source: Being)
- **Epistemology** – how the mind knows Reality as an experience by transcending the reason and rational, social ego so that the top levels 7–12 of consciousness can free themselves from Existence – detach themselves from the world of the senses – and know Being (source: Being/Existence)
- **Cosmology** – the study and description of the structure, science and theory of the universe approached from the universal being's awareness of the unity of the universe within Being (source: Existence)

I have long deliberated on the workings of the multi-levelled self. In *My Double Life 1: This Dark Wood*[8] and *My Double Life 2: A Rainbow over the Hills* I saw life in terms of episodes lasting two or three years, each of which contains a pair of opposites (such as family and war), and I saw the self's memories as reflecting these episodes. I saw the self in terms of a spruce cone, which has pairs of opposite scales arranged in clockwise and counter-clockwise spirals, with our earliest memories at the bottom. Consciousness clearly draws on these memories of the self in levels 6, 8 and 9.

We have seen that in metaphysics there is One Reality, the Fire or Light, which is perceived in many different traditions under different names, just as the sun is seen in many different countries under different names. We have seen that the four subdivisions of metaphysics have both rational and intuitional approaches to this Reality. In ontology (the study of Being), the rational approach sets out the structure of Being, or 'what is', in a theoretical scheme, while the intuitional approach *experiences* Being. In both approaches Being is a framework for cosmology (the structure of the universe). In psychology (what can be experienced of Being) the rational approach puts forward a theoretical scheme that includes the spirit's involvement in Being, while the intuitional approach is again about the experience of Being. In epistemology, there is again a conflict between rational and intuitional knowledge of Being, the first being theoretical, the second existential through direct experience. In cosmology, the rational approach sets out the structure of the universe perceived by the reason and the intuitional approach emphasizes the unity of the universe that is experienced in the universal being. But throughout metaphysics there is one Reality, the One, the Light, which, as I have just said, can be seen from within many traditions but is fundamentally 'the One' which features in the tradition of mystical experience (see pp 7–14) and orders the universe.

We must now turn to the metaphysical view of order in the universe.

THE METAPHYSICAL ORDER IN THE UNIVERSE: ORDER PRINCIPLE, LAW OF ORDER

Einstein wrote that there is 'a high degree of ordering of the objective world'.[9] He also said that physics inevitably leads to metaphysics.[10]

I have said (p 89) that the order may be conveyed in photons, and from the rational metaphysical viewpoint the universe is a system in which invisible substance has manifested into visible Nature. Energy from the invisible Being manifests into Existence, whose forms and systems bear witness to an orderly origin. Photosynthesizing growth is spurred on by photons and suggests organizing light behind it, just as shadows suggest a sun. The order behind the universe is concealed, just as the Chinese characters *Chin Hua*, 'Golden Flower', conceal a central character, *Kuang*, 'Light'. (In the 9th century it was heretical to speak of metaphysical Light in China, so the character for Light had to be hidden between two other characters.)

The universe can be seen as a system of light. The manifesting energy comes into the universe along with coded instructions for ordering phenomena which may be borne by light. These instructions may interact with DNA to release a drive for self-improvement or self-betterment in relation to the environment, so that each organism achieves and realizes the next stage in its development. The electromagnetic radiation interacts with matter. The electromagnetic spectrum reveals an ordered system. Wavelength is measured (in descending order) in kilometres, metres, centimetres, millimetres, micrometres, nanometers (previously known as millimicrometres or milimicrons), picometers and Angstroms. Until 1960 frequency was measured (in descending order) in kilocycles per second, megacycles per second and cycles per second. One cycle per second was renamed a hertz, and these units are now (in descending order) the terahertz, gigahertz, megahertz, kilohertz and hertz. To avoid confusion I shall stick with cycles per second. The nearest rays are long radio waves (with a frequency of $10–10^5$ cycles per second). Then come normal radio waves (10^6), then short radio waves ($10^7–10^{12}$). The cosmic microwave background radiation has a wavelength of 1.1mm and a frequency of 217 million cycles per second, which is over 10^8 cycles per second. Then come radar and TV, then infrared ($10^{12}–10^{14}$). Beyond is visible light (10^{14}). Each colour within the spectrum of light has a different wavelength. Beyond that is ultraviolet ($10^{14}–10^{16}$ cycles per second) and then X-rays ($10^{15}–10^{20}$) and gamma rays ($10^{18}–10^{23}$). The invisible substance that manifests from the infinite is beyond gamma rays.

We have seen that plants absorb light in chlorophyll, which is found in the elongated chloroplasts of cells and produces energy. They harvest sunlight through photosynthesis and, I contend, carry order. All photosynthesizing plants contain chlorophyll except for the *Halobacterium halobium*, which photosynthesizes by using a coloured protein resembling the visual pigment rhodopsin.

Animals and humans convert light to chemical energy in their light-sensitive cells and organs, after receiving light in their retinas. Eyes are not just for looking outwards and receiving images, they also receive light. The light-sensitive cells – the 120 million rod photoreceptors and 6 million cone photoreceptors in each retina (as we saw on p 89) – can transform light signals into a photochemical reaction which leads to electrical charges in cells and eventually nerve signals. Iguanas and lizards warm up by basking in the early morning sun. Sunlight penetrates through their eyes and radiates their internal circulatory system until their inner thermostat prevents the warming process from making them too hot. These animals are motionless until they have absorbed the light they require, and only then do they go about their daily business. Earthworms have light-sensitive cells within their skin, jellyfish have primitive eyes at their edge, starfish in their armpits and tube worms in their gills.

Light penetrates the light-sensitive or photoreceptor cells of humans even if they are blind and even if an eyeball is removed, so long as sufficient photoreceptors near the back of the eyeball are still intact.

Living things convert light into chemical energy universally throughout Nature via their eyes. The absorption of photons in their eyes initiates a photochemical reaction in the eye's fumaric acid and turns it into maleic acid, and vice versa, which leads to an electrical change in cells. Light-sensitive cells have to be combined with pigment-rich cells which extinguish light from one direction. Light also stimulates physical and chemical processes to have a profound effect on the direction of movement in animals and humans. In ways not yet known, it stimulates their inner clock and enables organisms to behave predictably as regards the time of the day and the time of the year. There is also a photobiology of the skin, which is nourished by light, and light's Vitamin D develops the skeleton. Too much or too little sunlight brings problems: too much sunlight can cause skin cancer, and light deprivation results in seasonal affective disorder (SAD). Sunlight is central to the vast biological ecosystem and local ecosystems, for it controls growth and an orderly way of life.

Evolution has taken place within biofriendly, orderly conditions amid a continuous process of manifestation of light – arguably, of metaphysical Light becoming physical light via the cosmological processes which created suns and our sun. It can now be said that the influx of light develops bodies and brains, and consciousness, with an order that attends to every need and deficiency. The universe is indeed an orderly system of light.

This order principle, order beneath apparent randomness and the uncertainty principle, may work with the four forces (the strong and weak forces, electromagnetism and gravity) as a fifth force, an expanding force of light that pours photons into all forms of life. This may manifest from Being as dark energy or subtle light that is invisible to the outer eye but conveys instructions into all creatures' retinas. A self-organizing order principle within Nature's system of ecology may work through the atoms, cells, photons, biophotons and 'mechanisms' revealed in cosmology, astrophysics, astronomy, biocosmology, physics, geology, palaeontology, biology, ecology, biochemistry and physiology. It is biofriendly to human life. The order principle may be carried in photon-like particles tinier than photinos, too small to have been found, like (until recently) Higgs bosons and the Higgs field that gives mass. It may be found within the photons of physical light as Newton suspected: 'Are not gross

Bodies and Light convertible into one another and may not Bodies receive much of their Activity from the Particles of Light which enter their Composition?' And, 'In the ether the spirit is entangled. This spirit is the body of light.' (See p 49.) As we have seen, these photons enter plants and as sunlight are converted to chlorophyll; and they also enter retinas. The order principle of light/photons may make all creatures grow.

The order principle may actually be a Law of Order.[11] A 'principle' in physics, such as the uncertainty principle, is 'a fundamental truth' or 'a highly general or inclusive theorem or "law" exemplified in a magnitude of cases' (*Shorter Oxford English Dictionary*). We have been considering a magnitude of cases in which a principle of order is at work. A 'law', as in 'the laws of Nature' or 'the law of gravity', is 'a theoretical principle deduced from particular facts, expressible by the statement that a particular phenomenon always occurs if certain conditions be present' and 'the order and regularity in Nature expressed by law' (*Shorter Oxford English Dictionary*). ('Regular' means 'conforming to some accepted rule or standard'.) I have already defined order as 'the condition in which every part or unit is in its right place, tidiness' (see p xvi), which covers how fish, birds, reptiles and animals share feeding and breeding sites to make the food go round. The 'magnitude of cases' exemplifying an order principle includes the 40 biofriendly conditions, symbiosis, physiological systems and medieval herbalism, and we are justified in referring to it as a Law of Order as order always occurs if certain conditions – the 'magnitude of cases', including the 40 biofriendly conditions – are present.

The Law of Order originates in the infinite, in the singularity, and orders the finite through manifesting light. It advances humans to higher consciousness in which they open to metaphysical Light which also pervades our solar system's corner of the universe along with physical light. It is my contention that the Law of Order manifests from the infinite into the universe, perhaps as a fifth force, and probably operates through light via the eyes of all creatures. It controls their growth, regulates their systems and pervades and controls their DNA. It creates organized, methodical, highly structural, complex systems. It is now for CERN scientists to discover evidence for a Law of Order in photons.

We have been examining an overview of the possible workings of a Law or Order in the scientific universe in which there is no likelihood – a likelihood of 10^{120} – that it could have begun by chance. However, as is to be expected when so much in the universe conforms to the algebraic +A + –A = 0, alongside the Law of Order (+A) is the Law of Randomness (–A), which states that the universe is also permeated by an unmethodical tendency for the energy of organized complex systems to deviate from their self-organized directions – either through adaptation or through faulty DNA replication. They may deviate into accidental mutations or into chaotic breakdown due to chance mishaps which may bring starvation and early sudden death. 'Random' can be defined as 'made, done without method or conscious choice' (*Oxford English Dictionary*).

Is there a teleological purpose behind the Law of Order in the universe? Aristotle declared in *Metaphysics* that a full explanation of anything must consider not only the material, formal and efficient causes, but also the final cause, the purpose for which the thing exists or was produced.[12] Teleology is 'the doctrine or study of ends or final causes, especially as related to the evidence's design or purpose in nature' and 'such design as exhibited in natural objects or phenomena' (*Shorter Oxford English Dictionary*). While order can be defined in terms of regularity and the functioning of a system in the present, it has other meanings which include (as we saw on p xvi) 'a state of peaceful harmony under a constitutional authority'. It is perfectly reasonable to ask the purpose of the present harmony. We do not know why Nature's system exists. We can only speculate on its end or final cause. If we are not careful, thinking about the purpose of the universe can take us readily from scientific description, philosophical exegesis and metaphysical rationalism – whose language is neutral – into theology, religion and faith, which are different categories of thought.

Nevertheless, the many examples of order set out in chapter 2 suggest there must be a teleological principle at work, for if the ordering had not been towards any end it would not have been successfully concluded. Logically, if the universe is ordered, it is purposive. Nature manifested from the infinite, and humankind has evolved in a partly ordered, not totally random, way; and there may well be a purpose linked to the infinite substance, 'ever-living Fire'. Given the 40 biofriendly conditions, the infinite must have manifested into Nature for a reason, and to the extent that evolution is controlled by order this reason must be associated with the evolution of humankind. It is therefore possible that each human being – whose source of growth is physical light and who is linked to the infinite by metaphysical Light – is fulfilling an infinite plan in his or her everyday finite living.

Whereas in the rational universe infinite Reality manifests and penetrates physical eyes and chloroplasts as an objective event, in the intuitional universe infinite Reality, the metaphysical Light, manifests and is received within the universal being or intellect as a subjective experience. In the Yogic practices of some forms of Hinduism and Buddhism, the Light travels up the spine through *chakras* or centres of the invisible subtle body to the crown *chakra*, which in Western thought is the intellect that receives illumination. In Western thought a sea of energy or latent Light enters the universal being or intellect which is detached from sense impressions and desires; and which opens, and like a mirror reflects the 'ever-living Fire', bringing serenity and 'peace that passeth understanding'. There is a Light-inspired drive of organisms through matter to higher and higher levels of self-organizing – and of the many-levelled self.

The intuitional self or consciousness perceives an intuitional universe in which consciousness may be transmitted as light or photons through the brain rather than being produced by the brain. Consciousness may be transmitted into the brain, which may act like a radio receiver. If so, the receiving probably happens in photons above the brain in a 'Bose-Einstein condensate' (a theory developed by Einstein and the Indian Satyendra Nath Bose in 1924–5, which accounts for the streaming of laser light). Photons satisfying Bose-Einstein statistics are called bosons. It is possible that the transmitted current of universal energy arrives on carrier bosons. Their energy stimulates neurons and pushes their electrical impulses into interconnectedness so that they bond with each other. Consciousness bosons may form a kind of halo squatting like a tenant in its home in the brain, which it may eventually desert on death to go elsewhere.

Natural light is, on this view, condensed metaphysical Light, and manifestation is a kind of condensation. A hidden network of manifested Light permeates humans all the time. Just as neutrinos pass through bodies as they have so little mass, so massless photon-like boson particles of manifested Light which may be tinier than neutrinos also pass through human bodies. All creatures are like sea-sponges living in a sea of Light. To change the image, Bohm held that matter is frozen light. He said that 'Light can carry information about the entire universe'[13], and he held that information can move at superluminal speeds, speeds faster than the speed of light (which is just over 186,000 miles per second).

As space-time emerged from a singularity (according to Penrose), something pre-existed the Big Bang. Manifestation from Nothingness to Non-Being, Being and Existence, which correspond to the four subdivisions of metaphysics, brought with it a system of information that seems to travel round the universe at speeds faster than the speed of light. It is now time to consider how this information, and order, came out of the Void and the quantum vacuum.

FORM FROM MOVEMENT THEORY: HOW ORDER CAME OUT OF THE VOID

I first set out my Form from Movement Theory on the origin and creation of the universe in *The Universe and the Light* and restated it in *The New Philosophy of Universalism*.[14] I have described (in *My Double Life 2: A Rainbow over the Hills*)[15] how I attended a conference on reductionism in Jesus College, Cambridge, during which I had discussions with Penrose, and how I formulated and wrote down the theory over dinner in Jesus' Hall with a young Norwegian mathematician, Henning Broten, on 4 September 1992. Some of the leading scientists of the age (including Penrose) were standing round and listening with broad smiles on their faces. My Form from Movement Theory explains how the origin and creation of the universe could happen in terms of the reversal of the algebraic formula I brought back from the East: $0 = +A + -A$.

My Form from Movement Theory holds that physical phenomena emerged from a pre-existing, moving, latent Fire, the Void. It looks back to Heraclitus's eternally moving, 'ever-living Fire' c500 BCE, which always existed, and to Anaximander's eternally moving 'boundless' *apeiron*. Aristotle was half-way to this position in seeing an 'unmoved mover' that 'will cause motion that is one and simple'.[16] Before dinner Broten asked me how I got from the Fire to Existence and said he would sit by me and write down a new maths to explain my theory. In Jesus' Hall I described manifestation passing through four stages, from Nothingness to Non-Being to Being and Existence.[17]

Nothingness had always been a self-entangled entity of virtual, infinite and irregular movement in all directions (although it preceded space-time and direction), a latent Oneness or metaphysical Fire or Light. The maths denotes this movement as M. A limitation of movement into regular movement occurred and possibly formed a spiral, Non-Being, which I denote as S. S is a subset of M in which both M and S are infinite. In place of Oneness there was now an apparent duality within the One, M–S versus S. M was larger than S and contained the whole of S.

From the creative tension and pressure between M–S and S new forms of order arose: symmetrical points or pre-particles. (Compare Edgard Gunzig's work on how pressure on a vacuum can create energy.) I postulated a pair of pre-particles, +p and –p. In sum they equal zero, so $S: +p + -p = 0$. (The colon can have the force of 'such that' in mathematics. S is still the spiral, Non-Being, formed as a limitation of movement from M, and this equation shows that S is such that it is, or can be regarded as, a pair of particles whose sum is zero.) I postulated that owing to the irregular movement of M–S upon S there was a reduction of symmetry and one of the pre-particles, –p, was annihilated and absorbed back into M. The other pre-particle, +p, derived energy from the movement of M–S upon S. It was an empty point or vacuum or singularity, and was Non-Being. It began to spread like a wave in all directions in the field of S and expanded. The point +p was gradually becoming Being. $S: +p \rightarrow B$.

Owing to the interaction between M–S upon B, B evolved more and more structure and was now activity within the quantum vacuum. B, which was implicit, evolved more and more explicit orders (see Bohm's implicate order), I_1, I_2, I_3... I_n (I_n being the most explicit order). Being (formerly +B) became Existence in a process in which potentialities became actualities, pre-particles became particles, pre-matter became matter, pre-organism became organism, pre-consciousness became consciousness, possibility became factuality. Existence can be denoted $E = I_{n+1}$, which was an event in M. I postulated one or more loops between these implicit orders, such as between I_{n+1} (the explicit order) and I_{n-2} (an earlier implicit order). I postulated a division between two manifesting orders, one leading up to explicit matter and the other to aware consciousness and creative intelligence.

So +p, the first pre-proton, expanded into Being and became pre-matter and perhaps pre-consciousness, and form was ready to rise from the infinite movement. Virtual particles emerged from the quantum vacuum (B in the field of S) in pairs. One virtual particle in each pair had the potentiality to become a real particle in explicit Existence if it drew energy from the pressure of M–S on S. Through quantum processes virtual particles derived energy from the pressure of M–S on S and merged into real particles in many regions of S, all over the expanded field of +p or B.

As a result of the proliferation of simultaneously emerging real particles, the process of the Big Bang or hot beginning, the creation of our universe, took place. Time then began, and there has been a succession of 10^{23} (10 thousand million million million) spatial events every second since the Earth cooled 4.55 billion years ago, and as the universe appears to be expanding forever (provided unevidenced dark matter keeps us accelerating) and is overlaid on the timelessness and infinity from which it emerged, time is not moving towards disorder in keeping with the second law of thermodynamics.

The processes behind my Form from Movement Theory can be set down mathematically:

$M \rightarrow M{-}S + S$. In S, $+p \rightarrow B$, which evolves $I_1, I_2, I_3 \ldots I_n$. $B \rightarrow E$, which is I_{n+1}. (M = movement; S = spiral; p = pre-particle; B = Being; I = implicit order; E = Existence.)

The origin of the universe as a whole can be stated as $0 = +A + -A$ in which 0 is Nothingness/Non-Being, +A is Being and –A is Existence. There are numerous pairs of opposites that can be traced back to 0, one pair being electrons (+A) and positrons (–A).

Towards the end of 2014 I lunched with a physicist who pooh-poohed colliders and told me that only two particles count, the electron and the positron, for when they collide they are annihilated and produce two or more gamma-ray photons. All other particles are offshoots of electrons and positrons. I told him that if 0 = +A + –A, electrons + positrons, then the Void could produce photons, light, almost instantaneously.

Is the process behind my Form from Movement Theory ordered or arbitrary and random? I have postulated that the invisible substance behind the universe manifests from infinity into finite radiation and physical light, into electrons and positrons which become gamma-ray photons, into the *yin-yang*-like symmetry of neutrinos and photons and the apparently ordered system of Nature.

The information network must have been part of the Big Bang and the first whoosh of inflation that led to the universe's expansion. The network of information has travelled among the photons of that expansion. The many examples of order we have detected and the Law of Order behind them all originated in the first moment of the creation of the universe and came out of that first second, and it does now seem that the order is the result of purposive rules and that the universe has purpose. The metaphysical moving Fire that burst into physical existence increasingly looks to have been purposive, and so the metaphysical order of the subsequent universe appears to be purposive and not a random accident.

The metaphysical perspective of order behind the scientific universe is an important aspect of America's spiritual vision that will appeal to the 4.6 billion religious world citizens who (as we saw on p 32) are in a nearly 6-to-1 majority over non-religious world citizens.

CHAPTER 4

THE SOCIAL AND REDUCTIONIST DENIAL OF THE METAPHYSICAL, AND ACCIDENT

The metaphysical outlook that dominated the thinking of such medieval followers of Plato as Anselm, William of Champeaux, St Bernard and William of Auvergne always co-existed with another outlook that was humanist. This can be traced back to Aristotle, who was more interested in the scientific outlook, and can especially be found in the classical period. Horace acknowledged the gods and acted like Augustus's Poet Laureate in writing *Carmen Saeculare* ('Song of the Ages'), which invoked Apollo and Diana for the *ludi saeculares* ('secular games') held on 31 May 17 BCE when Augustus sacrificed to the gods in Rome's Campus Martius. However Horace's poems have a humanist approach and only pay lip-service to the gods. When Virgil writes of Juno persuading Aeolus, god of the winds, to send an ill wind to scatter Aeneas's fleet in *The Aeneid*, one feels that his use of the two gods is a literary convention in the tradition of Homer rather than a matter of fundamental belief. Nevertheless, Virgil's universe is presided over by the gods. Ovid was banished by the divine Augustus and in his poems in exile he does not accept the divinity of Augustus, who was behind his unjust banishment. This classical humanism influenced the humanism of the Renaissance, which challenged the metaphysical outlook.

In the same way, latter-day American writers have a humanist outlook, as does Hemingway in his short stories. 'Hail nothing full of nothing, nothing is with thee,' the old man in Hemingway's 'A Clean, Well-Lighted Place' says ironically, expressing the nihilism and religious disbelief that was shaped by the horrors encountered during the First World War. A sceptical tradition has grown up alongside the Puritans' vision that confidently proclaimed 'In God We Trust', and in our time, as can be seen in contemporary American literature, this scepticism has turned assertive and agnosticism has actively denied the metaphysical outlook and morphed into atheism.

ATHEISM AND THE SOCIAL FRAGMENTATION OF WORLD CULTURE

We have seen (on pp xiv, 3 and 32) that the religious population of the world is 63 per cent of world citizens according to one survey and 84 per cent according to another survey; while 11 per cent of world citizens are atheists, agnostics, non-religious and non-theists – secular humanists – according to one survey and 15.35 per cent or 16.3 per cent according to two other surveys. In seeking to balance the conflicting metaphysical and secular approaches in each of the seven disciplines that have dominated world culture during the last 4,600 years, the American Universalist is confronted by the assertiveness of social atheism in each of the seven disciplines, its denial of the metaphysical and its insistence that the universe is a random accident. Atheism and the non-religious shades of opinion are in a minority of 1 to nearly 6 or 7. Liberty's vision of spiritual unity has to neutralize the challenge of fundamentalist atheism so as not to exclude the 4.6 billion followers of traditional religions.

Denial of the metaphysical is associated with atheism ('the theory or belief that God does not exist', *Concise Oxford Dictionary*): the denial of God as the first principle and opposition to any religion or worship of God. Atheism had been unknown in primitive societies and was rare in the Graeco-Roman world and in the early Christian era. The words 'atheism' and 'atheist' can be found in Plato's *Laws*.[1] *The Old Testament*'s Psalm 14 begins, 'The fool hath said in his heart, There is no God.' In other words, atheism is foolish. The *Letter to the Ephesians* enjoins 'Walk as children of light' in opposition to all non-believers. There are references to atheists in the Church Fathers St Ignatius of Antioch and Justin Martyr.

Atheism was unknown in the Middle Ages, during the genesis and growth of the European civilization. The Renaissance Humanists' interest in the Materialist Greek and Roman philosophers Democritus and Lucretius and in Roman paganism introduced scepticism into the European civilization, and in 1513 Niccolò Machiavelli advocated separating the modern state from religion in *Il Principe* (*The Prince*). Christopher Marlowe was accused of atheism in 1593, as was Sir Walter Raleigh, whose School of Atheism (or School of Night) had been the subject of a complaint in 1592.

But it was Descartes who opened the way to atheism. His *Cogito, ergo sum* ('I think; therefore, I am') placed truth in the free, thinking subject and in the evidence, and he explained natural phenomena in relation to mechanistic matter and motion. Deism and the British empiricism of John Locke advanced scepticism.

The 18th-century French Enlightenment of the *philosophes* Denis Diderot and Jean Le Rond d'Alembert fused British Deism and empiricism with Descartes' mechanism and rationalism. The *philosophes* praised atheism. Paul Henri Thiry, Baron d'Holbach, the author of *Christianisme Dévoilé* (*Christianity Unveiled*), wrote that an atheist is 'a man who destroys the dreams and chimerical beings that are dangerous to the human race so that men can be brought back to nature, to experience and to reason'. The French insistence on experience and reason was supported by the German Enlightenment, which opposed supernaturalism (belief in an order of existence beyond the observable universe). Kant, the founder of transcendental Idealism, was in conflict with the Church for his *Die Religion innerhalb der Grenzen der blossen Vernunft* (*Religion within the Limits of Reason Alone*) in 1793. In 1798 Friedrich Karl Forberg published an essay seeing God as the moral world order, and there was 'conflict over atheism' (*Atheismusstreit*). The German philosopher Friedrich Heinrich Jacobi attacked Johann Gottlieb Fichte and Friedrich Schelling as atheists who followed Spinoza, the 17th-century Rationalist who had identified God with the world (and was consequently accused of atheism). Hegel, the early 19th-century Idealist, wrote that 'without the world God is not God', a partial atheism. Ludwig Feuerbach and later Karl Marx extended atheistic thinking. Marx called religion 'the opium of the people' and held that religion exploited men. The 'will to power' of Friedrich Nietzsche carried the process forward. He proclaimed the need for 'the death of God' so the Superman could come into his own.

In the 20th century radical atheistic humanism saw man in terms of the behavioural sciences. Sigmund Freud saw spirituality and the quest for immortality as a consequence of neurotic frustration. Logical Positivism held that scientific knowledge is the only kind of factual knowledge, and that traditional metaphysical doctrines are meaningless. As the European civilization approached its unifying conglomerate (stage 43), its initial metaphysical vision was being dismissed by its new philosophers. The Reality of metaphysics was lumped in with the God of religion and denied – the Absolute was deemed to be a concept that had no meaning, or was unknowable – and the European civilization turned secular. The German Existentialists Karl Jaspers and Martin Heidegger did not deny religious transcendence, whereas the French Existentialists Jean-Paul Sartre and Albert Camus did. (Camus held that affirming God negated human reason.)

The North American civilization is still in its growing phase and affirms 'In God we trust'. But in 1933 the American Humanist Manifesto proclaimed 'the self-perfectibility of human personality'. The Manifesto grew out of Pragmatism, and was signed by the American philosopher John Dewey. The new humanism was a blend of the methods of natural science, evolutionism and vitalism (which emphasized the uniqueness of the life force). Man's ascent has left him the subject and source of human values. However, Max Planck, Einstein and Heisenberg all thought that the laws of the universe presupposed an infinite intellect, and that man merely discovers these laws.

In the 1960s a theology that emphasized imitating the life of Christ rather than revering God entered the European civilization under the influence of Paul Tillich and Dietrich Bonhoeffer, who was hanged in Flossenbürg in 1945. To the 1960s theologians, 'God' was a cultural category, and 'the death of God' had taken place. Reflecting on a letter by Bonhoeffer of 16 July 1944, Thomas Altizer and William Hamilton wrote that 'Bonhoeffer invites us to accept the world without God as given and unalterable'.[2] The impact of these German theologians reached the UK in John Robinson's *Honest to God* (1963), which rejected 'God out there' and saw God as 'the ground of being'. Robinson spoke of Bonhoeffer's 'religionless Christianity' and held that secular man requires a secular theology. The book was greeted with a storm of controversy as it seemed to be claiming that one could be a Christian without believing in the traditional God. Atheism seemed to have entered theology.

Both theoretical atheism – denial of the existence of God and of a concept of the world in which there is transcendence – and practical atheism – denial of God in one's conduct of private and public life – share a fundamental attitude. Unlike agnostics, who believe that nothing is or can be known about anything beyond material phenomena and are 'don't knows', atheists say there is no One or Reality or Light or Fire, and that (with the physicist I mentioned at the end of the Prologue) the Greek philosophers were all wrong, including Heraclitus. Atheists deny the existence of levels 11 and 12 of the multi-levelled self (which is set out on pp 91–2), including the universal being, and affirm the rational, social ego and the higher rational and intuitional consciousnesses (levels 8 and 9), which they regard as the highest. They deny all spiritual experience and experience of the divine. They see the universe as being formed of scientifically explicable phenomena and created by Materialistic processes. (We have seen that matter occupies just 4 per cent of the stuff of the universe, and that 96 per cent has not been found.) They believe that time began with the Big Bang and that the universe has no purpose and is an accident.

Until the 17th century, atheists were in a tiny minority. Now, despite being outnumbered in the world population by nearly 6 to 1, in secularized Europe they dominate the seven disciplines as we shall see below. Their names can be found in Wikipedia's 'Lists of atheists'. The atheists are listed under their surnames (A–Z) and also their professions, and the lists contain thousands of names. In contrast to the many European and Asian names, the list of US atheists is short. There is also a celebrity atheist list.

SECULAR, SOCIAL APPROACH IN THE SEVEN DISCIPLINES OF WORLD CULTURE

All atheists have a social approach. The impact of atheism has led to a social approach in the seven disciplines of world culture which challenges the metaphysical approach in each discipline (as we saw on p 7). Believing in the thinking reason of the social ego, social thinkers analyse the whole and fragment it into parts. Rational analysis perceives differences and makes distinctions, and social thinkers reduce the universe into pieces. We have seen that when the universe is seen as a whole, as One or the All, as a unity, its order is perceived along with a Law of Order. Analysing and reducing the universe into parts loses sight of the order that can be detected in the universe as a whole, the perspective that includes the 40 biofriendly conditions for life. The social view fragments the unified view of the seven disciplines of world culture into separate disciplines and challenges the traditional metaphysical view in each discipline, as we can now see.

MYSTICISM

The word 'mysticism' is derived from the Greek *muo*, 'close the eyes', and as we saw on pp 7–14 the mystical experience is 'what is seen behind closed eyes' – the Light. The social approach challenges and dismisses all mystical experience of God, the One, an invisible Reality beyond the senses, or the metaphysical Light, as a delusion. Atheists would argue that all the mystics listed on pp 11–12 were wrong, and that the mystics never had the experiences they claim. The reports of Augustine and Hildegarde of Bingen must be delusional. Atheists would argue that my own 93 experiences of the metaphysical Light (see *My Double Life 1: This Dark Wood* and *My Double Life 2: A Rainbow over the Hills*), all documented in written-on-the-day diary entries, must be a delusion as there must be an explanation acceptable to the atheistic reason.

'Mysticism' is also derived from closing one's lips, being a *mustikos* or initiate in one of the Greek mystery schools and concealing the truth they teach regarding the Light. The mysteries of Eleusis showed an ear of corn as a symbol of how the Light can make the soul grow, like the sun.[3] Social thinkers admit the initiates' social activity as acceptable to the reason, although they regard it as mistaken. We saw that there is an outer-world mysticism, seeing the phenomenal world as a unity. Richard Dawkins begins *The God Delusion* with a boy's overwhelming experience of the natural world but maintains: 'A quasi-mystical response to nature and the universe is common among scientists and rationalists. It has no connection with supernatural belief.'[4] The mystical experience is reduced reductionalistically to observation of Nature, and the sense of an orderly, unified universe is missing.

Social constructionism, a term from sociology and communication theory, is brought in to explain away mystical experiences as a family of different kinds of experience that are 'jointly contributed understandings of the world'. Mystical experiences are called 'contextualist', meaning that they are shaped by the concepts mystics bring to their experience. In other words, mystics contribute to, and 'misinterpret', their own experience. Such a social approach to mysticism views all mystical experiences as social reports on experiences that are not corroborated by rational, evidential scientific study. Secular scientists study mystical experiences and view them in social, secular – and often psychological – terms. They link mysticism to social transformation and social justice, a feeling for the world's poor. Atheist students of mysticism see it in exclusively social terms and are deniers of both traditional 'closed-eyes' and outer-world mysticism.

LITERATURE

In English literature, the atheistic social approach has challenged and dismissed the traditional metaphysical perceptions of the 17th-century Metaphysical poets. The rational 18th-century Augustans introduced their Neoclassical view drawn from the time and social values of the Roman Emperor Augustus and the poet Horace. Alexander Pope's social approach focused on society, as in *The Rape of the Lock*, but he was also aware of the order and harmony of the universe, virtues of the time of Augustus that Augustans admired. The later-18th-century and early-19th-century Romantic poets were deeply conscious of the metaphysical One, and their traditional quest for the One can be found in the Modernists W B Yeats and T S Eliot (who wrote 'And the fire and the rose are one' at the end of 'Little Gidding') and in the Neo-Romantic poets of the 1930s and 1940s: Dylan Thomas, John Heath-Stubbs, David Gascoyne and Kathleen Raine, who all looked beyond social realism. I knew the last three and had discussions with them. Kathleen Raine wrote *Defending Ancient Springs* which included essays on the Neo-Romantic poets Edwin Muir, Vernon Watkins, David Gascoyne and W B Yeats.

The social approach had been given impetus by the Bloomsbury Group of writers, including E M Forster, who met between 1907 and 1930 and based their values on personal relationships and friendship, a concept they took from the Cambridge philosopher G E Moore's *Principia Ethica*. The humanist view has been disseminated in the works of Forster and his followers, which suggest that life is meaningless except for social relationships

The Neoclassical English Movement poets of the 1950s challenged and attacked the Neo-Romantic poets. The atheist Kingsley Amis wrote in Robert Conquest's 1955 anthology, 'Nobody wants any more poems on the grander themes for a few years, but at the same time nobody wants any more poems about philosophers or paintings or novelists or art galleries or mythology or foreign cities or other poems.' In 'Against Romanticism' he challenged Neo-Romanticism: 'Over all, a grand meaning fills the scene.' In 'A Bookshop Idyll' he asks: 'Should poets bicycle-pump the human heart / Or squash it flat?' (The answer is that it is best to do neither and describe it as it is.) Philip Larkin wrote in Robert Conquest's anthology, '[I] have no belief in "tradition" or a common myth-kitty or casual allusions in poems to other poems or poets.' Donald Davie wrote in 'Remembering the Thirties', 'A neutral tone is nowadays preferred.' The Movement's social, provincial poetry took poetry away from the Neo-Romantic pursuit of the One and 'grandness' into social themes. The atheist Larkin's 'Church Going' was about the social pastime of visiting churches and dismissed the church's altar as 'the holy end'.

In *A New Philosophy of Literature* I tracked the challenge of the social view in world literature through ten periods (as we saw on p 15), culminating in the present time when literature has turned secular. Many of the poets and novelists condemn social follies and vices in terms of an implied universal virtue (as we saw on p 19), and many appear on the list of atheist writers – Kingsley and Martin Amis, Julian Barnes, Ian McEwan, Philip Larkin, Andrew Motion and Harold Pinter to name but a few. In social writers the quest for Reality has been replaced by social reality. The traditional quest for the One is in a minority. As I said on p 21, I have recently brought out *Selected Poems: Quest for the One* and *Selected Stories: Follies and Vices of the Modern Elizabethan Age*, in which Part Two is titled 'Quest for the One', and I sometimes think that in my poems and stories I am continuing the metaphysical tradition in literature single-handed, as Laurens van der Post told me I was in 1989.

In literary criticism too there is a social direction. The essays of Eliot have receded, and literary theory has dominated, including such social critical approaches to literature as deconstruction, gender criticism, Marxist criticism and historicism, all of which relate texts to their social or linguistic context. Only one distinguished social critic, Christopher Ricks, whom I have known for well over 50 years, has focused on literary principles rather than theory.[5] A Neoclassical critic and Empsonian who is known for his social approach and has described himself as an atheist, he has based his criticism on the principles of practical criticism and the Johnsonian principle of close reading and resonances of words. I too follow the principles of practical criticism and share his opposition to deconstruction, post-structuralism and postmodernism.

PHILOSOPHY

In philosophy, the social and empirical view of reality – the scientific approach – goes back to Aristotle, who challenged Plato's metaphysical hidden Reality. We have just seen that Descartes focused on the thinking social reason and opened the way for the empirical social philosophy of Locke and others. In the 20th century, the social challenge to metaphysics came from logical analysis or analytic philosophy, which had two branches: Logical Positivism and Logical Empiricism in the works of Gottlob Frege and Bertrand Russell; and Linguistic Analysis, which focused on the logic of language in the works of G E Moore and Ludwig Wittgenstein.

A school of Logical Positivism was declared at the University of Vienna in 1923, and meetings continued there as the Vienna Circle until 1938. Wittgenstein had stated in 1921 that the object of philosophy is the logical clarification of thoughts, and Logical Positivists focused on logic, language and perception. Rudolf Carnap helped shape the Vienna Circle's 1929 manifesto, *Wissenschaftliche Weltauffassung: Der Wiener Kreis* (*Scientific Conception of the World: The Vienna Circle*), which announced that philosophy should now be scientific and produce clear thinking. The universe, which Plato and Aristotle had studied and of which Einstein had so much to say, was declared a no-go area for philosophy, and traditional culture was demolished. Philosophy was fragmented into broken pieces. Logical Positivists refused to discuss the post-Einsteinian universe, and left a legacy of atheism. Whitehead, a pupil of Russell, had defected from Logical Positivism to metaphysics, and to the US, in 1924. Ernest Gellner's *Words and Things* (1959) attacked linguistic philosophy. It contained an epigraph from Russell on linguistic philosophers: 'The desire to understand the world is, they think, an outdated folly.' It should be noted that Linguistic Analysis had an impact on the new literary criticism of I A Richards and his pupil Empson – and on Empson's protégé Ricks.[6] Social and empirical philosophers have continued the Vienna Circle's challenge to traditional metaphysics.

REDUCTIONIST SCIENCE

In reductionist science, the social and empirical challenge began c1500, and grew with Galileo, Newton and Darwin. Scientific reductionism holds that the whole of reality consists of a number of parts and can be explained in terms of smaller entities, less complex and more simple phenomena. It holds that all more complex entities are combinations of simple entities. So biological and psychological phenomena are reduced, or simplified, to physics, chemistry and mechanistic explanations. The 19th-century mechanistic and deterministic T H Huxley reduced biological and mental events to physical events. Biological and medical reductionists have reduced the human body to a collection of atoms and chemically controlled cells. Reductionist geneticists have reduced man to a collection of genes, and reductionist brain physiologists and psychologists have reduced mind to physiological brain functions. In the 20th century, reductionist physicists have used classical physics to reduce the universe to granular atoms (atomism), and molecular biologists have reduced biology to physics and chemistry. Quantum mechanics has reduced chemistry to physics. Physiology has been reduced to physics and chemistry, and scientific psychology to neurophysiology and cybernetics. The behaviourism of John B Watson and B F Skinner has reduced consciousness to physical behaviour.

Scientific reduction to physical processes impacted on empirical philosophy and strengthened the challenge to traditional philosophy. Metaphysical ontology has been reduced to physical processes, and analytic and linguistic philosophers have analysed concepts and language and reduced all existing things to observable objects and sense data. Empirically verifiable statements have held man's religious aspirations to be meaningless. Mathematical axioms have been reduced to Kurt Gödel's incompleteness theorems, and religious truth to the anthropological theories of J G Frazer.

However, in the 20th century, reductionism, which had been based on observation, sense data, experiment and testing, was undermined by the mathematics of the relativity and quantum theories: the granular world of matter has been replaced by a sea of energies in which light can be both particles and waves, and electrons are best seen as events in a process in accordance with Heisenberg's uncertainty principle. Relativity and quantum theories show that the observer is a relational part of the universe he is observing, and mechanistic reductionism has been undermined from within science.

That was very clearly established at the conference on reductionism I attended at Jesus College, Cambridge, in 1992,[7] when challenging reductionists such as Michael Sofroniew, Patricia Churchland, Margaret Boden, Hao Wang and Peter Atkins were countered by metaphysicals including the philosopher Mary Midgley. In the presence of Roger Penrose, Peter Atkins's challenging view that the universe is a materialistic 'dung-heap' in his hubristic talk 'The Limitless Power of Science' was beaten back by Midgley's counter-attack entitled 'Reductionist Megalomania'.

The atheist Richard Dawkins challenged the metaphysical approach in his neo-Darwinist *The Selfish Gene* and in *The God Delusion*; and in his 'atheist bus campaign' run in 13 countries in early 2009 when, in conjunction with Ariane Sherine, he placed advertisements on buses proclaiming 'There's probably no God. Now stop worrying and enjoy your life'. His simplistic view of the metaphysical as being linked to the traditional Hell would not have been recognized by William Wordsworth or Samuel Taylor Coleridge, who do not appear in the index of *The God Delusion*. It must be remembered that, despite their posture of certainty and tone, no scientists witnessed the manifestation of the Big Bang, and the militant atheism of some scientists is as much a belief as the militant fundamentalism of Christians and Muslims.

HISTORY

In history the social approach grew through the Enlightenment and Gibbon. The challenge to the traditional metaphysical approach came through Marx, and the Marxist approach to history is still with us, in books and in magazines such as *The New Left Review*. There were many criticisms of the speculative, linear sweep of Toynbee's *A Study of History*. Social historians spurn the speculative, linear tradition that history has a teleological aim and looks beyond nation-states. The majority of historians today follow historical relativism, an approach prevalent since the 1960s which holds that there is no absolute truth and that a historical era can only be understood in its own terms that reject historical or cross-cultural comparison. My own study of 25 civilizations with 61 parallel stages would not find favour with their approach.

Social historians assign themselves to specific societies and periods, and interpret past social events, sometimes in terms of contemporary thinking. Social history studies the experiences of ordinary people in the past. Societal history studies the history of society, and there is also political, economic and military history, cultural history (which combines anthropology and history), diplomatic history and environmental history. Social history has subdivisions: demographic history, ethnic history, labour history, women's history and gender history; history of the family and of education; urban and rural history; and the history of religion. There have been distinctive French, German and Hungarian approaches to social history. A distinguished example of a social historian is Asa Briggs, whom I knew, an expert on the Victorian era and the Chartists and author of *A Social History of England*, a 5-volume *History of Broadcasting in the UK* and co-author of *Social History of the Media*, which examines the social impacts of the media.

COMPARATIVE RELIGION

In comparative religion the social, atheist approach strengthened as the civilizations of the main religions developed beyond their metaphysical growth and turned secular: Christianity in the European civilization (now in stage 43, loss of national sovereignty to a secularizing conglomerate, ie the European Union) as distinct from the North American civilization (now in stage 15, expansion into empire); Judaism in the renewed Israelite civilization (which had passed into the Arab civilization in 636 and re-emerged as a Western 'colonial state' in 1948); Islam in the Arab civilization (now moving into a federal stage 46); Hinduism, Buddhism, Jainism and Sikhism in the Indian civilization (now in the federal stage 46); and Taoism in the Chinese civilization (still in stage 43, having emerged from Mao's atheism). The higher religions all exist within secularized civilizations and have been buffeted by secular movements. Within Christianity, as we have seen, these have included the secularizing of English hymns (see p 31), the 'death of God' (see p 123), Dawkins's atheist bus campaign (see p 131) and the atheist scientists researching the origin of creation who, like Hawking, have a materialistic belief based on matter (which forms only 4 per cent of the universe).

The atheist challenge to mysticism has also challenged Christianity, Judaism, Islam, Hinduism, Buddhism, Jainism, Sikhism and Taoism. Secular atheists deny the common Light that shone through the distinctive gods (listed on pp 30–1) and shines through these higher religions today. Within each religion secular voices have spoken out in denial. All the higher religions have suffered from terrorism: Christianity from the IRA and other European terror groups; Judaism from the Zionist Irgun war against British troops, and from Brit HaKanain, the Kingdom of Israel group, Gush Emunim underground, Keshet, the Bat Ayin group and Lehava in the 1940s; Islam from al-Qaeda Jihadists, suicide-terrorists who call themselves the IS, Islamic State, despite being neither Islamic nor a state, who barbarously behead in the name of Allah; Hinduism from the saffron terror groups, the 65[8] terror groups active in India and Kashmir; Buddhism from the terror groups in Thailand, Myanmar (formerly Burma), Sri Lanka's war against the Liberation Tigers of Tamil Eelam, Japan and Tibet; and Sikhism from the Khalistan militancy, the assassination of Indira Ghandi by two Sikhs and the 38 terrorist incidents in the Punjab in the 1980s and 1990s. All these forces have pressured the higher religions into a social rather than a metaphysical approach.

INTERNATIONAL POLITICS AND STATECRAFT

In international politics and statecraft the traditional religion-based states were challenged long before the 20th century by growing nationalism and the emergence of nation-states, and also, as I showed in *The Secret History of the West*, by revolutions against Church-supported monarchies: the Reformation revolutions by heretics such as the Cathars, Savonarola and Luther; and the revolutions (backed by secret societies) in England, France, America and Russia. In the 20th century there were social challenges to the Church-supported monarchies by occultist Nazism and atheist Communism; and in the Cold War fought by proxies in the Middle East, Africa, Asia and Latin America there were social, Marxist revolutions: revolutionary social challenges to the old order in China, Vietnam, Cuba, Egypt, Iraq, Libya, Cambodia and Iran. The revolutions introduced rapid social change and, as in the French and Russian revolutions, large numbers of the upper and middle classes were put to death.

Now there is a post-Communist challenge to all nation-states and revolutionary republics to come together under a world government under an occultist New World Order (compare pp 34–5), whose covert god is Lucifer, the god of money and world revolution[9] and opposed to all religions. Across the world we see secular governments with a few reactionary theocracies such as Iran's government in the name of the Hidden Imam, the Taliban's Afghanistan and IS or ISIL (known in the Arab world as Daesh), which have revived the 7th-century cruelty of the Shariah law. As I have said (p 34), the New World Order is the project of self-interested, élitist families seeking to control all the gas and oil pipelines, and it would be better if the world's nation-states could come together in a democratic, partly-supranational World State that includes all civilizations and higher religions and their common essence and has nothing to do with the conflicting extremes of Luciferianism or Shariah law. Until steps are taken to create this paradise, the social challenge to the traditional states will continue to spread atheistic secularism.

WORLD CULTURE

In world culture works of art on the traditional theme of the quest for metaphysical Reality and immortality have been challenged by atheistic and social works of art. For example, the atheistic *Study for a Pope 1* by Francis Bacon (a distant descendant of the Elizabethan statesman, philosopher and essayist Sir Francis Bacon), whom I met several times at the Colony Room Club in London, is of a Pope with a twisted face against a black background. It was offered at auction in 2015 at a staggering estimated forecast price of £25–35 million (to many, an indication of the depths to which Western culture has sunk) but failed to reach that price or the reserve. During the 1950s and 1960s Bacon produced 45 Pope paintings based on Diego Velazquez's 1650 *Portrait of Pope Innocent X*, and one of his portraits fetched £89 million, the most expensive art work ever sold at auction. (To put world culture into perspective, Vincent Van Gogh, who was better, only sold one painting in his life, to his brother, and left nearly 900 unsold paintings and 1,100 unsold drawings at his death.)

All civilizations began with a unified culture as we have seen (on p 36), and an image of the unified European culture is: a tree with all the European nation-states as branches. The world culture can also be presented as such: a tree with all the world's nation-states as branches. The European culture's unified Christian trunk and national branches have thrust out offshoot-branches into 50 'isms' (as we saw on p 38), and all this secular multiplicity has made the European culture's original unity top-heavy and burdened it to splitting point. The same is true of world culture, which reflects these 50 'isms' or doctrinal movements that weakened the higher religions. All these 50 'isms' are known in America, but the traditional American unifying – and Universalist – trunk controls them, whereas in Europe the control of the unifying trunk has weakened and the 50 'isms' have broken away and compounded the anarchistic multiplicity and disorder of European values. In European and world culture, which includes all the advanced, increasingly secularized civilizations of the higher religions (as we saw on p 134), atheistic, social, secularized works of art about the 'outer world' which condemn follies and vices have challenged the traditional works of art which reflect the inner world and the quest for metaphysical Reality, the One.

World culture is now full of deniers of mysticism or outer-world mystics, social-approach writers, social-approach philosophers and Materialistic scientists, one-nation historians, nation-state politicians, social-form religious and secular cultural historians, who all fragment the whole and lose sight of the order within the whole perspective, as can be seen in each of the seven disciplines.

ACCIDENT AND CHANCE IN THE UNIVERSE: LAW OF RANDOMNESS AND LAW OF ORDER

I have already established (pp 95, 111–13) that the many examples of order in the universe suggest that the existence of the universe was not a random accident. The atheistic social approach sees the universe as just that: a random accident.

The argument for accident is that as space-time began with the Big Bang, we can only think of what came after the Big Bang, we cannot think back to a time before the Big Bang. As Hawking has written, 'The concept of time has no meaning before the beginning of the universe.'[10] Secular sceptics hold that, as we cannot go back before the Big Bang, there was no creation and the universe came into being by accident. Strangely, Hawking and Dawkins, proponents of this view, have indexes in their books that do not contain the words 'accident', 'chance' or 'randomness'. (It is important to keep separate the philosophical, religious and testable scientific categories, and Mary Midgley pointed out to general assent that Dawkins's 'selfish gene' metaphor slipped from scientific description to psychological egoism.) The argument for accident continues. The first atom of matter and the first cell came into being by accident, and so the Earth came into being by accident, and so man's place in the universe is a pointless accident. Evolution is a chance development, and every human being has been born by chance as in each act of conception one of more than a million eggs, each with a different genetic code, come into contact with one of 180 million sperm, each of which has a different genetic code, a point made by Brian Cox.[11] The argument for accident holds that our existence is an accident, and our minds and brains are just part of our random bodies. Intelligence is an accident. This was the view of randomness Atkins presented to the conference on reductionism.

However, there is a counter-argument to each of these points, emphasizing order. Thinking of what came before the Big Bang is perfectly admissible to metaphysics, which holds that 'the All' includes 'every known concept', and what was before the Big Bang falls within 'every known concept'. There is no evidence that the first appearance of matter (4 per cent of the universe) was an accident. We have seen (pp 53–69) that 40 conditions and 362 constants were exactly right for life. There is no evidence that the first cell or the Earth came into being by accident. There is no evidence that man's arrival was a pointless accident, and despite the 180 million sperm and more than a million eggs, there is no evidence that conception is a matter of chance. There is the order of the DNA cascades. There is no evidence that our existence is an accident or that our minds are dependent on brain function (despite Crick's hunch that the claustrum is the seat of consciousness).[12] There is no evidence that intelligence is an accident. We have seen (pp 93–5) that the probability rating against the universe being an accident and operating by chance is 10^{120}. This view of order counterbalances randomness.

In Heisenberg's new quantum mechanics of 1925, randomness or indeterminacy is fundamental, and identical electrons in identical experiments behave with apparent randomness. Einstein did not accept this randomness and proposed a 'hidden variable' that causes some nuclei to decay but not others, as underlying the indeterminacy and the uncertainty principle. Randomness ignores order, and to Bohm the apparent randomness, probabilities and uncertainties of quantum theory have order behind them, as tides order the sea.

I have suggested (on p 112) that a Law of Randomness that brings chaos, starvation and sudden accidental death is counter-balanced by a Law of Order, which describes an energy methodically organizing all creatures from birth into their rightful place within a system through light. I suggested that: +A (Order) + –A (Randomness) = 0. The two laws, though apparently in conflict, are two sides of a fundamental unity which reconciles all opposites. The Law of Order + the Law of Randomness = Being in Existence. To turn it round, Being in Existence is the Law of Order + the Law of Randomness.

PARTICLE PHYSICS, THE LAWS OF THE UNIVERSE AND THE STANDARD MODEL

Mechanical Materialism is a theory that holds that the universe consists of hard massy objects that are too tiny to see but resemble stones: the atoms of matter. The objects interact by impact and perhaps by gravitational attraction. The theory denies the existence of immaterial things such as minds and explains them as being material things or their motions. However, in modern particle physics, electrons and protons are not massy and stone-like, and the distinction between matter and energy no longer holds, and so particle physicists are physicalist materialists.

Physicalist Materialists today see the universe in terms of particles, which supply the laws of Nature. They see humans as particles within the universe of particles and deny the spiritual, or rather reduce that side of experience to physics and chemistry. Some Materialists exclude living cells and brains from being reduced to physical entities, but by and large Materialists reduce chemistry to physics and see biology as an application of physics and chemistry. However, they cannot account for intentionality, the mental capacity of human beings to point forwards through an intention, which non-mental processes are unable to do.

Materialist scientists assert that the origin of life on Earth came from the carbon in matter, and they speculate that this carbon originated on comets, one of which (they speculate) crashed into Earth bringing the building blocks of life. The European *Philae* lander on comet 67, a brilliant technical feat that began when *Rosetta* was launched on 2 March 2004 and arrived on 12 November 2014, promised the possibility of establishing that life came from a comet and that its ice created our seas. The *Philae* lander 'sniffed' organic molecules but was not able to take a soil sample of the comet's ice and dust. The *Philae* lander's battery was in shadow rather than sunlight, and ran down. But on 14 June 2015 the *Philae* lander 'woke up', and experiments may provide the European Space Agency with an answer as to whether life began on comets. At present there is no evidence that life on Earth began from a comet, and the idea is speculative. If evidence were found, the question would then become: how did the building blocks of life get into comets? The fundamental question of the origin of life on Earth would be pushed back by physicalist Materialist scientists from Earth to comets and the question would still remain unanswered.

Physicalist Materialist scientists assert that the laws of the universe and of Nature are those of chance, and that the order in the universe is the result of chance rules. The laws of the universe have been worked out by scientists and act as a framework. They include the Standard Model Lagrangian, a quantum field theory, the mathematical framework that describes all the 12 known particles of matter and forces other than gravity in a single equation which predicts the existence of the Higgs particle (discovered at a level of 3.8 sigma, a one in 10,000 chance that the results are false, in June 2013).

The Standard Model does not include dark matter, which has not yet been discovered and may turn out to be a new particle. The 12 matter particles are 6 quarks (up, down, charm, strange, top, bottom quarks) and 6 leptons (electron neutrino, electron, nuon neutrino, nuon, tau neutrino, tau), and the Standard Model theory explains the interactions between these and four bosons (strong-force gluon, electromagnetic-force photon and two weak-force bosons) – and the Higgs boson. It is a quantum field theory that describes all the known particles and forces other than gravity, and provides rules that allow probabilities to be calculated. It does not incorporate General Relativity and is not a Theory of Everything. There are many different versions of the Standard Model online. For the detailed workings of the Standard Model, see W N Cottingham and D A Greenwood, 'An Introduction to the Standard Model of Particle Physics'.[13] A simplified version can be found in Brian Cox and Andrew Cohen, *The Human Universe*, in which Ψ contains the 12 matter particles:[14]

$$
\begin{aligned}
\mathrm{L} = & -\frac{1}{4} W_{\mu v} W^{\mu v} - \frac{1}{4} B_{\mu v} B^{\mu v} - \frac{1}{4} G_{\mu v} G^{\mu v} \\
& + \overline{\psi}_j \gamma^{\mu} (i\delta_{\mu} - g\tau_j \cdot W_{\mu} - g' Y_j B_{\mu} - g_s \mathrm{T}_j \cdot \mathrm{G}_{\mu}) \psi_j \\
& + |\mathrm{D}_{\mu}\phi|^2 + \mu^2 |\phi|^2 - \lambda |\phi|^4 \\
& - (y_j \overline{\psi}_{jL} \phi \psi_{jR} + y'_j \overline{\psi}_{jL} \phi_c \psi_{jR} + \text{conjugate})
\end{aligned}
$$

The laws of the universe and of Nature also include Einstein's Theory of General Relativity, which covers the fourth force, gravity. Again there are longer versions but, opting for simplification, I follow Cox and Cohen:

$$
G_{\mu v} = 8\pi G T_{\mu v}
$$

Within the framework of the laws of Nature, many variations are possible. Cox compares these laws to the laws of cricket, which provide the framework for each game although within each game there are many variations and no two games are the same.[15] But the laws of cricket were not put together by chance, and the order the umpires enforce is not a chance order.

So the physicalist materialists' social approach to the universe in cosmology and astrophysics sees the universe as an accident; in biology sees genetics and the appearance of *Homo sapiens sapiens* and all evolution as an accident; and in physiology sees all bodily processes and mental events, the organization of the brain and consciousness, as an accident. All of these are seen in terms of physicalist particles. However, there is no conclusive evidence that the universe's atoms, the Earth, cells and human beings are accidental, chance, random events. The physicalist materialists' social approach is struggling in biocosmology on account of the 40 conditions and 326 constants; and in ecology on account of its food webs and food chains. The order in biocosmology and ecology seems too orderly to be an accident, and the probability for order and against there being an accident is 10^{120} as we saw on pp 93–5.

Physicalist materialist scientists spend their thinking lives within particle physics and, like the physicist I described at the end of the Prologue, have their own approach to the seven disciplines. They deny the inner experiences of mysticism and comparative religion and assert an aggressive atheism that reduces their inner experiences to physics and chemistry and their outer forms to social activities. They have a social approach to literature and see poetic feelings and human behaviour in terms of matter and particles. They disregard philosophy except for atomism and the views of the Vienna Circle. They see history in terms of the development of materialism in the Greek and Roman times. They see international politics and social political life in terms of the accidental, random existence of particles and the need for a society that assists social relationships. And they have a social, materialist approach to world culture. Theirs is a very fragmented view and does not see the whole and its pervasive order.

The tussle between the traditional metaphysical view that there is a hidden order in the universe and the secular, sceptical view of modern empirical scientists, philosophers and reductionists who deny the metaphysical view for a physicalist materialist approach has left the disciplines in separate pieces: internally broken and separated from each other and lacking order. Those who assert that the universe is an accident and champion a social, humanistic approach in the seven disciplines and world culture assert that life is meaningless except for social relationships and personal enjoyment: a form of hedonism.

To appeal to the traditionally religious population of the world, 63 per cent of the world's citizens, Liberty's vision of the spiritual unity of humankind has to neutralize the challenge of atheism by reconciling the conflicting approaches within the seven disciplines in accordance with +A + –A = 0: the reconciliation of Universalism, the philosophy that is surfacing in the current stages of the North American and European civilizations.

PART THREE

THE UNIVERSALIST SYNTHESIS: THE REUNIFICATION OF WORLD CULTURE

CHAPTER 5

UNIVERSALISM'S RECONCILIATION

As all presidents and prime ministers know, the way to keep a cabinet unified is to have an agenda that contains ideas that appeal to both wings: the traditional and the liberal, the pro-nation-staters and the internationalists. Roosevelt's New Deal that combated the Great Depression, the Truman Doctrine of combating subversion with Marshall Aid and Reagan's combative championing of liberty at the end of the Cold War all appealed to American nationalists and to internationalist supporters of the poor and the oppressed – supporters of Liberty, defender of the huddled yearning to breathe free.

To achieve the secret American destiny to bring in a World State that can unify humankind, Liberty has to project a vision of the unity of all humankind. A vision equally acceptable to Westerners and Easterners requires a reconciliation within the seven conflicting disciplines of world culture so that the 63 per cent of world citizens who are religious – the 2.2 billion Christians, 1.6 billion Muslims, 1 billion Hindus and 0.376 Buddhists – do not feel excluded from a secular view of world culture and the 15.35 per cent or 16.3 per cent of world citizens who are secular (some 1.1 billion) do not feel excluded from a purely traditional view of world culture. Only Universalism can achieve such a reconciliation.

Liberty holds the torch and is defined against New York's iconic buildings: the late-1920s Chrysler building whose seven terraced arches symbolize the Machine Age, and the One World Trade Center, the Freedom Tower, the tallest skyscraper in the Western hemisphere, which represents Liberty's triumph over 9/11 when the Twin Towers (jokingly nicknamed after Nelson and David Rockefeller) were brought down for this new skyscraper to rise phoenix-like from the ashes. Liberty shelters all poor and hungry, all homeless and oppressed, and the universality of Liberty makes her a symbol for, and presider over, the new Universalism in which all humankind is free and equal. Universalism is the study of the whole of humankind's activities (as we saw on p xv) and Liberty presides over humankind's activities for the Western world and with a global perspective.

Now that I move away from atheistic reductionism's denial of the traditional Reality and culture, I take up a position under Liberty whose torch of universal freedom shines out across the Western world and the entire globe, portending unity. America has a tremendous role to play in reunifying world culture and bringing in her own – and the world's – destiny.

THE UNIVERSALIST JOURNEY OF TRANSFORMATION

I have already established the unity and wholeness of the universe and the evidence of order (see chs 2 and 3). Universalism, which focuses on the universe, universality and the universal principle of order, examines the place of humans on Earth and in the universe, and of humankind as a whole in its seven disciplines. It teaches a way of looking that sees the unity of the universe and therefore of the seven disciplines of world culture.

This way of looking does not come from the rational, social ego but from the universal being, a deeper part of the self. I have described in *My Double Life 1: This Dark Wood* and *My Double Life 2: A Rainbow over the Hills* my journey along a 'perilous path' through a 'dark wood': 'the influences, belief systems, ideological conflicts and political causes of the 20th century.'[1]

As I progressed along the Mystic Way I came to understand that I could not reach the goal of my quest – Reality, the One – until I had undergone a transformation, a metamorphosis: a centre-shift from my rational, social self to my deeper self. I had to get behind my life of the five senses to a more reflective, contemplative self, a process that was a form of purgation. After earlier glimpses, illumination burst into my mind and cleansed my soul,[2] and this profound experience changed – transformed, metamorphosed – my way of seeing so that I found I now instinctively saw the universe as a unity behind all its differences.

The journey of transformation is a very important one, for it gets behind the social approach to life and opens up the traditional, metaphysical way of looking that was widespread in the 17th century but has slowly become lost: the ability to perceive the unity of the universe instinctively. It is because this faculty that used to be so widespread and prevalent has atrophied into relative disuse that world culture has settled into social-approach, atheistic Materialism. It is important that in the course of our education we all make a transforming journey – a quest for the One – by reading Wordsworth's *The Prelude* and Eliot's *Four Quartets* so that we open to awareness of this unity and live in unitive being, connected instinctively to the One.

We can all see the unity of the universe if we embark on the transforming process of the journey; and as the universities are filled with atheistic, social-approach lecturers and professors who live in their rational, social ego and the churches have social-approach vicars and priests who increasingly do not believe in God and no longer teach the way to one's deepest being, it is incumbent on Universalism to make the world's people aware of the vision of unity. Liberty's torch symbolizes the Light of illumination that opens the soul to this way of seeing unity.

The Universalist has made the journey from the ego to the universal being within that instinctively and intuitionally perceives the unity of the universe: that all living things including humans came out of the first cell and so are in oneness with Nature and the universe.

UNIVERSALISM'S ESEMPLASTIC VISION OF UNITY

Universalism counters the effects of rational analysis which, as we have seen, makes distinctions and perceives differences. The faculty that perceives unity Coleridge called 'the esemplastic power of the imagination'. As we have seen (p 74), 'esemplastic' comes from the Greek *eis en plattein*, to 'mould or shape, make into one'. Coleridge in *Biographia Literaria*, chapter X, wrote, 'I constructed it myself from the Greek words *eis en plattein*, to shape into one.' The *Shorter Oxford English Dictionary* derives the word from *eis en plassein*, 'to mould into unity, unify'.

The esemplastic power sees unity, it takes pieces and puts them together into a whole like an archaeologist piecing together fragmented potsherds that have been found in a trench, thereby restoring a vase. Universalists piece broken disciplines together into a whole, repair the broken fragments and restore the perception of order that is a response to the whole. They see literature and history as expressions of the whole, and philosophy as the study of the whole universe, Nature and man. Universalist metaphysical mystics, poets, philosophers, scientists, historians, religious leaders, international politicians and cultural historians piece the potsherds back together and restore the whole pot.

UNIVERSALISM'S REUNIFICATION OF SEVEN DISCIPLINES

Universalism presents a synthesis – a reunification – within each of the seven disciplines by combining the two opposites within each discipline – the +A + –A – as I have done in my work. It does this by presenting the antithesis in each of the pairs of opposites, the social, secular approach, within the context of the thesis, the ordering metaphysical approach. The social is presented as being within the metaphysical, so that +A (the metaphysical) + –A (the social) = 0 (the synthesis, reunification). We can see how this works within each discipline.

UNIVERSALIST MYSTICISM

In mysticism Universalism presents the natural, social, outer universe which in the mystic state is pantheistically felt to be a unity, one, within the context of ordering metaphysical Reality: the Light that I have documented in all cultures and civilizations over 5,000 years (in *The Fire and the Stones* and *The Light of Civilization*). The perception by the inner universal being that the infinite is behind the finite universe incorporates and contextualizes humanism, Materialism, Rationalism, Empiricism, scepticism, mechanism, positivism and reductionism and many other 'isms' in all disciplines. We can know infinite Being, or the One, beyond and behind the phenomenal world of the senses, rationally via the image of the surfer on the crest of the surging wave of the expanding universe, whose feet are in finite space-time and whose upper body and head breast the infinite; and intuitionally via the vision of the 'ever-living Fire' or metaphysical Light.

Within Nature – the splendour of flora and fauna, mountains, tossing seas, sunrise and sunset – is an order that is imperceptible to the careless eye but is perceptible when the universal being sees the universe as a whole. The view of the rational, social ego that each human being is a reductionist collection of atoms on a dunghill, physicalist particles and cells whose mind is mere brain function, a social ego that will cease to exist on death, is placed within a context of 12 levels of consciousness, including the universal being and its awareness of a possibly immortal spirit (or invisible body) within his or her visible body. The view of the rational, social ego that life and evolution are a chance, random accident, and that our DNA is a similar accident as there could have been 180 million × 1 million alternatives to our combinations of DNA, is placed within a context of the 40 conditions and 326 constants friendly to life which make it 10^{120} probable that the universe, and life, were not an accident.

This contextual approach of mystical Universalism can be summed up as +A (the infinite and order) + –A (the finite and accidental)

= 0 (the reunification of mysticism). The inner experiences of the infinite of the individual Christian mystics (listed on pp 9–10) and of the mystics of all cultures and civilizations (listed on pp 11–12) – experiences of ordering metaphysical Reality – are therefore a context for all the contemplative pantheism and views on the finite universe of the rational, social ego. The inner experience of the Light which is symbolized in Liberty's torch again co-exists with all the other views of the oneness of Nature, which have failed to replace it.

UNIVERSALIST LITERATURE

In literature Universalism presents condemnation of the follies and vices of humankind which can be found in the literature of the classical period within the context of the quest for the One, the literary theme of the quest for Reality that goes back to c2600 BCE. The balance between condemnation of follies and vices and the quest for the One, which I document in *A New Philosophy of Literature* as a tussle for dominance through ten literary periods, is now restored through Universalism.

The social condemnation of follies and vices in terms of an implied virtue exists within the context of awareness of the infinite that surrounds the universe, the Light and the universal principle of order that pervades the eight Universalist characteristics already described (pp 15–18). As all literature emerged from one point that preceded the Big Bang, from the first cell and the first instance of human literature, literary Universalism sees all literature as one, an interconnected unity that is one supranational literature. All nations' poetry is one universal poetry that, at its deepest, reflects the infinite and timeless One. Much literature in our time is of a Materialist and social-humanist outlook, but Universalist literature intermingles everyday life and social situations with epiphanies – revelations – of Being, as does Wordsworth in *The Prelude*. Universalist literature focuses on revelations of Being and their links to everyday lives.

Universalist literature appeals to the intuitive faculty and reflects the oneness of the universe, but it also appeals to the reason as it interprets intuitive experience rationally in a blend of the intuitional and rational, Romanticism and Classicism, and the opposites of sense and spirit in the Baroque Age. Universalist literature is the successor to Vitalism and Existentialism on the intuitional side and to empiricism on the rational side, as it emphasizes the empirical nature of the experience of Reality and the scientific view of the universe.

The Universalist poet reshapes and restructures the apparently chaotic universe into a structure of order in the act of writing a poem. He lets the universal order principle into his poem. He puts himself in readiness for the One and receives back from it a glimpse, a reassurance, that the universe is ordered with a purpose and meaning. The Universalist poet restates the order of the universe. Homer and Virgil showed a world presided over and ordered by the gods, Dante a world ordered by God. Shakespeare had a profound sense of order, the disruption of which affected 'the great chain of being'. (Similarly, in fiction Fyodor Dostoevsky's nihilists attempted to overthrow order and their defeat reinstated order; and Leo Tolstoy related war and peace to the order in society.) Marlowe saw order in terms of Heaven, Wordsworth in terms of the 'Wisdom and Spirit of the universe'. Percy Bysshe Shelley saw order in 'Adonais' – 'the One remains, the many change and pass' – and T S Eliot saw order in 'Burnt Norton': 'the still point of the turning world'. The pairs of opposites within the Neoclassical and Romantic positions that Universalist poetry reconciles (the Neoclassical first, the Romantic second) are:[3]

- Imitation, and inspired imagination
- Harmony, and the infinite
- Natural images, and symbols
- Genius that improves, and genius that is inspired
- Poetry as statement, and poetry as image

- Traditional stanzaic form, and organic form
- Poetry from the rational, social ego, and poetry from the soul
- Objective poetry, and personal poetry
- Materialist reality, and Reality as Light
- Personal and social reality, and metaphysical Reality
- Personal memory, and contemplation
- The historical, and the timeless
- The temporal, and the eternal
- Secular outlook, and metaphysical outlook
- Poetry of society, and poetry of the beyond
- Poetry of language, and poetry of the universe
- Structure (including grammatology and deconstruction), and symbolism
- Poetry of vices in relation to implied virtue, and poetry of the quest for Reality

Universalism has reconciled and synthesized five sets of contradictory traditions or approaches[4] in literature:

- The metaphysical and secular traditions
- The classical/Neoclassical and Romantic traditions
- Rational and intuitional approaches
- Linguistic and verbal imitative, and inspired imaginative, traditions
- Mystic and visionary traditions

In my poetry and writings[5] I have:

- Stated a metaphysical tradition in literature (the quest for Reality)
- Stated a secular tradition in literature (vices in relation to an implied virtue), which co-exists with the metaphysical
- Unified world literature by seeing it as a unity in relation to the dialectic of these two contraries

- Restored the metaphysical infinite to literature
- Restored the subjective vision of the infinite in literature
- Stated a synthesis of the metaphysical and secular traditions, Universalism
- Stated a Universalist literary tradition
- Reconciled classicism/Neoclassicism and Romanticism in the synthesis of Universalism
- Carried the Metaphysical Revolution, the 'Revolution in Thought and Culture' (described on p 171) into literature
- Stated a new direction for world literature

In these ten statements, restorations, unifications and revolutions, my Universalism reconciled the contradictions of literature by using algebraic thinking: +A + –A = 0.

The works of the Universalist man of letters reveal Being (as do my own *Collected Poems* and *Collected Stories*: see p 21). They try to investigate the universe with precise language and catch intimations of unity, of the presence of the One. They offer sudden revelations of Being and capture Being in the moment. Universalist epic relates the extremities of war and peace, and notions of Heaven and Hell, to the One (as I have attempted to do in my two poetic epics, *Overlord* and *Armageddon*). Universalist verse plays link order to government and the Being behind the divine right of kings and states, as do Shakespeare's history plays, and to the One (as do the five plays in my *Collected Verse Plays*). Diaries and autobiography link the everyday to growing awareness of Being and contact with the One (as do my *Awakening to the Light*, diaries, and *My Double Life 1: This Dark Wood* and *My Double Life 2: A Rainbow over the Hills*, volumes of autobiography).

The Universalist man of letters uses a variety of forms to probe and investigate the universe. Different forms and genres are like different drills miners use for different coalfaces. The Universalist man of letters drills several coalfaces of the universe. The universe is layered, tiered. Nothingness, the All or One, manifests through Non-Being to Being and Existence, and this process is reflected in layers or tiers or multiple states of Being and of consciousness: the 12 levels of the self which include the universal being as well as the rational, social ego. Humankind is presented against a layered, tiered universe and Universalism ranges over all lives and cultures and focuses on the inward Being of the 'ever-living Fire' or Light.

Universalism sees human order and organization creating one-world history, one-world culture and one-world literature and holds that the arts, including literature, should reflect the reunification of humankind. Literary Universalism reflects the multi-levelled self and multi-levelled cosmos and includes the depth of the perceptions of all the seven disciplines along with surface social follies and vices, and presents positive snapshots of the unity of the universe and its order.

UNIVERSALIST PHILOSOPHY

In philosophy Universalism presents empiricism within the context of evidenced and ordering metaphysical Reality. On the empirical side, Universalism reunifies linguistic and phenomenological philosophies. Phenomenology studies Being by 'bracketing out the object' – the source of Being – to focus on the data in human consciousness, a method Edmund Husserl devised in 1913 in *Ideen zu einer reinen Phänomenologie und phänomenologischen Philosophie* (*Ideas: General Introduction to Pure Phenomenology*). The data in consciousness can be reconciled with the linguistic approach to consciousness. (I should note in passing that in our time transcendental Husserlian phenomenology and ontological Heideggerian phenomenology have been reconciled by the British Universalist philosopher living in France, Christopher Macann, in *Being and Becoming*, 1998–2007.) On the metaphysical side, Universalism reunifies rational and intuitional metaphysics (as we saw on p 107).

Philosophical Universalism balances trust in reason – awareness of the finite universe, a view of Nature as order, clarity, balance, restraint, a sense of duty, a social view of humans via the rational, social ego – with trust in the intuition and the imagination: awareness of the infinite behind the finite, revolt against reason, the philosophical tradition, a view of Nature as organic dynamic process with a view of humans as individuals. In bringing together the conflicting traditions of reason and intuition, Universalism brings together the objective and the subjective, the empirical/scientific and the metaphysical, Classicism and Romanticism. Universalism sees the rational within the context of the intuitional. They complement each other, for they describe the whole from different parts of the self, one emphasizing the finite universe, the other the manifesting infinite in accordance with $+A + -A = 0$. The reunification of rational and intuitional Universalism[6] works through 12 opposite pairs (the rational first):

- Trust in the reason (analysed fragments of science) / trust in the intuition and shaping imagination (making the universe/Nature whole)
- Emphasis on the finite universe / emphasis on the infinite behind the finite
- A view of Nature as an ordered ecosystem / a view of Nature as an ordered system of organic dynamic process
- Emphasis on reason and mathematics / Expansionist revolt against reason, philosophical logic and language, and the fragmentation and reductionism of science
- Rational clarity about what is / intuitional experience of what is
- Sense of rational balance between the infinite and finite and all disciplines / revolt against past balance to return to the Whole
- Restraint in being objective about Nature / emphasis on being subjective about Nature
- Sense of the beauty of biofriendliness and symmetry / sense of

wonder at the phenomena of Nature
- View of humans as social in the concept of evolution / view of humans as individuals experiencing Reality
- Rational, social ego in social activities / universal being or intellect in solitary situations but at other times using all levels of self
- Focus on objectivity / focus on subjectivity
- Language used as an end to communicate socially / language used as a means to an end to reveal Being

The apparent dualism is reconciled within the unification of rational and intuitional Universalism, and is an amalgamation that both wings can support. It makes possible a manifesto of Universalism, whose 15 main tenets are:

- Focus on the universe rather than logic and language
- Focus on the universal order principle in the universe, a law which may act as a fifth force
- The idea that the universe/Nature manifested from the infinite/timelessness
- The idea that the universe/Nature and time began from a point and so everything is connected and one
- The idea that the infinite/timelessness can be known through universal being below the rational, social ego
- Reunification of man and the universe/Nature and the infinite
- Reunification of fragmented thought and disciplines
- Reunification of philosophy, science and religion
- Focus on the biofriendly universe, not a multiverse
- Affirming order as being more influential than random accident
- Affirming the structure of the universe as unique, its cause being the universal order principle from the infinite/timelessness/Void/Being/'sea' of energy
- Affirming the eventual reunification of humankind

- Affirming humankind as shaped by a self-organizing principle so that it is ordered and purposive
- Affirming all history and culture as being connected, and one-world government and religion
- Affirming that life has a meaning

Rational and intuitional Universalism can now combine to restate metaphysics as a blend and unification of their two wings:

- **Ontology** – studying a static concept of Reality in the rational, social ego, *and* experiencing Reality as a dynamic, moving process through the universal being or intellect
- **Psychology** – seeing the self in terms of the rational, social ego *and* seeing a multi-levelled self in a dynamic process whose variations can open to transpersonal spiritual experience
- **Epistemology** – how the mind knows Reality as a concept through the reason and rational, social ego, *and* how the intellect experiences and knows Reality as an experience of metaphysical Light
- **Cosmology** – the structure of the physical universe, *and* esemplastically shaping the fragments of scientific knowledge to return the fragments to a whole

In this reunification intuition is fundamental and reason works in the service of intuition. Intuition sees but does not know how to say what it sees. Reason says but is limited in what it says, and is reinforced by intuition.

UNIVERSALIST SCIENCES

In the sciences, Universalism[7] presents evidential Materialism within the context of ordering metaphysical Reality and the unity of the universe. The scientific view of 'what is' on the basis of our findings in chapters 2–4 can be expressed in simple terms:

> The finite universe manifested from an infinite, timeless, boundless Reality or Being which surrounds and permeates it and is both transcendent and immanent. Within the infinite, the photons of physical light stimulate all growth, creating biofriendly conditions for life through a Law of Order which works in Nature's local ecosystems, keeping all creatures in their place and driving to higher consciousness.

On the basis of our findings in chapters 2–4, scientific Universalism's view of the universe can be summarized as follows:

- Before the Big Bang there was an eternal, ever-moving boundless or timeless infinite Reality, the Void or One, an 'ever-living Fire'.
- The universe manifested from this infinite Reality as a point or germ, the first singularity, and, soon after the Big Bang, expanded by inflation; and the expansion has accelerated. A constant may save the universe from slowing down and perishing in a Big Crunch. The universe is finite and shaped like a shuttlecock or cone, open at the top. Space-time exists within it.
- Outside the universe, all round it (as well as within it), is the boundless, infinite Reality, a sea of energy which the surfer breasts. It consists of Light (Uncreated Light), and may be *aither* (ether) or dark energy. It is a moving process or flux and contains the latent possibilities of Being and Existence from which our universe was created. It manifests into a quantum vacuum, an emptiness filled with order.
- There is some evidence that there was a predisposition to order in the very early universe. This includes land mass and climatic conditions which favour life. There are 40 biofriendly laws and 326 constants and 75 ratios that were exactly right for life and

allowed human life to happen. The order principle can be detected at all stages in the universe's life and exists alongside the apparent randomness and uncertainty.

- The order principle, or Law of Order, has been associated with and may be contained within the photons of physical light, which may travel within metaphysical Light as Newton thought (his 'spirit' and 'ether'). This multi-layered Light may manifest into an expanding force of light that counteracts gravity, stimulates chemical composition and stirs plants and the bodies of organisms to growth. It also controls the four forces, the particles and all forms of matter.
- It is not clear how life began but the drive of evolution, an order and life principle, from one cell via apes and Ice Ages to modern *Homo sapiens sapiens*' body, brain and consciousness, has perfected many self-regulating, self-organizing physiological systems. It has developed higher (or deeper) consciousness, part of which can know Reality. The ordering thrust of evolution may be borne to cells by the information in photons, a tenet of Expansionism.
- All living things share oneness through DNA, and take part in a self-running, self-organizing system in which all creatures know their place and what to do. The order principle can be seen to operate through competition and co-operation: in the food webs, niches, symbiosis and healing plants of Nature's vast ecosystem. The focus of science is on the whole planet. The Earth is now in an interglacial within a continuing Ice Age.
- The constant of homeostasis is self-regulated in the self-organizing systems of both body and brain. Photons carrying information enter the brain through photoreceptor cells and are converted into chemical energy along neural circuits. There are 12 levels of consciousness. Mind may be partly an effect of brain and partly a system of light.

In each of the above points there are Materialist and metaphysical elements in accordance with algebraic thinking, +A + –A= 0: +A (metaphysics) + –A (evidenced Materialism) = 0 (the Universalist view of the unity of the universe). Henri Bergson in his *Introduction to Metaphysics*, 1903, called for 'a much-desired union of science and metaphysics'. Metaphysical science is science that connects to every possible concept, not just to every existing, evidenced concept, and which therefore relates to the infinite.

UNIVERSALIST HISTORY

In history, historical Universalism presents past events and social movements within the context of the ordering pattern of civilizations, which owe their genesis and growth to visions of metaphysical Reality. As all history emerged from one point that preceded the Big Bang and then from the first cell and the first human historical event, historical Universalism perceives history as one, an interconnected unity, a whole. My philosophy of history – Universalist history – is based on a movement away from partial history to 'whole history'. The history of a particular country cannot be studied in isolation from the history of the rest of the world, as that would be partial history. History is the combined events that have befallen humankind as a whole from the recorded beginnings to the present. And so history has a worldwide pattern.

Arnold Toynbee saw this and wrote of world history as a whole, following the linear tradition of Edward Gibbon and Oswald Spengler. He saw rising and falling civilizations in a regular pattern and attributed their motive force to 'challenge and response'. In 1954 he changed his 1934 scheme of civilizations, and wrote: 'I have been searching for the positive factor which within the last five thousand years, has shaken part of Mankind... into the "differentiation of civilization". ...These manoeuvres have ended, one after another, in my drawing a blank.'[8]

We have seen (pp 28, 30) that in my historical work[9] I have examined the rise-and-fall pattern of 25 civilizations and have found what I consider to be the law of history, that all civilizations go through 61 similar stages. Each civilization begins as a culture in which there is a vision of Reality as the 'ever-living Fire' or metaphysical Light (as we saw on pp 30, 36–7). A mystic (such as Mohammed, who saw the first page of the *Koran* written in Fire) receives a vision of the metaphysical Light. Followers gather round the vision, and a religion forms round it. A new civilization forms as the vision is taken abroad and its followers expand. The civilization grows as the vision is renewed among further followers. As long as the civilization follows its metaphysical central idea, its growth is strong. A civilization is healthy so long as the vision of the metaphysical Light is seen and is central.

My study of history shows that when a civilization ceases to experience its Reality, it turns secular and goes into a long decline which ends in conquest and occupation by foreign powers or other civilizations (as we saw on p 28–30). Eventually it passes within a successor civilization, whose gods replace its own gods. The civilization ends when it has passed into another civilization (as the ancient Mesopotamian and Egyptian civilizations passed into the Arab civilization).

In all civilizations, cultures and times, human beings have encountered similar problems. Although in the early stages of civilizations metaphysical visions of Being have been numerous, in the later stages of civilizations Being tends not to be seen. The prevailing climate then is one of scepticism, or secular atheistic materialism. Metaphysical or Universalist thinkers and men of letters keep their civilization alive by reminding their fellow-citizens of the 'ever-living Fire' or metaphysical Light that inspired their civilization's religion and therefore their civilization itself. They are against the trend of their day, the social approach, but they ensure that the civilization's fundamental vision is handed on to the next generation within the metaphysical-social matrix of Universalism. In the long term, such mystical thinkers and men of letters are fundamental to the health of their civilization. This view can be traced in my works.[10]

Universalist history charts the rise and fall of civilizations and their religions, and sees civilizations growing round their religions' vision of the metaphysical Light.[11] In my philosophy of history I have charted a historical approach to Being, which I see as central to religions and therefore to civilizations. Its philosophical approach is both rational (in setting out the pattern in history) and intuitional (in sensing the whole, esemplastically piecing the fragments of each civilization back into a whole 'urn'). The events and social movements within each civilization are described from a social approach, but the patterns within each civilization are related to stages connected with the metaphysical Light.

My philosophy of history is Universalist, since it shows the vision of Being that is central to religions (the 'ever-living Fire' or metaphysical Light) as being central to history. It is the motive force which Toynbee sought in vain. He looked for it within history but did not find it, because it is *outside* history: the Reality perceived by intuitional lone mystics which passes into a growing civilization's religion and is later obscured by kings, generals and their economists, whose struggles for succession, wars and material prosperity form the basis of most history books.

When a civilization's intellectual metaphysical vision becomes corrupted and turns secular, it gives rise to a more debased vision of Utopia (an imagined perfect place or state of things) which begins revolutions. In revolutions one class or part of a civilization tries to eliminate another class – as the French bourgeoisie and proletariat tried to eliminate aristocracy. Revolutions end in massacres (purges and guillotinings). The rational Enlightenment, which was embodied in the American Revolution, saw history as a rational progress towards perfection rather than a pattern of rising-and-falling civilizations.

Neo-Darwinists took up the view of Enlightenment progress and applied it to evolution, seeing history as driven by natural selection and therefore accidental, chance, chaotic and purposeless. This over-optimistic Enlightenment vision of progress was ended by the barbarity of the French Revolution, for rational progress had ended in mass killing.

The Universalist view that civilizations rise and fall – rise with a metaphysical vision and fall as a result of the fading of that vision – contradicts the thinking of the Enlightenment that history is perpetual progress. The Universalist view of history as having rising and falling civilizations in which there is progress for a while and then decay points to the hidden – secret – workings of the universal order principle that shapes the rising-falling pattern – and perhaps gives history a hidden purpose and meaning: to embody the idea of Being and metaphysical Light in religious buildings, such as temples, cathedrals and mosques. Universalist history focuses on all humankind's history and therefore on all civilizations, their patterns of rise-and-fall, their religions and how their stages affect human beings in their lives. It is history in which the vision of the 'ever-living Fire' or metaphysical Light is central to all cultures.

The vision of Being is known in all cultures and ages, and historical Universalism focuses on the impact such visions of Being have had on each civilization's stages and pattern. Each civilization has local customs, traditions and differences while reflecting a universal global theme, and the whole of history has a richly unified and varied pattern that can reunify the fragmented discipline of history. In our globalist world, historical Universalism's time has come, and Liberty is its torch-bearer.

UNIVERSALIST COMPARATIVE RELIGION

In comparative religion, Universalism presents the social observance of religions within the context of ordering metaphysical Reality, the

Light. We have seen (p 29) that the Light is common to all religions. As all religion emerged from the point that preceded the Big Bang, from the first cell and from the first appearance of organized religion, religious Universalism[12] affirms that all humankind will eventually be saved from the finite universe of time into infinite timelessness, not just members of one particular religion. Religious Universalism sees the prospect of all religions becoming merged into a one-world religion based on what all religions have in common: the infinite timeless Being that has been intuitionally glimpsed by mystics of all religions as the Light. All human beings are equal in relation to metaphysical Light that can fill their souls and order Nature's ecosystem.

The vision of metaphysical Light or Being is found in every generation and culture. It is a universal experience received in the universal being or intellect, and brings together Catholic, Protestant and Orthodox Christianity, Islam, Judaism, Hinduism, Buddhism, Jainism, Sikhism, Taoism and many other religions such as Zoroastrianism, which all share the experience. The universal experience of the Light can have regional and local applications. In the ancient Greek era, Zeus became identified with the local gods of religions in Asia Minor, and in the Roman era Jupiter became identified with local gods such as Zeus and Sol (who had taken over from Mithras in Asia Minor). A one-world religion, based on the one experience of the 'ever-living Fire' or metaphysical Light which all religions have in common, would merge God, Allah, Yahweh, Brahman, the Enlightened Buddha, Nirvana, Om Kar, the *Tao* and Ahura Mazda. The words of their prophets would be regional and local variations of the universal experience: the words of Christ, Mohammed, Moses, Shiva, the Buddha, Mahavira, Guru Nanak, Lao-Tze (or Lao-Tzu). For further details, see my thoughts on the prospect of a world Universalist religion based on the essence of all religions, the Light or Fire (pp 195–6, 201–2).

UNIVERSALIST INTERNATIONAL POLITICS AND STATECRAFT

In international politics, Universalism presents nation-states within the ordering context of regional empires and one World State that transcends nationalism. We have seen (pp 35–6) that a democratic World State with elected representatives from world constituencies would incorporate and subsume all the nation-states and solve the world's problems. As all politics emerged from one point that preceded the Big Bang, from the first cell and from the first human political organization, political Universalism[13] sees the whole world as being ordered as one political entity, an interconnected unity, a whole. As all humans are world citizens, they have human rights, which includes a human right to live under a world government that has abolished war, famine and disease. Political Universalism affirms a world government that is not totalitarian, respects the human right of all humankind to have a democratic vote and allows each human being the maximum freedom, and attacks poverty.

Our global identity is reinforced by the web created by Tim Berners-Lee, which theoretically allows each world citizen to communicate with all others (provided they are on email). The web symbolizes the interconnectedness of humankind just as the distinctive DNA signature of all world citizens symbolizes the uniqueness of each individual. (Compare p 73.)

Political Universalism minimizes the conflict that divides people. It eliminates divisions by negotiation. National borders in a World State would be like state borders in the US. Steps have already been taken towards a world government. Many trade institutions have been founded, and there is a structure of American, European and Pacific Unions, in different stages of advancement, which, it is intended, will eventually merge and form a one-world political structure with its own currency.

The age of global governance was ushered in when on 6 September 2000 149 heads of government and officials from other nations, representing 189 member states of the UN, attended the UN Millennium Assembly and Summit of World Leaders in New York and adopted a revised version of the UN Charter, the Charter for Global Democracy. In September 2005 there was another UN Summit, when a total of 191 UN states were represented. In September 2010 there was a further UN Summit on the millennium development goals, and in September 2015 there was yet another UN summit to adopt the post-2015 development agenda.

Since the gathering in September 2000, 9/11 has happened, and the invasions of Afghanistan and Iraq have led to turmoil in the Middle East, to the emergence of IS or ISIL and anarchy in Syria, Iraq and Libya. The troubles within Islam will have to be subdued and there will have to be changes in the outlooks of Russia and China before the inauguration of a world government can take place.

All the past world empires have been imposed by conquest by a civilization: the Roman Empire by the Roman civilization and the European empires by the nation-states of the European civilization, including the UK, which formed the British Empire. Each of these past world empires implemented a political Universalism that brought unity to the culture of their day despite suppressed anti-colonialist feeling in the colonies. For political Universalism to be established in a World State, all living civilizations including the Byzantine-Russian and Chinese civilizations would voluntarily have to place themselves under a world government, and the élitist families of the Syndicate would have to give up their self-interested ambition to loot the world's resources. Nevertheless, ahead is the Utopian prospect of a benevolent World State that spreads freedom and democracy and brings paradise to the Earth by abolishing war, famine and disease and liberating the poor from their poverty. Universalism will be the philosophy of a good globalist world government if one can come into being.

Connected with political Universalism is environmental

Universalism.[14] As the Earth and our environment emerged from one point that preceded the Big Bang, environmental Universalism sees all environmental developments as being aspects of one process and interconnected. Universalists perceive the Earth's environment as one and affirm a one-world, or one-universe, environmental movement.

An astronaut in space sees our planet as one, and to an astronaut the Earth may seem to have an environment that is a self-regulating equilibrium. Global warming, the depletion of the ozone layer by CFCs (chlorofluorocarbons) and human contamination of the environment will all be reduced by the global policy of a world government.

UNIVERSALIST CULTURE

In world culture's works of art, Universalism presents the secular, social perspective within the context of ordering metaphysical Reality, Being, the Light.

As all culture emerged from one point that preceded the Big Bang and from the first cell and (via life and consciousness) the first appearance of human culture, cultural Universalism perceives all cultures as one, an interconnected unity, a whole. A culture is a people's common way of living. Edward Burnett Tylor wrote in 1871: 'Culture ... is that complex whole which includes knowledge, belief, art, morals, law, custom and any other capabilities and habits acquired by man as a member of society.'[15] This 'complex whole' grows out of primitive family groups and includes a people's behaviour: their language, ideas, attitudes, values, ideals, traditions, beliefs, customs, laws, codes, institutions, tools, technologies, techniques, material objects and works of art, and also their rituals and religious or sacred ceremonies. It includes writing, tool-making, weaving, pottery, horror of incest and belief in spirits.[16]

The culture of a particular civilization is its people's customs and artistic and intellectual achievements, its symbolic forms of expression. Civilization, as distinct from culture, includes buildings, technology and all the material things that contribute to people's way of life. Universalism perceives all cultures as one, and therefore sees one supranational culture throughout the world. No local or regional culture can be studied in isolation from the cultures of the rest of the world. There has been one cultural impulse within civilizations, a one-world culture with common ground for all humankind and with local variations and differences.

I have said (p xv) that this study is not concerned with popular culture – people's common leisure activities and entertainment – but rather with the fundamental outlook of a people's common way of living: the rainbow with seven bands (or disciplines) they all share. World culture is one homogeneous entity.

We have seen (pp 4 and 36) that a civilization's culture is like a tree, and that the European civilization's culture is like a tree. World culture can also be seen as a tree. The trunk is all the higher religions, the branches all the 25 civilizations. The thrust of the sap from the trunk into the branches is metaphysical, and the ends of the branches that have turned dry and brittle are secular and are top-heavy with 50 'isms' (listed on p 38). The metaphysical Fire or Light has risen like sap from the roots through the trunk into each branching civilization, and that is cultural Universalism's[17] context: the vision of the metaphysical Light that is behind the genesis and growth of each civilization and its culture. All the cultures of the 25 world civilizations present their distinguishing features in relation to the metaphysical Light.

We have seen (p 36) that during its growth phase, when its vision of Reality or metaphysical Light is strong, a new civilization's culture is unified round the central metaphysical idea like branches growing from a central trunk which is the civilization's religion – in the European civilization, Christianity. During this early stage the trunk of the religion is fed with metaphysical sap and its branches – art, sculpture, music, literature and philosophy – all express a metaphysical vision of Being that is found in religion. Its leaves, individual works, express sap. There is unity of culture and 'unity of Being'. So in the European civilization, during the Renaissance the philosopher Marsilio Ficino and the artist Sandro Botticelli shared Dante's metaphysical and religious vision of Being.

The central idea of our European civilization and culture, and of all civilizations and cultures, is the metaphysical vision of Reality as the 'ever-living Fire' or Light (expressed in European art as the halo) which is beyond the world of the senses but knowable within the universal Whole. When the metaphysical sap stops flowing, the branches grow brittle and the culture is fractured and fragmented. Art, religion and philosophy cease to be filled with metaphysical sap and, deprived of natural vigour, start falling apart. When the sap fails, the branches turn dry, parched leaves fall, and the civilization and its culture declines.

The state of a local culture depends on the state of its civilization. When civilizations rise and are healthy, they embody the One, Being, which is reflected first in the mystical vision and later in rational philosophy. When civilizations lose contact with the One, the metaphysical Light, there is cultural decline and the arts, religion and philosophy turn secular, deal with surfaces and no longer embody the sap in the civilization's religious trunk. The culture becomes shallow and unhealthy, and declines.

In the European civilization the metaphysical sap of Christianity began to fail with the Renaissance and was drying up at the end of the 17th century. Since that time, secularization has advanced and the 50 'isms' or doctrinal movements (listed on p 38) have arisen. They represent secular, philosophical and political traditions; they indicate disunity and demonstrate the civilization's loss of contact with the One. These 50 'isms' or doctrinal movements were unthinkable before the Renaissance, because Christendom was unified by the medieval philosophy of the Church, which was founded on the metaphysical Light. The diversity of 'isms' reveals the multiplicity within which humans now live. The 'isms' are all ways of doing things or are based on one particular faculty of consciousness's many faculties and multi-levelled self. Deism, Rationalism, Idealism and Existentialism are all flawed because they engage parts of consciousness, not the whole of consciousness.

I have not included among the 'isms' fundamentalism, Unitarianism (which may provide routes back to the One) or Classicism or Romanticism (which are unified in and therefore aspects of Universalism and provide rational and intuitional ways to Reality). I have not included Expansionism for the same reason, and of course Universalism itself, which was an 'ism' before its new meaning of 'focusing on the universe, establishing the universal order principle, reunifying disciplines, focusing on humankind as a whole and, through universal intellect, contacting the One'. In its quest to restore contact with the universe, Nature, the One and unity, Universalism counteracts many of the other 'isms', and is the 'ism' that most offers a way back to Reality.

The Universalist counteracts the 'isms' by conducting a 'Universalist Revolution in Thought and Culture'. The Metaphysical Revolution is a restoration of the metaphysical, mystical tradition alongside science and in opposition to anti-metaphysical humanism, materialism, rationalism, empiricism, scepticism, positivism and reductionism, all of which are reconciled. The Universalist is discontented with the existing cultural order and opposes it. He or she calls for support to start a necessary change, a revolution in thought and culture, so that true values are reflected in the metaphysical-secular spectrum of our culture which should show symptoms of cultural health rather than terminal disease. The Universalist Revolution that restores the metaphysical tradition to world culture – which includes all disciplines – maintains and declares:[18]

- The phenomenal world of the senses is not ultimate Reality. The infinite is behind the finite universe. This perception challenges and sweeps aside the anti-metaphysical 'isms' we have identified: humanism, Materialism, Rationalism, Empiricism, scepticism, mechanism, positivism and reductionism in all disciplines. We can know infinite Being, or the One, beyond and behind the phenomenal world of the senses – rationally via what the surfer breasts, and intuitionally via the vision of Reality, of the 'ever-living Fire' or metaphysical Light.
- Each one of us is therefore not a reductionist collection of atoms on a dunghill whose mind is mere brain function or a solely social ego, but a being with 12 levels of consciousness and a possibly immortal spirit (or invisible body) within his or her visible body.
- Universalism states the universe in terms of the infinite and science, and particularly in terms of metaphysical Being, or 'ever-living Fire' or Light, which manifests into the structure of the universe. It is a science that studies the structure of the universal Whole, which includes every possible concept of the mind and the metaphysical layers of manifesting Being. It also studies perception of the One, the intellect's experience of the Fire or Light which can be reported phenomenologically (through a study of consciousness or perception) in 'self-reports' which are quasi-empirical. It is also a practical, contemplative, intuitional philosophy that 'existentializes' metaphysical Reality, whose universal energy can be known existentially in the contemplative vision. It contacts the universal energy of the 'ever-living Fire' or metaphysical Light, Reality, and applies its consequences to all disciplines.
- The central idea of all civilizations and cultures is the vision of Reality as 'ever-living Fire' or metaphysical Light, which is beyond the world of the senses but knowable within the universal Whole.
- This documented vision of Reality should be reinstated in

philosophy to reconcile, unite and move beyond Logical Positivism, Linguistic Analysis and Phenomenology.

- The vision of Reality has inspired the growth of all civilizations in history. History studies the universal Whole and should have a global perspective. The metaphysical vision which is common to all civilizations is the optimum basis for a common world culture.
- This vision of Reality should have a place in the spectrum of literature – novels, plays and poems – and literature that includes the vision should exist alongside and challenge secular, technique-oriented literature. Literature misleads if it conveys an exclusively surface view of life, if it assumes that appearances are all and does not hint at Being or Reality. Literature should be truth-bearing and glimpse or reveal metaphysical Being or Reality. Universalist literature is neo-Baroque as it combines the metaphysical and secular and unites the world of the senses and spirit by seeking the sunburst experience and unity. It reveals harmony between apparent opposites: sacred and profane, regular and irregular, order and disorder, stillness and movement, Being and Becoming, eternity and time. Universalist literature combines Classicism and Romanticism, statement and image, social situations and sublime metaphysical vision, traditional and organic form.
- Universalist philosophy, history and literature offer a vision of harmony, meaning and order in relation to the universal Whole after the *Angst* and anxiety of 20th-century thought, particularly in Modernist literature and Existentialist philosophy. Universalism emphasizes the contemplative gaze, union with the universal Whole and the rustic pursuit of reflection amid tranquillity, the vision of mystic writers, artists and sculptors.
- European artists – practitioners in painting, music, architecture and sculpture as well as in literature – should transmit the sap of the cross-disciplinary vision of the One, 'ever-living Fire' or Light in their works and connect themselves to the Universalist

Revolution's revitalization of the European civilization's central idea. (Vincent van Gogh's swirling starry night skies attempted to do this in his own way: 'I am painting the infinite.'[19]) They will thereby contribute to the return of a common, unified European culture that will affect the North American culture, which already has a Universalist outlook, and the whole of Western and global culture.

- European culture needs to be re-formed to restore (to use Matthew Arnold's words) the most perfect works from the best self, which constitute the highest expressions of culture, and to reconnect philosophy, history and literature to the tradition of the unity of vision of the 'ever-living Fire' or metaphysical Light. The Revolution will spread awareness of the consequences for world culture of the Revolution's fundamental shift in perception.
- On the Universalist principle that all the metaphysical ideas of all civilizations are essentially the same vision, a revival of the common metaphysical vision in one civilization and culture will be essentially the same as corresponding revivals in all civilizations and cultures, which, however, are at different stages of advancement. A revival within the European culture, which as we have seen in chapter1 is in stage 43, and in the American culture, which is in stage 15, can therefore inspire each other's civilization and culture and lead to an international Universalist movement. This can focus on the common metaphysical ground of all cultures and create a world culture, and be a force for world peace.

The implementation of this 12-point Universalist Declaration will have the following seven consequences in modern European and American thought and culture:[20]

- Renewal within the secularized, humanistic European and American cultures

- Restoration of a vision reflected in all the European arts over hundreds of years and in the American arts, round which all civilizations have grown and whose renewal revives and revitalizes the European and North American civilizations and cultures
- Identification of the unifying principle in the universe of physics and the formulation of a Form from Movement Theory (or a full Grand Unifying Theory)
- Renewal of philosophy through a new metaphysical philosophy, Universalism
- Introduction of a new global perspective in history through a new history which takes account of all civilizations and cultures, not just slices of nation-state history, and identifies the unifying principle in all civilizations
- Restoration of the essential vision in European and American literature through a new literature which mixes the metaphysical and secular, as did Baroque art (thus the new literature can be called neo-Baroque literature), draws on many disciplines and reflects our Age
- Revival of culture by a group of practitioners who draw on the essential vision in their work

The Universalist restores the harmony of the universe and its reconciled 'contradictions' to the culture of his or her own civilization and to world culture, and in doing so makes a contribution to restoring the health of world culture. The vision of Being in all cultures and ages is a combined tradition of contemplation and action that brings a sense of meaning and purpose to culture today.

Universalism restores a one-world culture as the common ground for humankind. By conducting a 'Revolution in Thought and Culture' against modern secularized culture with a view to making the metaphysical sap flow again in the trunks, branches and leaves of all the particular civilizations so that the metaphysical and the secular/social harmoniously co-exist, Universalism restores cultures to the health they once enjoyed. The common ground cultures share is: the concept and experience of Reality; the infinite; the scientific view of the universe and Nature's ecosystems; the metaphysical and scientific philosophical traditions; and the social approach and the shared experience of world history, its civilizations and cultures.

Universalism sees world history as a unity, so it sees world culture as a unity, a combination of all the civilizations' religions, philosophies and arts – a one-world culture. Its method of proceeding is both rational (in setting out a world culture of all civilizations) and intuitional (in sensing the whole, esemplastically piecing together the fragmented cultures into one world culture). Universalism's reunification of philosophy and science and its restoration of the metaphysical that surrounds and permeates the universe are themes of all cultures.

Universalism's reunification of the pairs of opposites in the seven disciplines of world culture is reunifying each of the seven disciplines, as Liberty, whose raised torch proclaims the unity of humankind, can see. In all seven, the finite is expressed within the context of the ordering infinite. In each discipline Universalism deepens the partial approach by seeing it within the context of ordering metaphysical Reality that proclaims the order in the universe. In each discipline Universalism has pieced together the conflicting social and metaphysical approaches.

Universalism also pieces all the fragmented disciplines together and combines and reunifies them into one, to restore the whole universe and its order. In all seven disciplines as a whole, the secular, social approach is united with the ordering metaphysical Reality from which it has become separated. As I have said (p xv), we can speak of seven separate Universalisms: mystical Universalism, literary Universalism, philosophical Universalism, historical Universalism, political Universalism, religious Universalism and cultural Universalism. But ultimately they are all aspects of one Universalism.

Universalism is like a rainbow with seven bands (as we saw on p xv), which symbolizes the experience of the metaphysical Light and the universal being's perceiving the oneness of Nature, the universe and the social world of humankind. It shines out the oneness of literature, philosophy and the sciences, history, comparative religion, international politics and statecraft, and world culture.

Universalists reconcile the contradictory pairs of opposites to reveal the pre-existing unity within the whole universe, and its order. The dialectic +A + –A = 0 can now be seen to be: metaphysical approach + social approach = reunified world culture through a perception of the unity and order within the universe. The Universalist Revolution can now be seen to be a Metaphysical Revolution, which has produced a metaphysical science; and we must now consider the metaphysical science's role in making the Universalist synthesis possible.

THE METAPHYSICAL REVOLUTION'S RESTORATION OF ORDER

Bergson called for 'a much-desired union of science and metaphysics' (as we saw on p 161). As metaphysical science connects to every possible concept, it relates to the infinite. In the Middle Ages science and metaphysics united.

Ontology is the study of Being and existence; epistemology is what can be known about Being. The foundations of most objectivist, positivist and reductionist science have a Materialist ontology, for most science sees the phenomenal world as the only reality. Its epistemology therefore depends on sense data and, more recently, mathematics.

The foundations of holistic science have a wholeness ontology, and see the wholeness of the finite universe and its interconnectedness as the only reality. Its epistemology depends on intuitional inner knowing of interconnectedness within the finite universe.

The foundations of a new metaphysical science, such as the one for which Bergson yearned, have a metaphysical ontology[21], for this science sees the infinite as the source of Reality, from which all else has manifested. Its epistemology depends on inner knowing of the metaphysical Light which manifests from the infinite. The foundations of a new metaphysical science, its ontology and epistemology, are quite different from those of reductionist and holistic science. A metaphysical science will carry metaphysics into many areas of science and philosophy and challenge 150 years of reductionism and Materialism in the sciences and philosophy. It will research, assemble evidence and do mathematics on the following ten hypotheses:[22]

- **The metaphysical origin of the universe**: seeing the hot beginning (Big Bang) in relation to the 'ever-living Fire' or metaphysical Light
- **Reality in the microworld**: seeing Newton's expanding force, Einstein's cosmological constant, dark energy (if it exists), the principle of hidden variability and the origin of mass (the Higgs boson) as effects of the manifesting *aither*-like metaphysical Light's varying intensities in different localities
- **Electromagnetic spectrum**: seeing the high-frequency, gamma end of the spectrum in terms of the neutrino-like or photino-like bosons of manifested metaphysical Light
- **Brain physiology**: seeing consciousness as a system of high-frequency brain waves of 4 cycles per second, boson light which connects to all rays on the electromagnetic spectrum in the region of 4 cycles per second
- **Mind-body problem**: seeing the mind and consciousness as transmitted photon-like bosons bearing coded information that are not dependent upon physiological processes but, having been transmitted, use the brain for their own metaphysical purposes, ie seeing the mind as independent of the body
- **Synchronicity**: seeing coincidences as evidence of a unified interconnectedness of matter and consciousness through the *aither*-like manifesting Light

- **Mysticism**: seeing religious experiences and mystical states of consciousness as contact with the metaphysical Light, which manifests into and pervades the universe, pouring universal energy into the universal being or intellect of humans; opening to pervading Reality
- **Order principle**: seeing the infinite and Being (the metaphysical Light which can be known intuitionally or existentially through contemplation) as an ordering principle which sends photons into retinas and plants' chloroplasts, whence they pervade DNA
- **Evolution**: within order as opposed to randomness, seeing all evolution in terms of the order principle and teleological evolutionary power of the neutrino-like, photino-like boson particles of manifested metaphysical Light, and its influence over a low-level 'mechanism' that controls DNA exchange and chromosome division and evolution's drive for self-improvement; seeing evolution as teleological
- **Philosophy**: seeing philosophy as subject to metaphysical science, as framing a system of general ideas that include all possible concepts, the whole universe at all hierarchical levels and life as a whole, in terms of the manifesting infinite's metaphysical Light

Through this agenda metaphysics returns science to its metaphysical foundations in the infinite. Metaphysical science will move science away from granular materialism since visible matter occupies only 4 per cent of the matter in the universe, and away from reductionism. The revealing of order in metaphysical science counterbalances reductionism. The discovery by CERN of the Higgs field, an ordering invisible reality in the microworld, has strengthened metaphysical science.

The Universalist synthesis finds evidence for order in the universe: for manifestation from Void to Non-Being to Being to Existence. The quantum vacuum and the Big Bang must be seen within this process of manifestation, a view shared by Bohm in *Wholeness and the Implicate Order*, in which he sees cosmology as manifesting from a sea of cosmic energy, an 'implicate order'.[23]

This process of manifestation can be found in my Form from Movement Theory (which we considered on pp 115–18).

Holding the torch of the Light, Liberty can see that the Universalist synthesis is reconciling all the pairs of opposites in the seven disciplines and all the seven disciplines of world culture into one rainbow-like Universalism. Universalism is also reconciling five sets of contradictions involving philosophy and the sciences:

- Science and metaphysics (whose union Bergson said was 'much-desired') through metaphysical science
- Science and philosophy, by reconciling the evidence of science set out in chapter 2
- The metaphysical and scientific traditions (Plato's and Aristotle's traditions) by reconciling infinite Reality and the scientific view of the universe set out in chapter 2
- The rational and intuitional philosophies within metaphysics, set out in chapter 3
- Linguistic and Phenomenological philosophies – by reconciling language and Being so that language can describe the infinite with precision and accuracy

These unifications may seem new, but when seen in the historical context of the last 2,500 years they can be seen to be *re*unifications. The reunion of science and metaphysics is a further step towards the reunion of science and philosophy. The reunion of the metaphysical and scientific traditions within philosophy and the reunion of the rational and intuitional philosophies within metaphysics, like the reunion of the linguistic and Phenomenological views within modern philosophy, are making significant contributions to the reunification of philosophy and science, which were unified under the 5th-century BCE Greeks.

It can now be seen that science, although it makes claims that can be disputed (the existence of new dimensions and of many universes cannot be proved outside mathematics), also affirms an infinite singularity – that is, infinity – from which the Big Bang came. It can be seen that the scientific universe is a manifestation of the Greeks' metaphysical 'boundless', and the Universalist philosopher now sees the same unity behind the universe that the Greeks saw. The union of the linguistic and Phenomenological philosophies will mean that language will seek to reveal infinite Being as well as finite existence.

The reconciliation of the pairs of opposites within the seven disciplines, and the reunification of the seven disciplines into one Universalism and the five reunifications involving science and philosophy, all taken together, amount to a Metaphysical Revolution. In so far as the reconciliations seem new, they constitute a Metaphysical Revolution that is in effect a counter-revolution against dehumanizing reductionism in philosophy and science and the social approach to which reductionism is linked. But when seen in the historical context of the last 2,500 years, they can be seen to be a Metaphysical Restoration – indeed, a restoration of order within the universe. I formulated a Metaphysical Revolution to return philosophy to metaphysics – and to the c1910 concerns of William James, Henri Bergson, T E Hulme (in his Bergsonian phase), Alfred North Whitehead and Edmund Husserl – as long ago as 1980 and declared it in 1991. The Universalist Philosophy Group of 12 philosophers which I led from 1993 to 1994 was arguably the first group of its kind since the Vienna Circle of A J Ayer and Ludwig Wittgenstein in the 1920s and 1930s. The Metaphysical Revolution will continue to work for the reconciliation of the five sets of contradictions, as will metaphysical science.

Of movements, Whitehead wrote in *An Introduction to Mathematics*, 1911:[24] 'Operations of thought are like cavalry charges in a battle – they are strictly limited in number, they require fresh horses, and must only be made at decisive moments.' The decisive moment is long overdue to effect a sudden and fundamental change in science and philosophy. Liberty can see this opportunity to bring about a reunification of world culture. The Universalist movement has begun at a decisive moment, and Liberty can see that the Metaphysical Revolution has a vital role to play in reconciling, synthesizing and reunifying world culture.

America, which has pioneered much science in the 20th and 21st centuries, is well placed to harmonize both the metaphysical-religious view of order we found in chapters 1 and 3 and the scientific view of order we have been examining in chapters 2 and 4 so far.

Being is unitary and perceived as One from the diversity of different cultures and disciplines, just as the one sun is perceived in different countries and has different names. The reunification of world culture can take place round this one sun.

Liberty knows that Universalism reconciles the conflicting approaches in the seven disciplines of world culture and with them the world's followers of the metaphysical and secular traditions. With a new Universalist philosophy that can unify world culture, Liberty can now turn to the democratic World State for which she yearns.

CHAPTER 6
PROSPECTS FOR WORLD UNITY

The American Declaration of Independence of 1776 affirmed all Americans' belief in 'Life, Liberty and the pursuit of Happiness'. Freedom has always been at the heart of American values, and during the Cold War America led the Free World in insisting on democracy, the rule of law and freedom of speech and of expression. When challenged on these issues, the Soviet tyranny collapsed and Chinese Communism morphed into a system founded on capitalism and the freedom of capitalist expression. At the heart of the secret American destiny is liberty. The secret American destiny is a vision of all the world's states living with democratic representation under the rule of law and with freedom of thought and expression.

LIBERTY AND AMERICA'S DESTINY

Liberty, a representation of Libertas, Rome's goddess of freedom from slavery, oppression and tyranny, has a more secret, hidden meaning not lost on the post-revolutionary French Freemasons who presented to the American people the statue that was dedicated in 1886 to celebrate the revolution that created the Declaration of Independence in 1776 and the federal principle that shaped the French Revolution in 1789.[1] Modelled (like the Colossus of Rhodes) on the Graeco-Roman sun-god Helios, a version of the sun-god Apollo on a marble tablet in the Museum of Corinth, Liberty wears the seven-spiked rays of the Roman sun-god Sol's radiate solar crown. She also stands for the Light as well as standing for freedom.

Now Liberty has come to symbolize the secret American destiny, and the seven spikes, besides representing the seven seas and seven continents,[2] symbolize the seven disciplines which can also be found in the seven terraces on the distant Chrysler building. Seven-spiked Liberty and her torch represent the Light in seven disciplines, and the distant One World Trade Center which has arisen from the ruins of the Twin Towers demolished after 9/11 stands for the coming one-world culture and government that will spread the American dream of prosperity throughout the world. It is America's secret destiny to turn Universalism into a worldwide philosophy and the UN General Assembly into a coming World State. We can now see what American Universalism can do.

Universalism, having balanced the metaphysical and social approaches into a new world outlook, can shine out like the torch in Liberty's right hand and proclaim a new outward-looking, anti-isolationist America's determination to re-form and unify world culture and unite all humankind into one political World State. The Universalist synthesis accords with the American vision of an ordered universe as expressed by the Founding Fathers, who took their cue from the Deism of Lord Herbert of Cherbury:

> Here is my creed. I believe in one God, Creator of the universe. That He governs it by His providence. That He ought to be worshipped. That the most acceptable service we render Him is doing good to His other children. That the soul of man is immortal and will be treated with justice in another life respecting its conduct in this. These I take to be the fundamental principles of all sound religion, and I regard them as you do in whatever sect I meet with them.
>
> As to Jesus of Nazareth, my opinion [of] whom you particularly desire, I think the system of morals and his religion, as he left them to us, the best the world ever saw [or] is likely to see; but I apprehend it has received various corrupt changes, and I have, with most of the present Dissenters

> in England, some doubts about his divinity though it is a question I do not dogmatize upon, having never studied it, and think it needless to busy myself with it now, when I expect soon an opportunity of knowing the truth with less trouble.[3]

George Washington was a moderate Deist who believed in an ordered universe and 'a Grand Designer along Deist lines',[4] of whom it was said:

> Washington can be classified as a Deist. ... The Supreme Being whose aid he counted upon Washington usually called Providence, Heaven or, to a lesser extent, God. ... He also made much use of such stock Deist phrases as Grand Architect, Governor of the Universe, Higher Cause, Great Ruler of Events, Supreme Architect of the Universe, Author of the Universe, Great Creator, Director of Human Events, and Supreme Ruler.[5]

In 1845 America's 'manifest destiny' was featured in an article by the journalist John L O'Sullivan in the *New York Morning News*, which argued that the United States had the right to claim 'the whole of Oregon':

> And that claim is by the right of our manifest destiny to overspread and to possess the whole of the continent which Providence has given us for the development of the great experiment of liberty and federated self-government entrusted to us.[6]

America's 'manifest destiny' in 1845 was to possess the whole American continent. This 'manifest destiny' has now spread to the whole world. The destiny has become globalistic. Samuel P

Huntington, the American political scientist, adviser and author of *The Clash of Civilizations* (1993), writing a few years before George W Bush became President, explained that culture follows power:

> The belief that non-Western peoples should adopt Western values, institutions and culture is immoral because of what would be necessary to bring it about. The almost-universal reach of European power in the late nineteenth century and the global dominance of the United States in the late twentieth century spread much of Western civilization across the world. European globalism, however, is no more. American hegemony is receding if only because it is no longer needed to protect the United States against a Cold War-style Soviet military threat. Culture, as we have argued, follows power. If non-Western societies are once again to be shaped by Western culture, it will happen only as a result of the expansion, deployment and impact of Western power. Imperialism is the necessary logical consequence of universalism.[7]

So if America can shape world culture again in accordance with its 'manifest destiny', it will have to increase its global power. As America is in stage 15 of the North American civilization (an expansive, imperial stage), it is possible that after Obama's retreat from American supremacy and hegemony a new anti-isolationist President will again challenge Soviet expansionism in Europe and Islamic terrorism and spread a new world culture of Universalism. As I have said,

> Not since the Roman Empire has one nation-state dominated the world to such an extent. There is a feeling abroad that America controls an empire, defined by the *Concise Oxford Dictionary* as 'an extensive group of states or countries under a single supreme authority, especially an emperor.'[8]

As the only superpower after 1991, America still has world influence over 'an extensive group of states or countries'.

WORLDWIDE CIVILIZATION AND WORLD STATE

Implementing Universalist statecraft, I have set out in *The World Government*[9] and *The Secret American Dream*[10] how a World State would look, how it can be created with American persuasion and how it could be financed. I set out the structure of the World State in a chart (see p 188) and have also set out a proposed representation based on the world situation in 2010 – in seats per country – for a World Parliamentary Assembly (850 seats based on the number of countries in 2010) and a World Senate (92 seats), and the 27 regions that could be represented on a World Commission.[11] See the three tables on pp 189–94.

I must emphasise that America's coming world role is to lead 'an extensive group of states or countries' into a coming democratic World State. America's role will be philanthropic in bringing in a federal association of world states that will transcend nation-states. Each nation-state will be independent internally like the US states but will externally be under a federal government that will be partly supranational and able to enforce disarmament and improve the lot of humankind. The US will not be reverting to self-interested imperialism but will be seeking to break the mould of rising and falling civilizations by creating out of all living civilizations a World State and universal peace that can be expected to last for a while before history reverts to its rising and falling pattern. In short, American leadership will be cultural and diplomatic. It will act as a midwife and bring to birth a new infant World State in a spirit of supreme benevolence, in order to benefit the whole of humankind, and will then step away.

THE STRUCTURE OF THE WORLD STATE

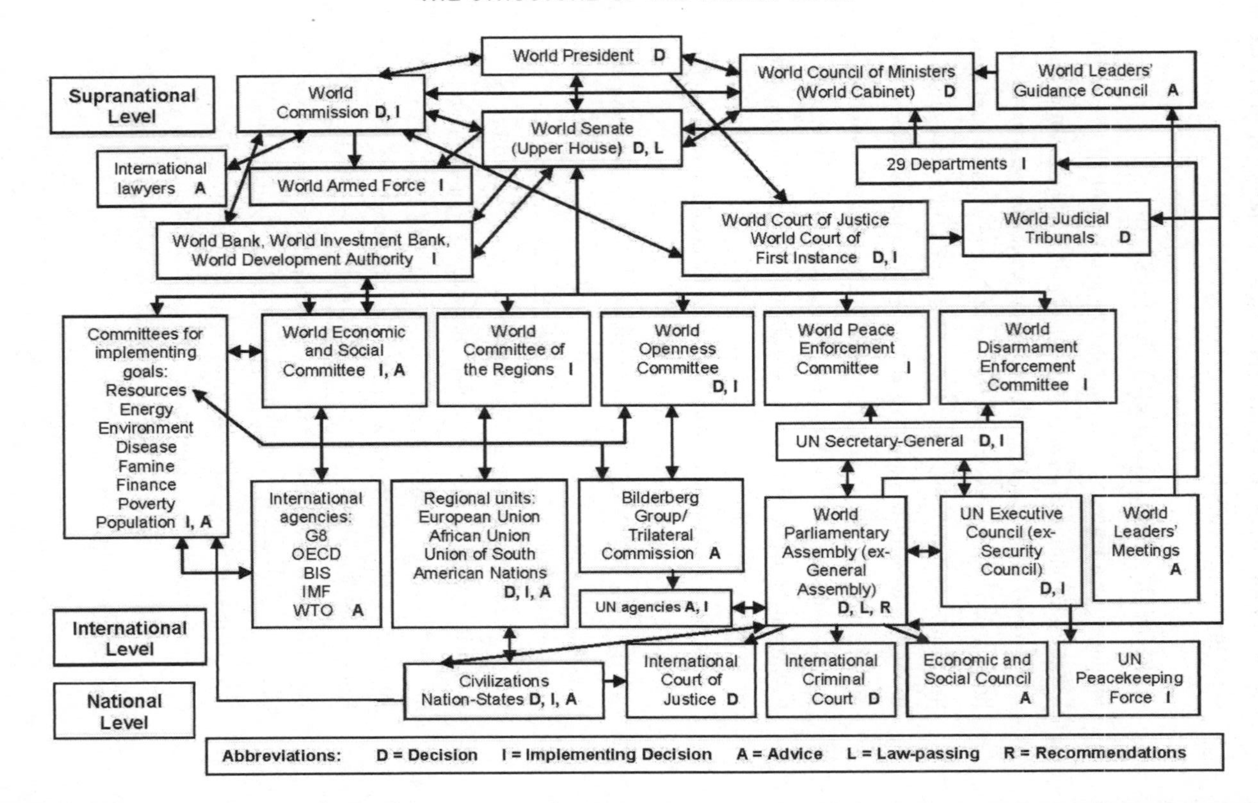

WORLD PARLIAMENTARY ASSEMBLY (WPA) REPRESENTATION

The proposed World Parliamentary Assembly has 850 seats, of which 816 are based on nation-states within the UN in 2010, 26 on dependent territories then outside the UN, and eight on formerly disputed territories.

Seats are allocated according to the size of populations but world influences have also been taken into account – in particular Permanent Membership of the UN Security Council. The four largest regions by population in 2010 (China, India, the EU, and the United States) have 30 seats each, while the three Permanent Members that are not among these four largest regions (Russia, France, UK) have 15 seats each. The ten largest countries after the largest four have 12 seats each and thereafter representation diminishes as populations get smaller.

Population percentages were based on the 1 July 2009 estimates by the UN Department of Economic and Social Affairs – Population Division.

The proposed World Parliamentary Assembly (WPA) has the following representation:

GROUP	COUNTRIES	WPA SEATS EACH PER COUNTRY	TOTAL NUMBER OF SEATS
A	THE 4 LARGEST: CHINA, INDIA, THE EU (ON THE BASIS OF 27 MEMBERS INCLUDING BULGARIA AND ROMANIA, EXCLUDING THE UK AND FRANCE, SEE B), THE UNITED STATES	30	120
B	3 PERMANENT MEMBERS OF THE UN SECURITY COUNCIL: THE RUSSIAN FEDERATION, UK, FRANCE	15	45
C	THE 10 LARGEST COUNTRIES AFTER THE LARGEST 4: INDONESIA, BRAZIL, PAKISTAN, BANGLADESH, NIGERIA, JAPAN, MEXICO, PHILIPPINES, VIETNAM, ETHIOPIA	12	120

D	THE 15 NEXT-LARGEST COUNTRIES: EGYPT, IRAN, TURKEY, THE DEMOCRATIC REPUBLIC OF CONGO, THAILAND, MYANMAR (BURMA), SOUTH AFRICA, SOUTH KOREA, UKRAINE, COLOMBIA, TANZANIA, ARGENTINA, KENYA, SUDAN (6) / SOUTH SUDAN (2), ALGERIA	8	120
E	THE 20 NEXT-LARGEST COUNTRIES: CANADA, UGANDA, MOROCCO, IRAQ, NEPAL, PERU, VENEZUELA, MALAYSIA, AFGHANISTAN, UZBEKISTAN, SAUDI ARABIA, NORTH KOREA, GHANA, YEMEN, TAIWAN, MOZAMBIQUE, AUSTRALIA, SYRIA, CÔTE D'IVOIRE, SRI LANKA	6	120
F	THE 30 NEXT-LARGEST COUNTRIES: MADAGASCAR, CAMEROON, ANGOLA, CHILE, KAZAKHSTAN, BURKINA FASO, NIGER, MALAWI, CAMBODIA, ECUADOR, GUATEMALA, MALI, ZAMBIA, SENEGAL, ZIMBABWE, CHAD, CUBA, TUNISIA, THE DOMINICAN REPUBLIC, GUINEA, HAITI, RWANDA, BOLIVIA, SERBIA, BELARUS, SOMALIA, BENIN, AZERBAIJAN, BURUNDI, SWITZERLAND	4	120
G	THE 40 NEXT-LARGEST COUNTRIES: HONDURAS, ISRAEL, TAJIKISTAN, PAPUA NEW GUINEA, TOGO, LIBYA, PARAGUAY, LAOS, JORDAN, EL SALVADOR, NICARAGUA, SIERRA LEONE, KYRGYZSTAN, TURKMENISTAN, ERITREA, SINGAPORE, NORWAY, UNITED ARAB EMIRATES, COSTA RICA, CROATIA, CENTRAL AFRICAN REPUBLIC, GEORGIA, NEW ZEALAND, LEBANON, BOSNIA AND HERZEGOVINA, REPUBLIC OF THE CONGO, MOLDOVA, LIBERIA, PANAMA, URUGUAY, LITHUANIA, MAURITANIA, ARMENIA, ALBANIA, KUWAIT, OMAN, JAMAICA, MONGOLIA, NAMIBIA, LESOTHO	3	120
H	THE 49 NEXT-LARGEST COUNTRIES: REPUBLIC OF MACEDONIA, BOTSWANA, GAMBIA, GUINEA-BISSAU, GABON, QATAR, TRINIDAD AND TOBAGO, MAURITIUS, SWAZILAND, EAST TIMOR, DJIBOUTI, FIJI, BAHRAIN, GUYANA, BHUTAN, COMOROS, EQUATORIAL GUINEA, MONTENEGRO, SOLOMON ISLANDS, SURINAME, CAPE VERDE, BRUNEI, BAHAMAS, BELIZE, ICELAND, MALDIVES, BARBADOS, VANUATU, SAMOA, ST. LUCIA, SÃO TOMÉ AND PRINCIPE, FEDERATED STATES OF MICRONESIA, ST. VINCENT AND THE GRENADINES, GRENADA, TONGA, KIRIBATI, ANTIGUA AND BARBUDA, ANDORRA, SEYCHELLES, DOMINICA, MARSHALL ISLANDS, ST. KITTS AND NEVIS, LIECHTENSTEIN, MONACO, SAN MARINO, PALAU, TUVALU, NAURU, VATICAN CITY	1	49

I	2 NON-UN-MEMBERS WITH LARGEST POPULATIONS: PUERTO RICO, PALESTINE	1	2
	TOTAL OF SEATS FOR GROUPS A-I		**816**
J	26 DEPENDENT TERRITORIES OUTSIDE THE UN WITH ASSOCIATE STATUS, AND SEATS HELD IN RESERVE, UNTIL THEY BECOME INDEPENDENT: MACAU (A SPECIAL ADMINISTRATIVE REGION OF THE PEOPLE'S REPUBLIC OF CHINA FROM 1999 TO AT LEAST 2049 WITH THE POTENTIAL TO BE DEPENDENT AFTER 2049), WESTERN SAHARA, NETHERLANDS ANTILLES, GUAM, US VIRGIN ISLANDS, ARUBA, JERSEY, NORTHERN MARIANA ISLANDS, ISLE OF MAN, AMERICAN SAMOA, BERMUDA, GUERNSEY, GREENLAND, CAYMAN ISLANDS, FAROE ISLANDS, TURKS AND CAICOS ISLANDS, GIBRALTAR, BRITISH VIRGIN ISLANDS, COOK ISLANDS, ANGUILLA, MONTSERRAT, ST. HELENA, FALKLAND ISLANDS, NIUE, TOKELAU, PITCAIRN ISLANDS	1	26
K	8 DISPUTED TERRITORIES NOT ON THE UN-BASED LIST: KASHMIR, ABKHAZIA, NAGORNO-KARABAKH, KOSOVO, TRANSNISTRIA, SOUTH OSSETIA, CHECHNYA, TIBET	1	8
	EVENTUAL TOTAL OF SEATS		**850**

WORLD SENATE REPRESENTATION

Within the World Regions are sub-regions or zones that form the basis of 46 constituencies, each of which elects two World Senators, making a total of 92 Senate seats.

The allocations of seats are based on population, topographical size and political significance – hence the making of Israel and Iran zonal regions. In the table below WPP means World Population Percentage (given to justify the problematic allocation of seats in China, India and Southeast Asia); PM means Permanent Member of the UN; N means nuclear/disarmament considerations for the representation (in the sense that a country possessing nuclear weapons needs to be represented so that it can participate in world disarmament negotiations); and R means regional considerations for the representation (in the sense that representation is partly determined by the country's regional importance).

The World Senate is represented as follows:

NUMBER OF WORLD SENATE ZONAL REGIONS OR CONSTITUENCIES	
CHINA: EAST, WEST, NORTH (INCLUDING MONGOLIA), SOUTH (PM, N, WWP 19.5%)	4
USA: EAST, WEST, NORTH, SOUTH, INCLUDING DEPENDENT TERRITORIES (PM, N)	4
EUROPE: 2 NORTHWESTERN (INCLUDING SCANDINAVIA, GERMANY), 1 EASTERN, 1 SOUTHERN (IE NORTHERN MEDITERRANEAN – SPAIN, ITALY, GREECE/AEGEAN)	4
AFRICA: NORTH, EAST, WEST (INCLUDING ATLANTIC OCEAN), SOUTH (NOTE: MIDDLE AFRICA DISTRIBUTED AMONG THESE 4)	4
RUSSIAN FEDERATION: EAST, CENTRAL, WEST (PM, N)	3
CANADA: EAST, WEST, NORTH (INCLUDING GREENLAND AND ARCTIC)	3
SOUTH AMERICA: NORTHEAST (BRAZIL, BOLIVIA, PARAGUAY), SOUTH (ARGENTINA, CHILE, URUGUAY, ANTARCTICA), NORTHWEST (PERU, ECUADOR, COLOMBIA, VENEZUELA, NORTH COAST)	3
INDIA: NORTH (INCLUDING NEPAL), CENTRAL, SOUTH (INCLUDING SRI LANKA, MALDIVES AND INDIAN OCEAN)	3
MIDDLE EAST: NORTHERN (INCLUDING TURKEY, IRAQ, PALESTINIAN AUTHORITY), SOUTHERN (INCLUDING EGYPT, SAUDI ARABIA)	2
CENTRAL ASIA: NORTH-CENTRAL (INCLUDING KAZAKHSTAN), SOUTH-CENTRAL (INCLUDING PAKISTAN)	2
EAST-CENTRAL ASIA (BANGLADESH, MYANMAR/BURMA, THAILAND, LAOS, VIETNAM, CAMBODIA)	2
EAST ASIA (JAPAN, NORTH/SOUTH KOREA, PHILIPPINES)	2

AUSTRALIA: EAST, WEST	2
UK (PM, N)	1
FRANCE (PM, N)	1
CENTRAL AMERICA, INCLUDING MEXICO	1
CARIBBEAN	1
ISRAEL	1
IRAN	1
SOUTH-EAST ASIA (MALAYSIA, INDONESIA, WPP 3.39%)	1
OCEANIA (NEW ZEALAND, ISLANDS AND DEPENDENT TERRITORIES)	1
TOTAL NUMBER OF CONSTITUENCIES (EACH OF WHICH HAS 2 SEATS)	**46**
TOTAL NUMBER OF WORLD SENATE SEATS	**92**

WORLD COMMISSION REPRESENTATIONS

The World Commission of 27 Commissioners is drawn from wider regions than the World Senate, taking into account population, topographical size and political significance – hence, again, Israel and Iran each have Commissioners, even though they are too small to warrant this in terms of their populations and topographical size. However, no nation-state may have more than one Commissioner. There is one World Commissioner per region (which is sometimes a nation-state).

The 27 World Commissioners represent the following regions:

1 China (PM, N, WPP 19.5%)
2 China's Communist/ex-Communist neighbours (Mongolia, North Korea [N], Laos, Vietnam)
3 Russian Federation (PM, N, topographically largest country in world)

4 Central Asia (ex-Soviet)
5 Canada (seat justified by topographical size of country regardless of world influence) and Greenland
6 USA (PM, N)
7 UK (PM, N)
8 France (PM, N)
9 Western Europe including Germany (R)
10 Eastern Europe (R)
11 Central America and Caribbean (R)
12 Northeast South America (including Brazil [N, R])
13 Southwest South America (including Argentina [R])
14 Northern Africa (R)
15 Southern Africa (R)
16 Arab Middle East (R)
17 Israel (N)
18 Iran (N?)
19 Pakistan (N)/Afghanistan (R)
20 India (N, WPP 17.23%)
21 West-Central and Southeast Asia (Bangladesh to Cambodia, R)
22 East Asia (Japan, South/North Korea, Philippines [R])
23 Indonesia (WPP 3.39%)/Malaysia
24 Australia/Oceania ([R], WWP 0.5%)
25 UN (secondment of executive expert)
26 World Bank (secondment of expert)
27 Agencies of global government (secondment of expert)

The power of such a World State would gather a world culture behind it. It is likely that a unified world culture would pre-exist the coming into existence of a World State. The World State would bring in what I have called 'a Golden Age of Universalism',[12] a Golden Age of peace, promise and prosperity. The unity of world culture and the seven disciplines would prepare the ground for and strengthen such a World State. Universalism would be the World State's philosophy and would reflect the unity of world culture and the seven disciplines.

AMERICAN UNIVERSALISM AND A ONE-WORLD MOVEMENT

The chart in appendix 1 shows 25 civilizations and cultures flowing into a one-world civilization, and vividly demonstrates the fundamental unity of world culture. The Universalist synthesis sees each discipline within the global flow of world history that leads to a worldwide civilization and offers the prospect, dear to Liberty, that each discipline and conflict between thesis and antithesis will lead to a one-world movement, as we can see by considering each of the seven disciplines:

ONE-WORLD MYSTICISM

The World State will bring in mystical Universalism's one-world view of mysticism. The Lights of the world's civilizations and cultures flow into a one-world civilization as shown in the chart in appendix 1. My study of history sees the North American civilization – and Liberty – as taking the lead in setting up such a worldwide civilization. As the civilizations and cultures are all based on the Light, it is possible that this one-world civilization will have a one-world mystical outlook set up by the North American civilization as an imminent stage in its growth.

My study of civilizations, to which I have often referred, also shows that stage-15 civilizations, like the North American, produce epic poetry (stage 16) and found a Light-based 'heretical' sect that plays an important role in stages 29 and 34. It is likely that the North American civilization's Puritan God of stage 4 and the Christ of radical ecumenical Protestantism of stage 15 will be challenged by a New Age movement championing the Universalist Light.[13] From the Christian point of view, the New Age is 'heretical' as it embraces all religions, and especially their mysticism. The New Age could mark the beginning of the heresy that can be expected to appear in stage 17. It looks up to the perennial philosophy, which surfaced in the Renaissance (as the *philosophia perennis*) and was set out in the Neo-Vedanta of Aldous Huxley and in Daisetsu Suzuki's works on Zen. According to the perennial philosophy, the mystical experiences of all religions are fundamentally the same, and this view has been conveyed at meetings of the New Age-minded Wrekin Trust and Scientific and Medical Network. Unitarian Universalism holds that there is truth in all religions besides Christianity, and that Christianity is not the only religion to have a loving God that redeems souls. William James's *The Varieties of Religious Experience* and the occult traditions of Theosophy, New Thought and the Fourth Way of George Gurdjieff and P D Ouspensky are all in accord.

The New Age Universalist Light has begun the syncretistic blending of religions to reveal their essence, the mystic Light. An American Universalist movement in an early phase of stage 17 could create a one-world mystical movement from the mysticism within the world's higher religions: Buddhism's Shingon, Vajrayana and Zen mysticism; Christianity's mysticism including Quakerism (which is on the list on p 10); Hinduism's Vedanta, Yoga, Bhakti and Saivist mysticism; Islam's Sunni, Shiite and Sufi mysticism; Jainism's Moksha mysticism; Judaism's Kabbalah and Hasidic mysticism; Sikhism's oneness mysticism; and Taoism's harmony mysticism. The mystery religions – for example, the Eleusinian mysteries – also had their own mysticism. All these follow the Light – see my comprehensive *The Light of Civilization* – and could be unified into a one-world mysticism based on the metaphysical Light.

Universalism is looming ahead in both the European and North American civilizations (as we saw on pp 5–7). In the European civilization, now in stage 43 (loss of national sovereignty to a secularizing conglomerate, the European Union), stage 44 – the next stage – is one of syncretism and Universalism as religious sects draw together under the new conglomerate, the European Union. The Christian sects have all gravitated towards each other, and there is more of an ecumenical outlook today than there was 70 years ago. Universalism surfaced in the European civilization in stages 15, 29 and 34, and the principle is well established as the European civilization progresses towards stage 44. The North American civilization's Universalism that has surfaced in the New Age sects and movement and is groping towards the 'heretical' mystic Light of stage 17 will draw strength from the European civilization's Universalism. The two civilizations either side of the Atlantic will be well placed during the next ten years to create a one-world mystical movement, whose time is nigh. Such a one-world mystical movement led from America would follow the tradition of all the mystics (listed on pp 11–12).

ONE-WORLD LITERATURE

Literature in its primary meaning is 'literary productions as a whole, the writings of a country or period or of the world in general' (*Shorter Oxford English Dictionary*). World literature is therefore the writings of all civilizations and cultures in verse or prose. It includes all genres, such as: religious texts; mythology; philosophy; epic, lyric, elegiac, pastoral and didactic poetry; drama, including comedy and tragedy; history; satire; and oratory. 'Literature' also has a qualitative nuance suggesting the highest literary standards, depth, complexity, beauty of form, emotional effects and the like. Literature is supranational. It transcends nation-states, and world literature is the aggregate of all the writings detailed above and elsewhere at all times.

On pp 14–19 I referred to my study *A New Philosophy of Literature*, which sets out the fundamental theme in world literature: a dialectic between a metaphysical aspect based on a quest for the One (Reality and immortality) and a social aspect based on condemnation of follies and vices. In the dialectic $+A + -A = 0$: quest + vices =

fundamental theme. Also: metaphysics + secularism = Universalism. I set out 12 Universalist characteristics as the metaphysical aspect of the fundamental theme of world literature and followed eight of them through 10 literary periods.

A one-world literature will not just reflect the writings of all civilizations. It will also reflect the one-world movement that is looming for all the seven disciplines. It will reflect aspects of the one-world movement which will result in a World State, including attempts by a self-interested élite to rule the world through a New World Order. (I endeavoured to reflect attempts to create a New World Order in Hitler's time in *Overlord* and in our post-9/11 time in *Armageddon*.)

Literary Universalism is caught up in the political, historical, religious and philosophical movement towards a World State, and the man or woman of letters must monitor the cultural consequences of the deeds of ambitious leaders. T S Eliot, writing in 1944 when Fascism and Communism had ambitions to rule the world, stated in *The Man of Letters and the Future of Europe* that the man of letters must champion the cultural health of Europe and scrutinize the actions of key figures for their cultural consequences:

> The man of letters as such, is not concerned with the political or economic map of Europe; but he should be very much concerned with its cultural map … The man of letters … should be able to take a longer view than either the politician or the local patriot. … The cultural health of Europe, including the cultural health of its component parts, is incompatible with extreme forms of both nationalism and internationalism . …The responsibility of the man of letters at the present time … should be vigilantly watching the conduct of politicians and economists, for the purpose of criticizing and warning, when the decisions and actions of the politicians

> and economists are likely to have cultural consequences. Of these consequences the man of letters should qualify himself to judge. Of the possible cultural consequences of their activities, politicians and economists are usually oblivious; the man of letters is better qualified to foresee them, and to perceive their seriousness.

In our time global developments have overtaken Eliot's perspective of the European civilization, and the man of letters has a duty to scrutinize the conduct of the élite running the world today, which I have done in *The Syndicate*. Eliot was concerned at the cultural consequences of leaders' actions. The current book is in the tradition of Eliot's *Notes towards the Definition of Culture*, and Eliot would have approved of my concern regarding the seven disciplines of world culture.

Besides monitoring our rulers, the man of letters can now chart a new direction for one-world literature and world culture. This will involve a return by poets, dramatists, novelists and cultural essayists to the inspired metaphysical vision, which is received during the quest for Reality and immortality. As I said on p xx, I describe 93 instances of this vision which I recorded in my on-the-day *Diaries*, in *My Double Life 1: This Dark Wood* and *My Double Life 2: A Rainbow over the Hills*, which quote from my *Diaries*, and many of these visions can be found in my poetic works. A new one-world literature will reflect the reunification of humankind and the new world culture such a reunification will make possible, and focus on the universe and the infinite that surrounds it, the context for a united humankind.

Besides making possible a new understanding of the past, Universalism makes possible a new view of the imminent and pressing future in which the arts, including literature and especially poetry, will convey the reunification of humankind.

ONE-WORLD PHILOSOPHY AND SCIENCE

Philosophy has been marginalized since it retreated into logic and language, and its traditional view of the universe has been replaced by science, which has explored the origin of the universe and assembled evidence for a Materialistic view that it was an accident, as we have seen, while at the same time offering evidence for the order of the universe. The new cosmological science has a one-world following and place in world culture.

Universalism seeks to restore the universe and Nature to the foreground of a one-world philosophy, where it was for the early Greeks. As the North American civilization attempts to form a political World State and champions Universalism as it approaches stage 17 and the European civilization champions Universalism as it approaches stage 44, the new philosophy of Universalism's appeal in the West will be strengthened. As an outlook that reunites the metaphysical and scientific traditions within philosophy, the rational and intuitional philosophies within metaphysics and the linguistic and phenomenological views within philosophy, philosophical Universalism can provide a one-world philosophy that derives strength from being interconnected with mystical, literary, historical, religious, political and cultural Universalism.

I have set out (in *The One and the Many*)[14] how philosophical Universalism can offer a new spiritual vision for all humankind and how the experience of the Light could act as common ground for a worldwide civilization. An American-led worldwide civilization with its own World Parliamentary Assembly, World Senate and World Commission would work with its philosophy of Universalism to broaden and strengthen the common ground of all humankind. This democratic model would be recognizable throughout the UN. Within the context of the coming World State, a new one-world philosophy of Universalism lies ahead.

ONE-WORLD HISTORY

The World State will bring in historical Universalism's one-world view of history, which regards history as the record of all humankind's activities during the past 5,000 years. Central to this is the rise-and-fall pattern of 25 civilizations (see pp xvii and 163–4) and their progress to a worldwide civilization, the flow that can be monitored by following the arrows on the chart in appendix 1. Also central to this is the seven-foot (just over 2m) long chart involving 25 civilizations going through 61 stages that accompanied *The Fire and the Stones*, which can also be found at the end of my work *The Rise and Fall of Civilizations*.[15] At the start of each civilization's genesis and growth is the mystical vision of the Light on which its religion is founded, the common essence of all civilizations and religions.

ONE-WORLD COMPARATIVE RELIGION

The World State will bring in religious Universalism's one-world view of religion. We have seen that the New Age sees a common essence in all religions, and a one-world religion would be a 'tent' for all humankind, who could bring their local Lights to its altar. Stage 44 of the European civilization, a stage of Universalism and syncretism, will see religious Universalism strengthening. It may be hard to believe that Islamic fundamentalism can take part in such religious Universalism, but in my Baghdad lecture room in 1961–2, when the Arab civilization was in stage 43, the Sunnis, Shiites and Kurds co-existed relatively peacefully despite tensions.

At present the Arab civilization is in stage 45: rejection of the present and yearning for the lost past of its own civilization, revival of cultural purity. The Taliban in Afghanistan, al-Qaeda in Iraq and Islamic State (or Daesh) all yearn for the 'cultural purity' of the 7th century. When the Arab world enters a federation of Arab states (which will retain their own sovereignty) the yearning for a lost past will recede. All the religions and all the words of their prophets will syncretistically merge under religious Universalism (as we saw on pp 164–5), and there will be a new 'perennial philosophy' based on the mystic Light that formed the basis of all religions during their civilizations' genesis and growth.

ONE-WORLD INTERNATIONAL POLITICS AND STATECRAFT

The World State will bring in political Universalism in the form of a one-world worldwide civilization that includes all previous civilizations. The structure for such a World State is in place. It straddles three Unions: the American Union of all countries in North, Central and South America; the European Union (which became a superstate with its own legal personality following the Lisbon Treaty of 2009); and the Asian-Pacific Union. I set out details of the Unions in *The Syndicate* (2004),[16] and details of the institutions of global governance in *The Secret American Dream*,[17] in which I summarized the progress in setting up regional trade groupings:[18]

- The 1994, 34-state Free Trade Area for the Americas (FTAA), which is an extension of NAFTA (the North American Free Trade Agreement), CAFTA (the Central American Free Trade Agreement), and LAFTA (the Latin American Free Trade Association, created in 1960 and replaced in 1980 by LAIA, the Latin American Integration Association), and was set to pass into an American Union
- The 2008 Union of South American Nations, which replaced the South American Community of Nations (created in 2004) and was also set to pass into an American Union
- The CARICOM (the Caribbean Community), which grew out of CARIFTA (the Caribbean Free Trade Association) in 1973
- The EU (European Union, with a legal personality that overrides its 27 [*sic*] member nation-states), which grew out of the EC (European Community), whose roots were in the EEC (European

Economic Community) and before that the ECSC (the European Coal and Steel Community)
- The AU (African Union), which grew out of the OAU (the Organization of African Unity)
- The APEC (the Asia-Pacific Economic Co-operation), a forum for 21 Pacific Rim Countries that was growing into an AEC (Asian Economic Community) and was set to pass into an Asia-Pacific Union
- The SAFTA (South Asian Free Trade Area), which was also growing into an AEC (Asian Economic Community)

The European Union has since expanded to 28 member nation-states with the advent of Croatia. From these Unions and free-trade groupings it can be seen that political Universalism is advancing towards a World State (even though it may sometimes seem that fragmentation is in the air with talk of the UK leaving the EU, of Scotland leaving the UK and of Catalonia leaving Spain).

Global organizations for trade include the 12-nation Trans-Pacific Partnership (TPP) and the US-EU Transatlantic Trade and Investment Partnership (TTIP), which seek to merge the US and EU regulatory systems to create a new common market. The Trade in Services Agreement (TiSA) covers most of the global economy and seeks to give the UN's World Trade Organization (WTO) control of the world's service sector. The TPP–TiSA–TTIP trinity excludes the five BRICS countries, which in 2015 brought a new dimension to banking.

On 8–9 July 2015 the BRICS nations (Brazil, Russia, India, China and South Africa) brought the New Development Bank (NDB) into existence in Shanghai. It seemed to be an alternative to the US-dominated World Bank and International Monetary Fund (IMF) which were created under the Bretton Woods Agreement after the Second World War that made the US dollar the world's reserve currency. The NDB offered an alternative to the international banking cartel owned and controlled by the Rothschild family. This financial challenge was backed by the Shanghai Cooperation Organization (SCO) – comprising China, Russia, Uzbekistan, Kazakhstan, Kyrgyzstan, Tajikistan, India and Pakistan, with Egypt and Iran interested in joining – which offers military co-ordination and support. (The 2015 US deal with Iran has to be partly seen within this context, as heading Iran off from the SCO.) However, with Brazil's credit rating downgraded, Russia in recession and China and South Africa on the brink of recession, in 2015 the BRICS economy was crumbling before a strong dollar.

In *The Secret American Dream* I demonstrated that the world is crisscrossed by US- and Russian-controlled oil and gas pipelines. In that work I showed a map[19] of the oil and gas pipelines already in place.

The key pipelines affecting international politics and statecraft (and scheduled completion dates, some of which have passed, reflecting delays in some projects) are:[20]

- The US TAPI gas pipeline from Turkmenistan through Afghanistan to India, completion date unknown
- The US North American Denali natural gas pipeline from Alaska north slope to Alberta, Canada, and US mid-west, completion date unknown
- The IGI Poseidon gas pipeline from Greece to Italy, scheduled to be completed in 2015
- The North American Keystone oil pipeline from Alberta, Canada, to Illinois and Oklahoma, three phases in operation, the fourth awaiting US government approval
- The Russian Mozdok gas pipeline from Azerbaijan to North Ossetia, scheduled to be operational 2015

- The Russian Altai gas pipeline from Russia to China, scheduled to be completed 2011–15, subsequently re-routed farther east and renamed the Power of Siberia gas pipeline
- The Russian South Stream gas pipeline from Russia to Austria and Southeast Europe, scheduled to be completed 2015
- The Russian Nord Stream gas pipeline from Russia to Sassnitz, Germany, scheduled to be completed 2011
- The US Trans-Caspian natural gas pipeline from Turkmenistan to Azerbaijan, completion date not yet announced
- The US White Stream gas pipeline from Georgia to Romania and West Europe, scheduled to be completed 2016
- The US Nabucco gas pipeline from Turkey to Austria and Southeast Europe, scheduled to be completed 2015
- The SCO Growth Kazakhstan-China oil pipeline from Kazakhstan to China, completed, further portion scheduled to be completed 2011
- The ESPO oil pipeline from Russia to China and potentially Japan, scheduled to be completed 2014
- The Iranian Pars gas pipeline from Iran to Turkey, scheduled to be completed 2014
- The Iran-Pakistan-India gas pipeline from Iran to India and Pakistan, scheduled to be completed 2015
- The Russian Trans-Ukrainian natural gas pipeline from Russia through Ukraine (Urengoy-Pomary-Uzhgorod in the Ukraine), also known as the Trans-Siberian pipeline, completed in 1982–1984, and several subsequent pipelines from Russia to Europe through Ukraine, some to the Black Sea
- The Mosul-Haifa oil pipeline from Kirkuk, Iraq to Haifa, Israel, begun in 1927, built by the British Iraq Petroleum Co. between 1932 and 1935, operational in 1935 and reactivated by the US Bechtel Co. after 2003

The Mosul-Haifa pipeline had reached Al-Hadith in 1934. It then forked. One branch went through Syria south of Palmyra to Tripoli (Lebanon), the other to Haifa. In 1952 Western oil companies built two new pipelines through Syria and the pipeline to Haifa fell into disuse and decayed. One reason why George W Bush invaded Iraq in 2003 was to resurrect the branch of the pipeline to Haifa. Just as there was fighting in Afghanistan, where the TAPI pipeline passed through Herat and Kandahar, so from 2011 to 2015 there was fighting in Syria where two new oil pipelines cross south of Palmyra.

The Trans-Ukrainian natural gas pipeline from Russia also crosses a region (south of Kiev) where there has been fighting, as do several other pipelines from Russia through Ukraine. In 2004 Ukraine's 'Orange Revolution' transformed independent Ukraine from a pro-Russian ex-Soviet republic into a pro-NATO US satellite and potential member of the EU. The 'Orange Revolution' was ended in February 2010 when Ukraine's Electoral Commission declared the pro-Russian Viktor Yanukovych the winner of new presidential elections. Since then, West Ukraine has returned to pro-EU rule while East Ukraine has been fought over by Russian-backed militias and Russia has seized the Crimea. In 2011 Russia opened the Nord Stream pipeline to bypass Ukraine. On 16 June 2014 Russia limited the supply of natural gas to Ukrainians owing to non-payment, and the next day the original pipeline was damaged by a bomb.

In Afghanistan, Iraq, Syria and the Ukraine the extent to which fighting is linked to oil or gas pipelines is not clear.

With the structure of institutions and pipelines that now crisscross the world, a World State does not seem far off. In *The Secret American Dream* I set out Obama's ambition to move away from American hegemony and military superiority towards a peaceful, humane World State in which all humankind could benefit from the American Dream. Since that work came out in 2010, the banking crisis and its attendant recession have slowed down Western economies. Obama has withdrawn American troops from Afghanistan and Iraq and was reluctant to provide anything other than a supporting role in Libya and Syria, and consequently the terrorist organization Islamic State (or Daesh) has been allowed to take root and flourish as would not have happened had George W Bush been President. Obama has made peace with Iran, and with Cuba. Following the Lisbon Treaty, the European Union has emerged as a superstate, not as powerful as the US but still a German-led force for peace. Russia has seized Crimea, is defending it with nuclear weapons and is fighting clandestinely in East Ukraine, and in March 2015 mounted an exercise in the Baltic to rehearse the capture of islands from Denmark, Sweden and Finland with a view to sealing the Baltic and re-taking Estonia, Latvia and Lithuania to join up with its Russian Kaliningrad exclave between Poland and Lithuania, where it was siting nuclear weapons.

The Pentagon has moved troops, artillery and Abrams tanks into Poland, Slovenia and the countries that have borders with western and southern Russia or the Black Sea – Estonia, Latvia and Lithuania, Romania and Bulgaria – and in 2015 there was a stand-off between naval forces in the Baltic and Black Sea. The Pentagon has also increased its surveillance capabilities in Europe, including the drones in NATO's arsenal, and high-altitude spy-plane flights over Russia. There has been concern that war could erupt from these exercises and unease that there is a potential nuclear confrontation across the Arctic of intercontinental ballistic missiles aimed at cities.

The Baltic states seem to be threatened, and recently new information has come to light[21] as to how they passed under Soviet influence in the first place. Eastern Europe was carved up as a result of the 1939 Molotov-Ribbentrop (that is, Stalin-Hitler) Pact, whose 'secret protocol', authenticated by US government stamp, divided Central and Eastern Europe into Soviet and German spheres of influence. Finland, Estonia and Latvia were assigned to the Soviet sphere of influence, Poland was partitioned and Lithuania was assigned to the German sphere of influence. A second 'secret protocol' reassigned the greater part of Lithuania to the USSR. The Pact and its protocols allowed Hitler to invade Poland (causing the UK to declare war on Germany) and divide it with the Soviet Union. The spirit of the pact survived in the Tehran Agreement of 1943, which perpetuated the Soviet sphere of influence.

Following the evacuation of the German Foreign Office from Berlin in 1943, copies of the Pact turned up in the West. Soviet officials and scholars presented the protocols as Western forgeries, but in 1989 Gorbachev set up a commission to investigate them. The commission concluded that the protocols were genuine, that they violated peace treaties between the Baltic states and the USSR in the 1920s and 1930s, and that the Soviet occupation of the Baltic states was illegal. The Congress of People's Deputies of the Soviet Union subsequently passed a declaration confirming the existence of the protocols and denouncing them, and this declaration paved the way for the independence of Estonia, Latvia and Lithuania and led to the unravelling of the Soviet Union. This Soviet declaration confirmed my call in the 1970s and 1980s for FREE (Freedom for the Republics of Eastern Europe) and my defiance of the 1943 Tehran Agreement in a broadcast behind the Iron Curtain on 4 November 1986,[22] for the Soviet occupation of much of Eastern Europe was subsequently proved to have been illegal.

Many observers believe the world is becoming more disorderly: the internecine warfare in Syria, Iraq, Yemen and Libya, the spread of IS (which was reputed to have somewhere between 20,000 and 100,000 foreign troops fighting in Syria and Iraq – the lower figure according to CIA sources, the higher figure according to Jihadists – but by September 2015 had shrunk to 10,000, and is fanatical enough to use a dirty nuclear bomb) and al-Qaeda (which has 25,000 foreign troops from 100 countries); the unrest in Africa (where Nigeria's terrorist movement Boko Haram has used looted Libyan arms) and on the borders of Israel; and the war of attrition in Ukraine, involving East Ukrainian militias and Russian support. (This activity within the Arab civilization is a reflection of its stage 45, revival of cultural purity, and this activity within the Russian Federation is a reflection of the counter-thrust at the beginning of the Byzantine-Russian civilization's stage 46.) There were also terror groups in India, Kashmir and Pakistan, and in Thailand and Myanmar (formerly Burma).

IS has a grandiose plan to restore the early Arab Caliphate on a grander scale, and to occupy all the territory from East India to Spain, and from the Balkans to the African equator, an enlarged version of the Ottoman Empire. It wants to lure the West into conflict but so far is confined to Iraq, Syria and Libya. Its strategy is to use terror to drive into unstable areas in the ex-Ottoman nation-states and then join up the 'blots' and try to suck the West into battle by provocative acts in the manner of the 1914 assassination of Franz Ferdinand and the 2001 9/11 attack (both of which started a war) to bring about 'the end of days' and Armageddon. (This was bin Laden's strategy as I outlined in my poetic epic about 9/11, *Armageddon*.)

A major issue of our time is refugees fleeing conflict, massive population upheavals that recall the *Völkerwanderung*, the 'barbarian' migration of Germanic and Slavic peoples from the 2nd to 11th centuries that shook the Roman Empire and destabilized the Dark Ages: the Germanic tribes of Goths, Vandals, Angles, Saxons, Lombards, Suebi, Frisii, Jutes and Franks; the Huns, Avars, Slavs, Bulgars and Alans; and later the Viking, Norman, Hungarian, Moorish, Turkic and Mongol invasions. In the biggest refugee crisis since the Second World War, hordes of refugees from the Middle East and Africa fled to Europe in inflatables or unseaworthy boats, aided by people traffickers. Refugees, asylum seekers, economic migrants and some illegal immigrants poured across the Mediterranean from wars and Islamic terrorism in Libya, Syria, Iraq, Afghanistan and Yemen and from sub-Saharan poverty in Eritrea, Ethiopia, Somalia and Sudan.

The UN estimates that by 2015, 7.6 million of around 23 million Syrians had been displaced.[23] By July 2015 more than 4 million Syrians had fled to neighbouring countries such as Turkey (1.8 million, at a cost to Turkey of more than $5 billion over four years), Lebanon (1.1 million registered), Jordan (630,000), Iraq (250,000) and Egypt (132,000).[24] Most of these were in UN refugee camps: over 4 million Syrians had registered or were awaiting registration with the UN High Commission of Refugees (UNHCR).[25] Half of all Syrians, some 11 million, had had their homes destroyed but many had stayed on in the ruins.[26]

Many Syrian refugees have been fleeing from chemical weapon attacks by both Assad's and IS forces. Assad's forces are thought to have dropped chlorine gas bombs in 31 raids on Idlib between March and June 2015, according to a dossier presented to the US Congress.[27] There are reports that IS is 'making and using' mustard gas and used it in Marea 25 km (15½ miles) north of Aleppo in April 2015 and on at least three other occasions. In Marea doctors treated more than 30 patients with suppurating blisters following an attack by artillery shells in April 2015, and similar artillery attacks have been made on Kurdish Peshmerga forces near Sultan Abdullah, raising fears that IS have pillaged chemical stockpiles of sulphur mustard (mustard gas) – perhaps 200 tons of mustard agent missing from Assad's declaration to the UN,[28] or perhaps Saddam Hussein's hidden stockpiles the Americans could not find after the 2003 Iraq War.[29]

Saddam used mustard gas in Halabja on 16 March 1988, killing 3,200–5,000 civilians (more than were killed in 9/11), and it was his assumed possession of these chemical weapons that triggered the 2003 Iraq War. IS may be using Saddam's hidden supply of mustard gas in Syria. IS are pro-Saddam Sunnis who passed into 'al-Qaeda in Iraq' and broke away as ISIL before calling themselves IS. Their first mass execution in Tikrit took place 100 metres (320 feet) from Saddam's Water Palace and the executioners shouted 'Persians' as they shot Shiite prisoners, echoing Saddam's derogatory word for Shiites on the scaffold, 'Are you Persians?', and indicating their support for Saddam's cause. The secret of the whereabouts of the missing chemical weapons of mass destruction may have passed from Saddam's entourage to *their* successor organization 'al-Qaeda in Iraq' and thence to their successor organization IS.

Five hundred thousand refugees from civil wars and dreadful conditions arrived on the borders of the European Union in the first eight months of 2015 – 200,000 in Greece (50,000 in one month), 150,000 in Hungary and 120,000 in Italy – including 94,000 Syrians, 26,000 Afghans and 32,000 Eritreans. As many again were expected in 2016 unless an EU deal with Turkey, that it will seal its borders in return for Turkish citizens having free access to the Schengen Area, could stem the flow. These migrants are thought to have included some IS terrorists seeking to penetrate European countries, and some associated with increases in thefts, murders and rapes. There was some resentment that they were depleting their hosts' food, medical provisions and taxpayer-funded benefit systems. The scale of population movements was huge: there were as many as 60 million refugees in the world in 2015, 38 million of whom were forcibly displaced by violence within their own country, according to UNHCR.[30]

The global refugee problem could arguably be laid at the door of: the US and Israeli wars of aggression (perhaps to establish a 'Greater Israel' and 'Greater Khazaria', like the empire of the Khazars which used to include the Ukraine and Crimea); the murderous policies of Assad (who has used suffocating chlorine chemical weapons against Syrian civilians) and IS (which has used mustard gas chemical weapons against Syrian civilians), which compelled people to flee for their lives from Syria and Iraq; and the NATO air strikes which left Libya in a state of anarchy and allowed arsenals of Gaddafi's weapons to fall into the hands of terrorists. There is scope for this refugee problem to continue from Africa as, according to the UN, Africa's population of 1.1 billion in 2013 will double to 2.4 billion by 2050 and nearly double again to 4.2 billion by 2100, while food in Africa will not double and may be reduced because of climate change.

European rules require refugees to be given asylum in their country of entry. Some countries of entry could not cope with the massive influx: nearly-bankrupt Greece was faced with 200,000 new mouths to feed. Germany (which needs migrants, as its low birth rate will reduce the population by 25 per cent by 2050) was set to take in 800,000 refugees in 2015 alone and may have taken in 1.5 million, and Angela Merkel called for all EU countries to share the asyluming and settling of migrants. The UK had admitted 22,000 of the 200,000 Hungarian refugees who fled the Soviet invasion in 1956 and 27,000 of the 55,000 Ugandan Asians expelled by Idi Amin in 1972, and was set to admit 20,000 Syrians from UN refugee camps over five years on top of being the world's second-biggest contributor to the refugee camps. Europe was set to admit hundreds of thousands of Syrian refugees. Eurostat, the EU's statistical office, showed that from April to June 2015 only 21 per cent of those claiming asylum in Europe were from Syria (44,000 out of 213,000). Some poorer countries (such as Hungary) did not welcome migrants, seeing them as Muslim terrorists or economic parasites who had no jobs and few language skills and expected to live on welfare benefits paid for by European taxpayers, and attempted to close their borders with razor-wire. The Schengen open-borders system was challenged, and in September 2015 Germany took the unprecedented step of imposing border controls with Austria after 50,000 refugees poured in during one week, and Austria, Hungary, Holland, Slovakia, Slovenia, Croatia and Bulgaria also imposed border controls.

Universalists regard all migrants as world citizens and like the UN Secretary-General Ban Ki-moon feel their suffering. They recognize the impotence of the UN, which is 'inter-national' in the sense of being an organization *between* nation-states without supranational powers, and grasp that a World State would create safe havens near the countries (such as Syria) whose chaos had caused the exodus in the first place, and eventually pacify those countries with a peace-keeping force. With global planning, a partly-federal World State would be able to control the movements of populations far more effectively than can the present system of inter-national nation-states and a powerless UN.

Observers say that Obama's foreign policy has been weak, not appreciating his long-term goal of resolving conflicts in preparation for a World State and his support for multilateral nuclear disarmament, which Russia has slowed by introducing nuclear weapons in the vicinity of the Ukraine. Some believe that US influence abroad has declined and that there may have to be more intervention to sort out the disorder.

However, a balanced view of global order shows that, the Middle East and North Africa aside, there is peace in much of the rest of the world: in Europe, North and South America, China, most of the ex-USSR, Oceania, much of Africa (the struggles of the liberation movements of the 1960s and 1970s now pacified), India and Asia (the struggles in Vietnam in the 1960s and 1970s and in Sri Lanka now pacified and the terrorist movements connected with Kashmir and Palestine contained). Obama, who received the Nobel Peace Prize in 2009, has pursued a policy of pacification in preparation for a World State.

From this perspective the whole world is ready for a World State except for pockets of bellicosity in the Middle East, North Africa and the western border of Southern Russia, and if these spots of unrest are sorted out by interventions in the coming years – the US and Russia may not be able to manage and contain IS and al-Qaeda and may have to destroy them (the Romans' approach to Carthage) rather than contain them – the world will be more peaceful than it has been for a century. The time for a World State is right.

However, progress towards a World State has been slow, and Obama said in a speech in Seattle on 23 July 2014:

> But whether people see what's happening in Ukraine, and Russia's aggression towards its neighbors in the manner in which it's financing and arming separatists; … what's happened in Syria – the devastation that Bashar al-Assad has wrought on his own people; … the failure in Iraq for Sunni and Shia and Kurd to compromise – although we're trying to see if we can put together a government that actually can function; … ongoing terrorist threats; … what's happening in Israel and Gaza – part of peoples' concern is just the sense that around the world the old order isn't holding and we're not quite yet to where we need to be in terms of a new order that's based on a different set of principles, that's based on a sense of common humanity, that's based on economies that work for all people.[31]

We are in a time of transition, as Obama said. The old order has ceased to be hegemonistic and militaristic, and the more human new order based on common humanity and economies that work for people has not yet taken shape. The 2015 deal with Iran is based on the principle that a more human order is emerging in which Iran should be included. (Iran promptly behaved in the old militaristic way by conducting a nationalistic ballistic missile test and showed ballistic missiles queuing on trailers in an underground tunnel.) The new order transcends nation-states and works for international harmony and accord as in the Iran deal – and for the coming World State that will create a 'one-world' worldwide civilization.

ONE-WORLD WORLD CULTURE

The World State will bring in cultural Universalism's one-world view of world culture (which we considered on pp 175–6). This will unite all the civilizations and cultures on the chart in appendix 1, which shows the Light as the common ground for humankind. By restoring the metaphysical tradition to the secularized culture in the West, Universalism will bring about the 'Revolution in Thought and Culture' that will make the metaphysical sap flow again in the trunk, branches and leaves – religion, seven disciplines and artistic works – of all living civilizations and unify world culture.

To change the image to that of a rainbow, as we have seen (pp xv and 177), world culture has seven bands: the seven disciplines which can be unified in accordance with the dialectic +A + –A = 0. The prospect ahead is of a world culture that includes works of art that express metaphysical Reality, the Light, as did Van Gogh's swirling skies that attempt to catch the energy in the universe and its infinite, ordered source. The seven disciplines unite in reflecting the mystic Light, which is known both intuitively and rationally in philosophy and is reflected in literature, and in one worldwide civilization and religion within a political World State and world culture that shows man as a citizen of the world and of the universe rather than of his own nation-state.

Universalism's synthesis has pieced together all the broken disciplines like potsherds and reassembled them into one interconnected patchwork vision. All opposites and contradictions are reconciled. Within the shuttlecock-shaped expanding universe, all living things appear to be subject to a universal order. Liberty's torch shines out for freedom from tyranny and for world unity within a unified world culture in which mysticism, literature, philosophy and the sciences, history, religions, international politics and culture are bands in one metaphysical-and-secular rainbow.

Individual disciplines taught at the universities reflect parts – slices

– of the whole view, so that undergraduates leave with a partial view. Universalism should be taught as a new discipline in its own right so that undergraduates leave with a whole view of the universe and of the social approach – and of the prospects for world unity. Such a course would include modules on: cosmology, astrophysics, physics, biology, geology, plate tectonics, Ice Ages, ecology, biochemistry, physiology, psychology and, most importantly, early Greek and Universalist philosophy. But it is not just a whole view of disciplines and modules which needs to be taught. The perspective that has most unified world culture is *the vision of order* in the universe and world culture.

Liberty knows that American Universalism can reunify the seven divided disciplines of world culture, and that a reunified world culture can accommodate both religious and secular world citizens and emphasize the order that brings spiritual unity and support for a democratic World State that can abolish war, famine, disease and penury.

PART FOUR

ORDER AND AMERICA'S DESTINY

CHAPTER 7

RESTORING THE METAPHYSICAL VISION OF ORDER IN WORLD CULTURE

St Augustine's *The City of God* showed human Christian society as an association of souls that reflected the harmonious gathering of the deceased in the Christian Heaven. To the early Christians, Heaven was an orderly place. Utopias sought to reflect and recreate Heaven on Earth, and from Sir Thomas More's *Utopia* to the Marxist socialism of the 19th and 20th centuries, social thinkers have dreamed of an orderly paradise in which the poor, hungry and diseased, and the refugees from war, could enjoy a peaceful, harmonious life that reflects the orderliness of the spiritual life of the soul.

From Nelson Rockefeller to George Bush, American proclamations of a New World Order have begun to disseminate such a vision, though their New World Order has been confused by the unhumanitarian ambitions of an élite, 'the Syndicate' (a group of influential dynastic families seeking to advance their own global wealth).

America's contemporary vision of the spiritual unity of humankind, which can be found in New Age thinking, is an expression of the metaphysical order in the universe, and we should pause briefly to remind ourselves of what has been established about the order in Nature, in the sciences and in the seven disciplines.

ORDER IN NATURE

We are most aware of the order in Nature when we study the four ecosystems that surround ponds, woodlands, lakes and oceans and their food chains and food webs. I have given (pp 77–9) some examples of the food chains in and around ponds, of the food web of ponds and wetlands and of co-operative behaviour in woodlands. More examples cannot fail to astonish. First, the food chain in lakes:

> In and around a lake ecosystem, the food chain is algae-fish-bird. Algae and phytoplankton are eaten by zooplankton, which are eaten by herbivores and insectivores such as freshwater shrimps, which are eaten by carnivores (carnivorous fish) such as bleak, which are eaten by perch, which are eaten by northern pike, which are eaten by ospreys. Also, plants are eaten by caterpillars, which are eaten by lizards, which are eaten by snakes. Also, dead animals or carrion are fed on by blowfly larvae and carrion beetles, which are eaten by centipedes and ravens. Also, earthworms, nematodes and bacteria decompose organic matter in the soil while dead wood and rotting plants are eaten by detritivores such as pill bugs and fungi. The dead material in a lake exceeds the living material, and detritivores and decomposers thrive.[1]

Secondly, the food web in oceans:

> In the sea or marine-littoral zone food web, large seaweeds are eaten by herbivorous fish such as grey mullet, which are eaten by carnivorous fish such as pollack. Large seaweeds are also eaten by flat winkle, which are eaten by edible crabs, which are also eaten by pollacks or herring gulls. Tiny seaweeds are eaten by limpets and by sea urchin, and all are eaten by edible crabs, and sea urchins and edible crabs are both eaten by herring gulls. Limpets are also eaten by lobsters and dog whelks. Plankton is eaten by common mussels, barnacles and common prawns. Mussels are eaten by lobsters, and prawns by herring gulls and seals, which are eaten by polar bears. Also, in the marine food web, phytoplankton is eaten

> by sardines and Atlantic herrings, which are eaten by man. And benthic (ie bottom) detritivores' organisms are eaten by algae, which are eaten by phytoplankton, which are eaten by zooplankton, which are eaten by planktivorous fish such as shad, which are eaten by piscivorous game fish. The large predators at the top of the marine food web include tuna, seals and some species of whales.[2]

And lastly, the co-operative behaviour or symbiosis in oceans:

> In the ecosystem of oceans some fish feed at the top (such as blue marlin, Pacific sailfish, yellowfin tuna and dolphins), while some fish feed at the bottom (such as catfish, flatfish, flounders, soles and stingray), and so there is enough food to go round. In the UK, cormorants (*Phalacrocorax canbo*) and shags (*P. aristotelis*) share a nesting habitat on cliffs and can feed in the same water. Cormorants dive and catch fish on the seabed, such as flatfish, whereas the smaller and slimmer shags feed on surface-swimming fish such as herrings. As they feed differently, they have different niches and so there is enough food to go round. It is amazing that most cormorants and shags have an oil gland in their backs which secretes oil. They wipe their beaks on the oil and then wipe oil on their feathers, making them waterproof so they can fly when their feathers are wet after diving. This device enables bottom-feeders to feed co-operatively at the bottom, and the intricacy of this device is yet another sign of an orderly system.[3]

Wherever we look, the adherence to levels and niches suggests that the Whole is a vast system which works because each living creature has a 'right' place in it and is programmed through its DNA to operate – top-feed or bottom-feed, eat or be eaten – as it is supposed to do.

ORDER IN THE SCIENCES

Discovering the order within the universe, which is hidden and not apparent at a cursory glance, is an important aspect of restoring the metaphysical tradition within each of the seven disciplines. In the conflict within each discipline, order counterbalances accident, chance and the random.

Order is in each of the sciences we examined in chapter 2. It is in cosmology and astrophysics: the events of the first three minutes after the Big Bang (which are covered on p 45 and in the Timeline on pp 256–8), the revolutions of the planets and the order of the stars. It is in physics: Newton's gravity and light and Einstein's photons, relativity and cosmological constant. It is in biocosmology: the 40 biofriendly conditions, and the 326 constants and 75 ratios which are listed in an appendix in *The New Philosophy of Universalism*. It is in biology: the self-organizing principle in the genes and evolution's adaptations. It is in geology: plate tectonics and the pattern of Ice Ages. It is in ecology: the food chains and webs and symbiosis, as we have just seen, and mutualism, parasitism and commensalism (as we saw on pp 79–81); and Nature's astounding checks and balances which keep populations stable. It is in physiology: the homeostasis of body and brain.

We saw (on pp 93–5) that the probability of the 40 biofriendly conditions for life happening by chance is 10^{120}, many more times than the total number of all the atoms in the observable universe (10^{80}). In other words, despite claims by sceptical materialists that life won a 10^{120} lottery (as if there had to be a winner in the universe's lottery), it is extremely improbable that the biofriendly conditions for life happened by chance.

ORDER IN THE SEVEN DISCIPLINES AND WORLD CULTURE

Order is similarly to be found in the seven disciplines. It is in mysticism: the manifesting Light of the One Reality and the ordering it brings to lives that have opened to it, their drive and achievements. It is in literature: in their poems Universalist poets reflect the order in the universe, and the order in rhymed stanzas and literary forms instinctively replicates the order behind Nature. It is also in the unity of world literature as demonstrated in the fundamental theme of world literature, the dialectic between a quest for the One and condemnation of follies and vices. It is in philosophy: the manifestation from Nothingness or the Void to Non-Being to Being to Existence, and the vision of unity. It is in history: the law of history that all civilizations pass through 61 stages has a beautiful order in its symmetry. It is in comparative religion: that the essence of all religions is the vision of the Light. It is in international politics and statecraft: that all civilizations and cultures pass into a worldwide civilization and World State that will end war, famine, disease and poverty. It is in world culture: the unity of all the world's cultures on the flow chart in appendix 1 and the pervasive simplicity of $+A + -A = 0$: the metaphysical approach + the secular approach = world culture.

Order has contributed to the metaphysical vision in all the sciences and disciplines because its origin can be traced back to metaphysical manifestation: the order emerged at the same time that existence emerged from Being immediately after the Big Bang.

The concept of order within the universe that has affected each of the seven disciplines, as we have just seen, has contributed to the reconciliation of the conflict within each discipline and therefore to the unity of world culture. Universalism, the new 21st-century philosophy of reconciliation, has restored the metaphysical approach and with it the metaphysical vision of order in world culture. Once again, the order within the universe, which in recent times has been widely overlooked and become something hidden, a secret, is taking its place in world culture and can be universally acknowledged.

America's World State will emphasize the order in Nature, the sciences and the seven disciplines, and the order within the governance of the World State. America's vision of the spiritual unity of humankind is inextricably linked to its vision of order, which is in turn inextricably linked to the manifestation of existence from Being after the Big Bang. Emphasis on the order within the universe resonates with both the religious who follow the metaphysical tradition and with atheists who follow the evidence of science, and contributes to healing the fissure in world culture.

CHAPTER 8

AMERICA'S WORLD VIEW AND WORLD UNITY

Each civilization early on in its rainbow-shaped development has a sense of its own destiny. In Homer's *The Iliad*, destiny and fate are supreme forces, and the outcome of the Trojan War is partly the making of the gods and partly due to the heroes' choices. Virgil wrote of Rome's destiny in *The Aeneid*: Aeneas had to leave Dido to found Rome. The European Crusaders felt it was their destiny to liberate Jerusalem from the infidel. At key moments of the European civilization's development, Napoleon, Hitler and Churchill had a sense of being destined to change the international situation and redraw the map of Europe.

George Washington had a sense of American destiny when he chaired the Constitutional Convention that created the United States in 1787 – his chair had a rising sun with 13 rays representing the colonies, as can still be seen in Philadelphia's Independence Hall. We have seen (p 185) that America had a 'manifest destiny' c1845: to spread throughout the American continent. But these powerful intimations of American destiny are as nothing besides the secret American destiny that lies ahead.

AMERICA'S EXPANSIONIST PHASE

America's destiny is to understand its coming global role, to implement the structure of a World State that will export the American Dream of freedom and prosperity to all humankind. America needs to grasp the stage the North American civilization is in, and the parallels for such a course of action in other civilizations when they reached the same stage.

America's stage-15 expansionist phase – the stage that begins a long expansion in its civilization that lasts until stage 41 – began c1913 with Woodrow Wilson's inauguration as President. The pattern of stage-15 expansion within the rising-and-falling civilizations is as follows:[1]

STAGE-15 EXPANSION OF 25 CIVILIZATIONS

	CIVILIZATION	DATE OF EXPANSION	EXPANSION
1	INDO-EUROPEAN KURGAN	c2550–c2200 BCE	FUNNEL-NECK BEAKER FOLK
2	MESOPOTAMIAN	c1950–c1750 BCE	OLD BABYLONIAN EMPIRE
3	EGYPTIAN	2110–1786 BCE	EMPIRE OF MIDDLE KINGDOM
4	AEGEAN-GREEK	c1650–c1450 BCE	MINOAN EMPIRE ON MAINLAND GREECE
5	ROMAN	c341–218 BCE	ROMAN EMPIRE IN ITALY
6	ANATOLIAN	c1471–c1300 BCE	HITTITE EMPIRE IN SYRIA/ CANAAN
7	SYRIAN	c1471–c1360 BCE	UGARITIC HEGEMONY IN CANAAN
8	ISRAELITE	c1140–c960 BCE	ISRAELITE EMPIRE TO DAVID
9	CELTIC	c337–c250 BCE	CELTIC LA TÈNE EXPANSION
10	IRANIAN	c280 BCE–10 CE	PARTHIAN EMPIRE
11	EUROPEAN	c951–1244	EUROPE'S EXPANSION INTO MEDITERRANEAN
12	NORTH AMERICAN	c1913– c2250?	AMERICA'S WORLD EXPANSION
13	BYZANTINE-RUSSIAN	c677–1071	BYZANTINE EMPIRE (INCLUDING BALKANS)
14	GERMANIC-SCANDINAVIAN	c38–c170	EXPANSION OF GERMANIC TRIBES
15	ANDEAN	c350 BCE–c300 CE	EXPANSION OF NAZCA/MOCHE
16	MESO-AMERICAN	c350 BCE–c100 CE	POST-OLMEC EXPANSION
17	ARAB	790–1055	ABBASID CALIPHATE EXPANSION

18	AFRICAN	c370–c540	AKSUM EMPIRE
19	INDIAN	c120 OR c290–c750	GUPTA EMPIRE
20	SOUTHEAST ASIAN	c850–c1100	SEVEN SOUTHEAST ASIAN EMPIRES
21	JAPANESE-GREEK	c710–c1000	IMPERIAL STATE RULED FROM NARA/KYOTO
22	OCEANIAN	c850–c950	POLYNESIAN EXPANSION
23	CHINESE	c354–907	SUI/TANG EMPIRES
24	TIBETAN	c1247–1481	TIBETAN EXPANSION
25	CENTRAL ASIAN	c1–c950	EXPANSION UNDER XIONGNU (HSIUNG-NU) ETC

We can see that the young North American civilization's expansion, which has taken it to two world wars and three anti-Islamic wars (Iraq twice and Afghanistan), to globalization and remoter space – NASA has now sent spacecraft to every planet in the solar system, including the ex-planet Pluto in the Kuiper Belt, débris left over from the solar system's formation 4.56 billion years ago – is not yet finished. It may continue from the North American civilization's stage 15 to stage 41, for several hundred years. (Compare pp 243–4.)

There are 14 living civilizations: the European, North American, Byzantine-Russian, Andean, Meso-American, Arab, African, Indian, Southeast Asian, Japanese, Oceanian, Chinese, Tibetan, and Central Asian.[2] During the next few hundred years the North American civilization can be expected to lead the other 13 living civilizations into a World State with a partial federal rule in seven areas (see p 230), a Golden Age of freedom from war, famine, disease and poverty. This Golden Age will last for a while, perhaps several hundred years, until all the 14 living civilizations leave and history returns to its rise-and-fall pattern.

This is the view of political and historical Universalism. It can make forecasts because historical Universalism's pattern of rising-and-falling civilizations has order. The orderly law of history reflects the order within the universe, and the orderly parallel stages within all civilizations allow forecasts to be made.

THE EIGHTH PATH TO THE SECRET AMERICAN DREAM

In *The Secret American Dream*[3] I identified seven paths that America has followed at different times of its civilization's short life. I said that President Obama could have reverted to one of these. He could have:

- Followed federalism and formed a federal association of many states in Central America and in the Caribbean
- Expanded further westward into the Pacific islands
- Built a benevolent empire in the Caribbean and Pacific
- Been isolationist from the Middle East and succumbed to the clamour for American decline and withdrawal
- Continued imperial hegemony by continuing Marshall Aid and protected free nations from a new Russian expansionism
- Demonstrated American supremacy in an even wider world empire with more bases
- Created a new political network to enact American commercial pipeline interests

Obama could have continued the American foreign policy he inherited in 2008 which (with different emphases at different times) followed the last three paths of hegemonistically protecting Europe from Russian expansionism; conquering tyrannies in Syria and Iraq (Assad and IS); and delivering a New World Order to the self-interested élites. Instead, Obama chose an eighth path, to pursue the secret American Dream and bring the universal values of 'Life, Liberty and the pursuit of happiness' to all humankind. That is the path of delivering the World State.

Political developments may have advanced progress to a World

State. The US-led deal between six powers and Iran has prevented Iran from developing a nuclear weapon and could improve the harmony in the Middle East if Iran helps to silence IS and calms Syria, and gets the region working together. The deal may have moved the Middle East away from war, closer to peace – despite opposition from Israel, Saudi Arabia and the Gulf States whose perspective is their own nation-state's rather than Obama's perspective of bringing in a peaceful World State. Russia's belligerent intentions towards ex-USSR territories will have to be countered.

SEVEN FEDERAL GOALS OF A WORLD STATE

A World State, a supranational authority with legal power to declare war illegal, President Truman's dream, could pursue seven federal goals:[4]

- Bringing peace between nation-states, and disarmament
- Sharing natural resources and energy so that all humankind can have a raised standard of living
- Solving environmental problems such as global warming, which seem to be beyond the capability of self-interested nation-states
- Ending disease
- Ending famine
- Solving the world's financial crisis
- Redistributing wealth to eliminate poverty

STRUCTURE OF WORLD STATE OR WORLD FEDERATION

Again implementing Universalist statecraft, I have said[5] that the structure of a World State, which can be followed on the chart on p 188, could be as follows. A World Federation would exist at partly inter-national (between nation-states) and partly supranational (federal) levels.

At the inter-national level (between nations):

1 The UN General Assembly could be converted into an elected World Parliamentary Assembly of 850 seats. This would be a lower house at the inter-national level. It would legislate supranationally in conjunction with the World Senate, acting as a global legislature in some sessions, as well as representing individual nation-states' parliaments.
2 All the offshoots of the UN General Assembly would continue to operate: the Economic and Social Council, the International Criminal Court, the International Court of Justice, and the UN organs (UNDP, UNHCR, UNICEF and UNEP) and specialized agencies (FAO, UNESCO, WHO and WTO).
3 All members of the new Assembly would belong to one of the world political parties: a World Centre/Left or Social Democratic Party, a World Centre/Right Party, a World Socialist Party, a Liberal-Centrist Party, a World Green Party, a Far Left Party, a Far Right Party, and a Party for World Sceptics.
4 The UN Security Council would be converted into a veto-less UN Executive Council of five Permanent and 12 Non-Permanent Members.

At the supranational level:

1 A World Commission of 27 Members drawn from all regions of the world would be established.
2 A World Senate of 92 Senators would be set up. This would be an elected upper house like the US Senate. Senators would belong to World Parties. The Senate would work with the World Parliamentary Assembly in the same way that the upper and lower houses work together in the US Congress. The World President would have a power of veto similar to that of the US president.

3 There would be World Senatorial Committees to monitor the implementation of the seven federal goals.

4 A World Openness Committee, a World Senate committee, would control the agencies of the élites. The Committee would scrutinize all candidates for world officialdom in terms of their possible links to the Syndicate. The Committee would receive advance copies of all agendas of meetings of Syndicate agencies such as the Bilderberg Group and Trilateral Commission, and would receive all minutes of their meetings. Two members of the Committee would attend all meetings of these agencies and report back to the Commission. Thus, the Syndicate would be allowed to go on functioning but their activities would be controlled and they would be excluded from secret decision-making and subject to investigation by the civil police and to law enforcement.

5 A World Council of Ministers would represent 29 World Departments, each of which would work closely with a Senatorial committee covering its field: World Finance; World Treasury; World Peace; World Disarmament; World Resources; World Environment; World Climate Change; World Health (ending disease); World Food (ending famine; crop-growing programmes); World Regions, Communities and Families; World Labour (or World Work and Pensions); World Housing; World Economic Development; World Regional Aid and International Development (ending financial crises); World Poverty (eliminating poverty by introducing a minimum entitlement of $10 per day for all world citizens); World Population Containment (as opposed to reduction); World Energy Regulation; World Transportation (world aviation, roads, shipping and rail); World Law; World Oceans; World Space; World Education; World Citizenship (law and order); World Culture and History; World Sport; World Unity in Diversity; World Dependent Territories; World Foreign

Policies (liaising with nation-states' Foreign Ministers); and World Human Rights and Freedom (guaranteeing individual freedoms, including freedom from population reduction under the new system).

6 A World President would be elected every four years, like the President of the United States. Candidates for World President would be nominated by each of the world political parties. There would be eight candidates (if the number of parties is as I have proposed) and each would be vetted by the World Commission and the Senatorial World Openness Committee. The President would lead the World Cabinet of the World Council of Ministers and be responsible for achieving the seven federal goals.

7 There would be a World Guidance Council of elder statesmen and distinguished world figures. They would meet every three months to advise the World Commission, World Senators and World Council of Ministers.

8 There would be World Leaders' Meetings for heads of nation-states or their foreign ministers. There would be a Regional Leaders' Meeting for the leaders of the 13 main regions, which are based on the 14 living civilizations (because South America includes two living civilizations; see below): North America; Europe; Japan; Oceania; China; Tibet; the Russian Federation; South America (which includes the separate Andean and Meso-American civilizations); Islam (representing Muslims in West, Central, South and Southeast Asia and North and Northeast Africa, and focusing on Indonesia and India which have the world's largest Muslim populations); Africa; India; Southeast Asia; and Central Asia.

9 The World Bank and World Investment Bank would be overhauled to operate at a supranational level. The World Bank would continue to make loans to poorer countries for capital programmes to reduce poverty.

10 An executive of international lawyers would help the World Commission, World Senate and World Parliamentary Assembly (the world lower house based on an elected UN General Assembly) turn the World Commission's proposals into international laws. It would liaise with the World Peace Enforcement Committee and the World Court of Justice.

11 The World Court of Justice would have 25 judges and would hear acts brought by the World Commission against nation-states for breaking a directive. It would rule on legal disputes between nation-states. A World Court of First Instance would exist alongside it to hear actions against the World Commission for deeds or failure to act. World Judicial Tribunals would hear cases in which world law needed to be enforced, and would enforce international laws.

12 The World Armed Force or World Rapid Reaction Force of 200,000–400,000 troops would serve the World Commission, the World President, the World Senate and the World Court of Justice. There would be a reserve force of 300,000–600,000.

FUNDING AND PEACE DIVIDEND

The funding would be afforded out of the existing budget of the UN. Funding of the UN General Assembly would be switched to the World Parliamentary Assembly. There would be a peace dividend, a phasing out of the global military spending by nation-states which totalled $1,472.7 billion ($1.4727 trillion) in 2008 and $1,745 billion ($1.745 trillion) in 2012,[6] of which $1,049.8 billion ($1.049 trillion) was spent by NATO alone in 2008 and $1,020 billion ($1.02 trillion) in 2013.[7]

Nearly $1.5 trillion per annum minus the cost of financing the World Armed Force plus the saving from not having to replace nuclear weapons could be diverted to benefit humankind.

LIFE UNDER THE WORLD STATE

I have presented elsewhere a picture of life under the World State.[8] War has been abolished, peace is enforced by the World Court of Justice and the World Armed Force and its international bases on every continent. The World Commission moves in a regular roster between 11 cities. Television comprehensively shows the activities of the World Commission, the World Senate and the World Parliamentary Assembly. Gas and oil pipelines supply gas and oil to all nation-states and there is a network of nuclear power stations. The World Cabinet (the World President and Council of Ministers) controls pollution. Diseases are under control, the world's citizens are being moved from conditions of squalor, rehoused and guaranteed access to pure water and medical care. There is no military expenditure; annual world budgets finance economic growth and public spending. There is one global currency and one worldwide central bank. Access to mortgages and jobs is universal. Migration is freely conducted, subject to quotas. The 13 regions based on the world's living civilizations (see point 8 on p 233) send regional leaders to the Regional Leaders' Meeting, but the main world regions are now: the American Union; the European Union; the West Asian (or Middle Eastern) Union; the Central Asian Union; and the East Asian-Pacific Union.

13 REGIONS, 14 LIVING CIVILIZATIONS AND THE WORLD STATE: FEDERATIONS AND WORLD FEDERATION

Twelve of the 13 civilization-based regions (excluding the North American) – and 13 of the 14 living civilizations (excluding the North American) – are all either within stage 43 or stage 46. The five stage-43 living civilizations are: the European; the Japanese; the Oceanian; the Chinese (which entered stage 43 in 1949); and the Tibetan. The conglomerates or unions of all the stage-43 civilizations and their dates, which assume no World State, are:

CIVILIZATIONS LOSING SOVEREIGNTY TO CONGLOMERATES

	CIVILIZATION	LOSS OF SOVEREIGNTY TO CONGLOMERATE, WHICH ACTS AS SECULARIZING FOREIGN INFLUENCE	DATE
1	INDO-EUROPEAN KURGAN/OLD EUROPEAN	UNETICE-TUMULUS PEOPLE'S EMPIRE IN WEST WITH TRADE IN CORNWALL, IRELAND, CENTRAL EUROPE AND THE BALTIC	c1550–c1400 BCE
2	MESOPOTAMIAN	CYRUS'S ACHAEMENIAN PERSIAN EMPIRE WHICH WAS UNITED WITH BABYLONIA INTO A CONGLOMERATE	c539–331 BCE
3	EGYPTIAN	SAITE DYNASTY'S ASSYRIAN-BACKED CONGLOMERATE UNDER THE ASSYRIAN VASSAL PRINCE PSAMTIK I OF SAIS, WHO TOOK THE ASSYRIAN NAME NABUSHEZIBANNI IN 663 BCE	c664–525 BCE
4	AEGEAN-GREEK	PERSIAN-BACKED PELOPONNESIAN LEAGUE CONTROLLED BY THE PERSIAN GREAT KING; ATHENS REVIVED AGAIN FROM C378 BCE BUT WAS CHECKED BY THE PERSIAN ARTAXERXES III OCHUS AND LOST A SECOND ATHENIAN EMPIRE, WHILE THE REST OF GREECE WAS A PERSIAN-CONTROLLED CONGLOMERATE	c404–337 BCE
5	ROMAN	EMPIRE OF THE GERMAN CHIEFTAN ODOACER, WHO DEPOSED THE LAST ROMAN EMPEROR IN THE WEST IN 476 AND ESTABLISHED A KINGDOM OF ITALY; VISIGOTHIC KINGDOM IN SPAIN AND FRANCE; VANDAL KINGDOM IN NORTH AFRICA, SICILY, SARDINIA AND CORSICA; AFTER 488, RULE OF THE OSTROGOTHS WHO INVADED ITALY, BESIEGED RAVENNA AND OVERTHREW ODOACER	c476–540
6	ANATOLIAN	CYRUS'S ACHAEMENIAN PERSIAN EMPIRE	c546–334 BCE

7	SYRIAN	CYRUS'S ACHAEMENIAN PERSIAN EMPIRE (LANGUAGE SPOKEN: IMPERIAL ARAMAIC)	c538–333 BCE
8	ISRAELITE	CYRUS'S ACHAEMENIAN PERSIAN EMPIRE	c538–333 BCE
9	CELTIC	SECULAR INTERNATIONALIST SAXON RULE SPREADING FROM EAST BRITAIN TO WEST BRITAIN	c540–687
10	IRANIAN	ARAB CALIPHATE IN IRAN	c642–821
11	EUROPEAN	EUROPEAN UNION WITH ITS OWN LEGAL PERSONALITY AFTER THE LISBON TREATY, DEVELOPING INTO A UNITED STATES OF EUROPE EVENTUALLY COMPRISING 50 STATES[9]	FROM 1992 (EU)/2009 (EU AFTER LISBON TREATY)–c2150?: CONGLOMERATE CREATED WHEN AN EXPANDED, ECONOMICALLY INTEGRATED EUROPEAN COMMUNITY LED VIA A EUROPEAN UNION TO A USA-INFLUENCED, POLITICALLY UNIFIED UNITED STATES OF WESTERN, CENTRAL AND EASTERN EUROPE
12	NORTH AMERICAN	NONE	
13	BYZANTINE-RUSSIAN	CONGLOMERATE OF USSR BASED ON AN INTERNATIONALIST FOREIGN MARXIAN IDEOLOGY	c1918–1991
14	GERMANIC-SCANDINAVIAN	REUNIFICATION OF THE FRANKS UNDER MAYORS OF THE PALACE, BEGINNING WITH PEPIN II AND CHARLES MARTEL	c687–843
15	ANDEAN	INTERNATIONALIST SPANISH COLONIAL EMPIRE	c1572–1810

16	MESO-AMERICAN	INTERNATIONALIST SPANISH COLONIAL EMPIRE	c1542–1810
17	ARAB	ARAB WORLD PASSED INTO INTERNATIONALIST EUROPEAN COLONIAL EMPIRES WHICH SECULARIZED ISLAM IN NORTH AFRICA AND THE MIDDLE EAST	c1881–c1980 (SEMI-COLONIAL OCCUPATION IN IRAQ AND AFGHANISTAN 2001–2006)
18	AFRICAN	INTERNATIONALIST EUROPEAN COLONIAL EMPIRES WHICH SECULARIZED AFRICAN RELIGION FOLLOWING SCRAMBLE FOR AFRICA	c1914–c1980
19	INDIA	INTERNATIONALIST BRITISH EMPIRE (BRITISH RAJ), UNIFICATION OF INDIAN STATES INTO ONE INDIA	c1818–1947
20	SOUTHEAST ASIAN	EUROPEAN COLONIZATION AND EMPIRES IN SOUTHEAST ASIA (BY BRITISH, FRENCH AND DUTCH)	c1876–1947
21	JAPANESE	AMERICAN OCCUPATION OF JAPAN UNDER GENERAL MACARTHUR IN 1945–51, THEN UNIFIED CONGLOMERATE OF 47 PREFECTURES OR PROVINCES	c1945–c2050?
22	OCEANIAN	WESTERN (EUROPEAN AND NORTH AMERICAN) COLONIZATION AND EMPIRE IN OCEANIA	c1900–2007 (FEDERATION OF OCEANIA BEGAN IN 2007. SOME ISLANDS STILL UNDER WESTERN RULE)
23	CHINESE	CONGLOMERATE OF PEOPLE'S REPUBLIC OF CHINA BASED ON AN INTERNATIONALIST FOREIGN MARXIAN IDEOLOGY, DEVISED BY A GERMAN JEW IN EUROPEAN LONDON	c1949–c2050?
24	TIBETAN	EUROPEAN INTERNATIONALIST CHINESE OCCUPATION WHICH HAS SECULARIZED TIBETAN RELIGION	c1951–c2050?
25	CENTRAL ASIAN	CHINESE MANCHU OCCUPATION OF MONGOLIA (CONQUEST COMPLETED IN 1759)	c1644–1911

If the five stage-43 living civilizations pass into a World State, their conglomerates or unions will be superseded by the World State and will pass into the World Federation.

The eight stage-46 living civilizations are: the Byzantine-Russian (which passed into stage 46, the Russian Federation, in 1991); the Andean and Meso-American; the Arab; the African (which entered stage 46 with the advent of the African Union); the Indian (a federation since 1947); the Southeast Asian; and the Central Asian. The stage-46 federations of all the 13 living civilizations (excluding the stage-15 North American civilization) and their dates, which assume no World State – that is, projected dates for the federations of the eight currently in stage 46 and for the eventual federations of the five still in stage 43 – are:

LIVING CIVILIZATIONS PASSING INTO FEDERATIONS

	CIVILIZATION	DATE	STAGE 46: FOREIGN FEDERALIST INFLUENCE
11	EUROPEAN	c2150–c2250?	FEDERATION OF EUROPEAN NATION-STATES?
13	BYZANTINE-RUSSIAN	c1991–c2100?	FEDERALIST POST-COMMUNIST RUSSIA LINKED TO COMING UNITED STATES OF EUROPE
15	ANDEAN	c1810–c2050?	PAN-AMERICAN FEDERALISM IN LATIN AMERICA UNDER US (NOW THROUGH THE 1948 ORGANIZATION OF AMERICAN STATES, THE 2005 FREE TRADE AREA OF THE AMERICAS, OR FTAA, OF 34 NATION-STATES INCLUDING THE US, AND THE 2008 UNION OF SOUTH AMERICAN NATIONS)

16	MESO-AMERICAN	c1810–c2050?	PAN-AMERICAN FEDERALISM IN LATIN AMERICA UNDER US (NOW THROUGH THE 1948 ORGANIZATION OF AMERICAN STATES, THE 2005 FREE TRADE AREA OF THE AMERICAS, OR FTAA, OF 34 NATION-STATES INCLUDING THE US, AND THE 2008 UNION OF SOUTH AMERICAN NATIONS)
17	ARAB	c1980–c2100?	COMING FEDERATION OF ARAB AND ISLAMIC STATES THROUGH THE 1945 ARAB LEAGUE (WHICH IN 2004 PROPOSED AN ARAB UNION THAT IS STILL BEING DISCUSSED)?
18	AFRICAN	c1980–c2100?	COMING FEDERATION OF AFRICAN STATES (STARTING WITH THE ORGANISATION OF AFRICAN UNITY, OR OAU, 1963–2002 AND BASED ON THE AFRICAN UNION, OR AU, OF 54 STATES FOUNDED IN 2001)?
19	INDIAN	c1947–c2050?	INDEPENDENT FEDERAL INDIA UNDER WEST?
20	SOUTHEAST ASIAN	c1950–c2050?	COMING FEDERATION OF SOUTHEAST ASIAN STATES BASED ON THE 1967 ASSOCIATION OF SOUTHEAST ASIAN NATIONS (ASEAN) (EVENTUALLY PACIFIC COMMUNITY)?
21	JAPANESE	c2050–c2150?	COMING FEDERATION OF JAPANESE PACIFIC TERRITORIES
22	OCEANIAN	c2007–c2100?	FEDERATION OF OCEANIA BEGAN IN 2007
23	CHINESE	c2050–c2150?	FEDERALIST POST-COMMUNIST CHINA LINKED TO COMING FEDERATION OF SOUTHEAST-ASIAN STATES?

24	TIBETAN	c2050–c2150?	COMING FEDERATION OF SOUTHEAST ASIAN STATES (EVENTUALLY ASIA-PACIFIC COMMUNITY)?
25	CENTRAL ASIAN	c1911–c2050?	FEDERALISM UNDER RUSSIA AND CHINA, AND COMING FEDERATION OF ARAB AND ISLAMIC STATES?

If the eight stage-46 living civilizations pass into a World State, these federations will be superseded by the World State and will pass into the World Federation.

As the North American civilization is in stage 15 (as can be seen in the table on pp 227–8) – in the same stage that the Roman civilization was in before 218 BCE when it expanded its Republican Empire in Carthage, Macedonia, Greece and Spain as a result of the Punic Wars, and before its expansion during Caesar's campaigns into Gaul, Britain, Dacia, Armenia, Assyria and Mesopotamia – it can harness all the stage-46 federations and can organize the stage-43 unions into entering an American-initiated World State or World Federation for the 13 living civilizations other than the North American civilization. As the only superpower, the North American civilization would preside over the World Federation just as the Roman civilization presided over the world state of its day, the Roman Empire. However, the North American civilization would preside in a non-imperial way, over a Federation as a system of interconnected federations.

From the dates it looks as if three of the stage-43 living civilizations, the Japanese, Chinese and Tibetan, will enter federalism c2050, which could also be when the World State comes into being. The European civilization looks as if it will enter federalism later, c2150. It looks as if five of the stage-46 civilizations, the Andean, Meso-American, Indian, Southeast Asian and Central Asian, will end their federalism c2050 and then undergo foreign occupation, while the Arab, Byzantine-Russian and African civilizations will end their federalism in 2100 and then undergo foreign occupation.

If the World State or World Federation is formed over a period of time, then the living civilizations we have just looked at can be expected to enter in batches by consent, like nation-states entering the EU – some c2050, and some c2100. It is possible to see how a World State could take shape by studying the living civilizations' patterns of union (stage 43) and federation (stage 46).

The World State or World Federation would be *partly* federal in limiting itself to seven supranational goals (see p 230): bringing peace and disarmament between nation-states, sharing resources and energy, solving environmental problems such as global warming, ending disease, ending famine, solving the world's financial crisis and redistributing wealth to eliminate poverty. It would be partly federal in loosely allowing nation-states and civilizations to continue at local regional level outside these seven policy areas.

DISARMAMENT

As part of the peace dividend, the War on Terror would be discontinued and the nuclear powers would surrender their nuclear warheads. The USSR alone had 45,000 nuclear weapons in 1985. There were 23,574 nuclear warheads throughout the world in 2009 (12,987 of which were in the ex-USSR).[10] Since 2009 nuclear weapons have been dismantled; and in 2015, after seven years of Obama's eighth path, there were 15,695 nuclear weapons, 93 per cent of which belong to the US (7,100) and Russia (7,500).[11] The US and Russia maintain around 1,800 of their nuclear weapons on high-alert status, ready to be launched within minutes of a warning.[12] Each of the above-mentioned nuclear weapons is many times more powerful than the two atomic bombs dropped on Japan in 1945.

WORLD POPULATION

Money saved on armaments would be spent on funding the secret American Dream: raising the standard of living of the world's poor. Under a World State the world's population can be controlled. Without a World State the world's population will increase from 7.33 billion in 2015 to 9.4 billion by 2050[13], and the 2 billion increase in the world's population, nearly a quarter more mouths to feed, would place a strain on the world's resources, especially food and water. (The US Census Bureau projects that the biggest population gains will be in Africa. Nigeria's population, 166 million in 2015, will exceed 400 million by 2050, and Ethiopia's population, currently 91 million, will be 278 million by 2050.)[14]

According to John R Wilmoth, the director of the United Nations (UN) Population Division, speaking on 10 August 2015, models of demographic change derived from historical experience estimate the global population as 9.7 billion in 2050 and 11.2 billion in 2100, and give a highest estimate of the world's population in 2100 as 16 billion and a lowest estimate as 6 billion, depending on future wars, diseases, famines and fertility rates.[15]

There will be shortages. There will have to be central planning (and perhaps some form of rationing) to cope with such a huge rise in world population, which may double in the course of the 21st century, whereas the availability of food will not double. Without a World State the world will be dominated by the élitist New World Order which will continue to profit from energy and banking.

HOW LONG THE WORLD FEDERATION WILL LAST

The World State will only last as long as the North American civilization's expansionist phase lasts. The Roman Empire lasted beyond the Roman civilization's stage 15, to its stage 37 when in 410 Rome was sacked by the Visigoths, and beyond its sack by Vandals in 455 and its sack by Odoacer in 476 in stage 41. The World State could last until the North American civilization's stage 41, for several hundred years. (It took just under a thousand years for the European civilizations to pass from the beginning of its stage 15 in 951, through the expansion of the Crusades, to its stage 41 in 1914.)

When the expansionist phase of the North American civilization ends, the World State will break up and all 13 living non-North American civilizations will leave the World Federation and resume the stage in their rising-and-falling pattern they have reached, as will the 14th living civilization, the North American. Apart from the seven federal areas, the living civilizations will have continued their rising-and-falling pattern at local regional level, and their return from the World State to the patterns of stages will therefore be seamless. The civilizations that are at present in stage 46 can expect to be occupied by invaders in stage 49.

US LEADERSHIP

Without America's inspiration and leadership, there can be no World State. President Obama has abandoned military supremacy in much of Near Asia, the Middle East and Africa and has done useful groundwork in preparing for a World State and the secret American Dream.

America will remain true to its revolutionary roots and spread liberty and the benefits of the American Dream to all humankind – and not pursue military supremacy. It will build on Obama's legacy of the eighth path. But America cannot be led by events. Sometimes there will have to be reluctant intervention to impose peace within the 13 regions (13 of the 14 living civilizations). Liberty must approach the world with a view to creating a benevolent world government of unified humankind, which, under American leadership, will be good for the US. When any nation or terror group acts aggressively and threatens world peace – whether it is Russia, or IS or al-Qaeda – America must be prepared to surround and isolate it while the conditions are put in place to create the 13 regions.

The chaos in Syria and Iraq in 2015 remains to be cleaned up before IS produces (and detonates in Europe) a dirty nuclear bomb – with help from Russia, Iran or through another Western interventionist sending of special forces to be used in conjunction with moderate (but divided) Syrian ground troops fighting near Raqqa, for example the Free Syrian Army (an isolated supremacist initiative). When order is eventually restored and the World State happens, the *Pax Americana* will stand out as a Golden Age, as did the *Pax Romana* under the Emperor Augustus.

WORLD CULTURE

Those living under the World State will share a world culture that includes the metaphysical aspect of all the higher religions – most notably Christianity, Buddhism, Hinduism, Jainism, Sikhism and Taoism – and the social aspect of the secularized and secularizing nation-states' State. In each discipline the world's citizens will be able to find some common ground: in mysticism, literature, philosophy and the sciences, history, comparative religion, international politics and statecraft, and culture.

It will then be seen that the unification of world culture in the seven disciplines created a world population that was ready for a World State. The unification of world culture will not be seen as a consequence of the World State, but as the common ground on which the World State will be welcomed and allowed to flourish.

The Universalist approach to the seven disciplines and focus on an ordered universe will be seen to have established this common ground on which the unification of humankind can take place in a World State. And, of course, after the World State has been set up, the Universalist unification of the seven disciplines and world culture – the world view that did so much to help bring the World State in – will also seem to be a reflection of the new world unity of humankind.

GLOBALISM AND WORLD ELECTION

In my lifetime, globalism has come to dominate trade and world thinking, and the internet has made it possible for everyone to contact everyone else. The guide who showed me round Iran in 2007 can find me years later and send me a message, as can any reader. Hundreds of television channels cover every nook and cranny of the Earth simultaneously. Skype and mobile phones can take me into any room in the world. Technology has made all these things possible in my lifetime, and it is only logical that we should move to one-world elections, in which world citizens can be elected to a World Parliamentary Assembly whose representatives share a common world culture based on the seven disciplines.

LIBERTY AND *Pax Universalis*

Liberty will preside over the setting up of a limited supranational authority that will abolish war, disarm nations and bring in a *Pax Universalis*. Universal peace is Universalism's greatest gift and accords with the peaceful, contemplative vision of the metaphysical Light. Universal peace transcends the institutional competitiveness of social religions that are in conflict with each other and have utilitarian secular values. Liberty applauds when the poor and homeless are assisted in their countries of origin before they become refugees to America's shores, when 'Life, Liberty and the pursuit of happiness' (the words in the Declaration of Independence in which the American Dream is rooted) is exported to the downtrodden and oppressed in the 13 other living civilizations, in the other 12 of the World State's 13 regions.

'Liberty' suggests separation and independence from a previous condition: liberty from poverty, liberty from oppression. 'Freedom' suggests a state of belonging to a community, as in 'the Free World'. The Freemasonic *Novus Ordo Seclorum*, or 'New Order of the Ages', which is on the Great Seal of the United States and on the back of the dollar bill and refers to the birth of a 'New Atlantis' in the New World, a free community, passed into the 'New World Order' acclaimed by Nelson Rockefeller in 1962 and 1968 and became tarnished by association with the Syndicate's self-interested policies. Liberty will revive the original universal spirit of the *Novus Ordo Seclorum* (the pre-Syndicate, universal 'New Order of the Ages'), which will live on in the World State.

LIBERTY'S SUPRANATIONAL DESTINY

'Destiny' has featured in American expansion ever since 'manifest destiny' surfaced in 1845: the idea that the United States had a special, divinely ordained, predetermined and providential destiny to lead the world, that the ideals of liberty in the Declaration of Independence placed it above all other nations. The political Universalism of an American-led World State may seem divinely ordained but it can be freely chosen. As Obama said at the end of his Prague speech on 5 April 2009, 'Human destiny will be what we make of it.' America's Universalist destiny is what America makes of it.

The present structure of global governance is 'inter-national', based on the relations *between* nations. It is not supranational. The UN, World Bank, IMF and G20 will need to be fundamentally reformed to accommodate the World Commission, World Senate and World Parliamentary Assembly. The US President would have to go before the UN General Assembly and make the case for a World Constitutional Convention to bring in the supranational structure of a democratized World State – similar to what the Lisbon Treaty did for the then 27 (now 28) members of the supranational European Union. The World State would live by the rule of law, which Eisenhower called for. The rule of law that a World State would introduce has been called for by Einstein, Russell, Truman, Eisenhower, Churchill, Gandhi and Pope John Paul II.

The religious Universalism that would accompany the political Universalism of a World State would also be supranational (and 'suprareligional'), and would focus on the common Light, which can be found in the Christian Light of the World and transfiguration, the Islamic lamp-like Light of Allah, Buddhist enlightenment (Mahayana *sunyata*, Zen *satori*), Hindu Yogic *samadhi*, and the Taoist Void of *Tao*. It would also take note of Freemasonry's syncretistic roots in the early Egyptian, Canaanite and Israelite religions.

The supranational World State would transcend and transform civilizations. For 5,000 years history has been a story of inter-national rising-and-falling civilizations, and Universalist history has focused on the vision of the metaphysical Light that has passed into the religion of each inter-national civilization at a very early stage. Samuel P Huntington wrote of the 'clash of civilizations' – between the Arab and North American civilizations – at the inter-national level. The history of civilizations would continue at the inter-national level within the 13 civilization-based regions, but the World State would transcend it even though it is within a stage in each civilization's development. Being supranational, the World State would be above civilizations. This was how Francis Fukuyama envisaged the culmination of political development, a permanent liberal democracy, which he called 'the end of history' in Hegel's sense of 'end-state'. Fukuyama should have seen this liberal democracy as a temporary stage, perhaps lasting 230 years (c2020–c2250, within the North American civilization's stage 15; see p 227). America, the most powerful living civilization and the only living civilization in its inter-national stage 15, the stage in which worldwide empires are founded, would be breaking the mould and doing something utterly and fundamentally new by founding a supranational *Pax Americana*, a *Pax Universalis* that would legally resolve all inter-national level conflicts at the supranational level.

LIBERTY'S DREAM OF ORDER

Supranational considerations aside, Liberty's dream – her secret American Dream – is ultimately of the unity of humankind. It accords with the vision of order: an ordered universe, the structure of a World State that is a framework for the orderly living – without war, famine, disease or poverty – of all human beings regardless of which part of the Earth they inhabit. Universalism is the new 'heretical' philosophy that has featured in other civilizations and (in the case of religious Universalism) a new approach to religion that can help to create a World State. In stage 26 of the North American civilization, Universalism will create a new 'Universalist' people. In its stage 27 (when a new people graft a heresy onto their civilization's central idea) new 'Universalists' will graft religious Universalism onto the American Protestant Light, and they will introduce a new religious focus during the expansion of American civilization in stage 29. The 'new people' can be outsiders or insiders, or members of the civilization who see the world in a radical new way, as did the Renaissance Humanists in the European civilization which grafted Protestantism onto the Catholic Light.

Liberty towers above the world with her torch, a symbol of the Light that spreads Universalism and the unification of humankind. She wears her seven-spiked solar crown that symbolizes the unity of the seven disciplines and world culture. Her left foot tramples on the broken shackles of the nationalism of nation-states as she calls for a supranational World State. Beyond her Roman face and spiked crown, a rainbow's seven bands symbolize the seven disciplines of world culture that are united in one rainbow: world mysticism, world literature, world philosophy and science, world history, world religion, world international politics, and world culture. Her stature and torch proclaim an ordered universe and call for a supranational end to war, tyranny, oppression, homelessness, hunger, disease and penury. Once war has been abolished and disarmament becomes universal, the peace dividend will fund a new paradise, a new Golden Age.

ATTEMPT AT A NEW WORLD STATE

World Universalists have begun to come forward. The Russian Igor Kondrashin, President and CEO of the Athens-based World Philosophical Forum (WPF) which is modelled on the World Economic Forum that meets annually at Davos, has set out 'Transuniversalism' as a secular 'universal ideology of humanity'. A dialectical Materialist and secular humanist, he has worked with UNESCO[16], and has drawn up a Constitution for a coming secular World State. Aware of my books, he invited me to attend a conference and Constitutional Convention in Athens in October 2015.

I saw that both my Universalism, which includes metaphysics and the 4.6 billion religious world citizens and is not therefore a partial Universalism, and my democratic World State had (if I looked hard) some features in common with his equivalents, and that we both followed dialectical thinking. I saw that his Constitution looked back to Plato and Aristotle and aims to reach all humankind. Sensing that unless I acted swiftly and made something happen, the opportunity to create a World State might be lost for another generation, I made common cause and was asked to write a paper, which immediately appeared on the WPF website (see appendix 6). I was made the WPF's 'Special Envoy to the UN' to visit the Secretary-General Ban Ki-moon and request a special session of the UN General Assembly. That would allow me to raise the benefit of introducing a limited, supranational World State to declare war illegal, begin disarmament and solve specific problems – in short, to set out the seven-point agenda (p 230) and the ideas in this book. Recalling T S Eliot's insistence that the man of letters should monitor the cultural consequences of international political action (which can be found on pp 198–9), I decided to go to Athens.

On account of the contribution made in my books, I was asked to chair the Constitutional Convention of international philosophers (most of whom had already been registered as global citizens, Citizens of the Earth) that, in an act of political Universalism, created and established a new administrative World State, the Universal State of the Earth (USE). George Washington chaired the Constitutional Convention that brought into being the USA, and I chaired the Constitutional Convention that brought into being the USE. I read aloud a Declaration in which I called on the 7.3 billion inhabitants of the Earth to join the new World State by becoming global citizens in accordance with the UN's global citizenship education policy. I had been instrumental in bringing the new administrative World State to birth on 7 October 2015, and I now found I was listed on the WPF website as 'responsible for the USE'. I was also Vice-President of the WPF and Acting Chairman of the USE's highest body, The Supreme Council of Humanity (SCH), which was to act as a collective Presidency. This was a supranational body, equivalent to the administrative World Commission of point 1 in my 12-point scheme (which can be found on pp 231–4).

I had set up an embryonic, parallel version of the World Commission. The attempted supranational World States of Aristotle's pupil Alexander the Great, Julius Caesar, Genghis Khan, Napoleon, Adolf Hitler and the Communist International had all been based on conquest and had collapsed, but the World State I envisage, like the League of Nations and the United Nations, which were at the nation-state rather than the supranational level, is peaceful and based on consent. Socrates had said incorrectly, 'I am a citizen not of Athens or of Greece, but of the world' (Plutarch, *On Exile*). What he should have said was, 'I am a citizen of Athens and of Greece, *and* of the world.'

There were two views of the USE's legality. One view (stated by Igor Kondrashin) was that all societies have five different social levels, namely family, local, regional, country (or nation-state) and global; that at the global or supranational level there has never been any supranational law and so there is no legal precedent, and we had just created a precedent that would have universal application; that the USE was therefore a legal entity approved by an assembly of properly registered, global-level Citizens of the Earth. The other view is that the USE was a legal entity applying only to the tiny number of Citizens of the Earth who approved it, and that until people become Citizens of the Earth in great numbers the USE is an embryo whose representation, and therefore legal basis, is dubious. For a constitution to stand in history, it must be broadly based and thoroughly discussed. It took the American Constitutional Convention 127 days to discuss and create the American Constitution, and the UN conference two months to sign the Charter (or constitution) of the United Nations. For a supranational body to declare war illegal, it must be supported by a great power such as the US that can provide a peace-keeping force and enforce peace and disarmament, and because of its dubious legal basis the USE may not attract that support.

I remain convinced that the way forward is through the UN General Assembly whose delegates, representing 193 nation-states, can be asked after deliberations (as during the creation of the United Nations in 1942 and 1945) to consider my 16-point plan with a view to signing a Declaration and then a Charter to bring in a bicameral, partly inter-national, partly supranational democratized world government.

It is nevertheless interesting that following my calls for a UN Constitutional Convention to establish a World State (first made in *The World Government* in 2010 and then in *The Secret American Dream* in 2011), the Russian President of a world body of international philosophers aware of my books asked me to chair a Constitutional Convention in Athens in 2015 and bring in a universal ideology akin to my Universalism and a Constitution for a 'Universal State of the Earth' akin to my World State – and to create and establish an embryonic World State.

The 2016 US Presidential Election may show that in the coming years the world's only superpower will resist the temptation to turn inwards, ignore the rest of the world's problems, citing the limits of American power, while pursuing the national interest of 'Little America'; and that instead it will resume its global leadership, shape the world order and continue to spread universal political and economic freedom.

UNITED FEDERATION

Liberty hopes that America, a nation-state, will take active steps to adopt the coming World State's supranational seven-point agenda (see p 230) and, making use of the UN General Assembly, found a world government with a 16-point part inter-national, part supranational structure that includes a World Commission, World Senate and World Parliamentary Assembly. As I see it, the supranational USE I set up is a dress rehearsal for a coming World Commission that can bring in a fully operational, democratized world government whose 16-point inter-national and supranational structure can be found on pp 231–4. I am now overseeing the writing of a legal constitution whose articles will turn the United Nations of nation-states into a United Federation (a World Federation).

LIBERTY'S VISION OF A PARADISE

Liberty has the vision of the secret American destiny: to create a new paradise on an ordered Earth in which all human beings can flourish and prosper, and be free. This can happen. I have set out the vision of how a unified humankind can live as one, and the structure of a world government. The vision now needs to be put into practice. A World Commission now needs to be founded and form new institutions.

An American President now has to place the power of the United

States' nation-state behind a supranational World State or World Federation. The US has to support a new UN-based Constitutional Convention and a peacefully created World State that will represent all citizens of the Earth, a supranational body that is above all nation-states, including America.

Obama has taken the world along the eighth path towards a World State, but progress has been slow. Liberty sees hordes of refugees cross the Mediterranean to Europe. She cannot wait any longer and urges the UN Secretary-General to organize a plea to the UN General Assembly to set in motion the process of forming a World State whose supranational approach can solve the world's immediate problems. She is shaking her torch in exasperation at the delay. She wants to know that an American President will press the UN General Assembly to set up a democratized, bicameral world government and proclaim the secret American destiny throughout the world.

TIMELINE

Origin of the Universe and Life on Earth, and the Evolution of *Homo sapiens sapiens*

Billion years ago	Event
Before 13.798	Moving infinite Void
13.798 (+/– 0.037)	Big Bang
	Seconds after Big Bang:
	10^{-43} Gravity separates at 10^{32}K, mass-energy becomes the observable universe. Universe begins to expand by a factor of 10^{54} faster than the speed of light
	10^{-36} Inflation begins, lasts until some time between 10^{-33} and 10^{-32}. Expansion in process
	10^{-35} Leptons and quarks form
	10^{-12} Electroweak forces separate from strong at 10^{15}K
	10^{-4} Weak and electromagnetic forces separate from electroweak forces
	10^{28} Strong force separates
	3 minutes after Big Bang:
	Universe has cooled from 10^{32}K to 10^{9}K (1 billion degrees)
13.79762	Electrons orbit nuclei and create atoms, glow of cosmic background radiation
13.32	Matter era begins, galaxies and stars have formed
5.5	Formation of the sun
4.6–4.55	Formation of Earth
4.4	Liquid water first flows on Earth, first oceans
4.2/3.96/3.9	First rocks
4–3.8	Life begins on Earth, first cell

3.8	LUCA (the Last Universal Common Ancestor)
3.8–3.5	First prokaryotic cells
3.7/3.5	First fossils of primitive cyanobacteria
2.7	First chemical evidence of eukaryotes, first stable isotopes
2.7–2.3	Huronian Ice Age
2.6	Bacteria living on land
2.5–2	First multicellular eukaryotic cells
1.9	Oxygen atmosphere develops
1.8	Oldest multicellular fossils
1.5	First photosynthesis

Million years ago

850–630	Cryogenian Ice Age
800	First multicellular life
700/575	First animals
543	First shelled animals
533–525	Cambrian explosion
520	First land plants
500–450	First fish, insects and other invertebrates move on land, first colonization of Earth by plants and animals
460–430	Andean-Saharan Ice Age
400	First vascular and seed plants, and insects
365	Tiktaalik moves onto land
360	Four-limbed vertebrates move on land
355	First reptiles
350–260	Karoo Ice Age
320	First amphibians
290	First conifers
250/225	First mammals and dinosaurs
200	Dinosaurs dominate

160	First birds
135	First beaked birds, first flowering plants
65	Large dinosaurs extinct, mammals dominate
60	First primates
40/33.7–present	Our Ice Age
35	First apes
15	Apes diverge from other primates
14	Orangutans diverge from other apes
8–6	Gorillas diverge from chimpanzees, bonobos and ancestors of humans
5.3–5	Ancestors of humans diverge from chimpanzees and bonobos
4.43	First hominids
2.5	Bonobos diverge from chimpanzees, first stone tools
2.3–2	Early *Homo*
1.8	*Homo erectus*

Thousand years ago

400–250	First archaic *Homo sapiens*
250	First *Homo neanderthalensis*
200	Glacier advance peaks, ancestors of modern Cro-Magnon *Homo sapiens* leave Africa
150–130	Anatomically modern humans (*Homo sapiens sapiens*) arise in Africa
115	Glacier advance peaks
100–50	Modern *Homo sapiens sapiens* leave Africa
40/35–10	Cro-Magnon man in France
29/27	*Homo neanderthalensis* extinct
11.5	Holocene interglacial begins
10	First domestic animals
5	First writing and civilization

APPENDICES

APPENDIX 1

25 Civilizations and Cultures: From One to One, the Fundamental Unity of World Culture

APPENDIX 2

The Rainbow-like Parabola: 61 Stages in a Civilization's Life Cycle

APPENDIX 3

Numbers in Powers of Ten

Very large and very small numbers contain many zeros. These are sometimes referred to in words, but the powers-of-ten notation is also used in which, for example, 10 multiplied by 10 six times (giving 1 with six zeros) is written as 10^6 and 1 divided by 10 multiplied by 10 six times (giving 1 with 6 zeros) is written as 10^{-6}.

APPENDIX 4

Image Showing How the Universe Began and the Shuttlecock-like Shape of our Expanding Universe

APPENDIX 5

Universalism's View of the Structure of the Universe

This graphic shows manifestation from the metaphysical One of the physical universe and all life forms, demonstrating the fundamental oneness of all creation.

APPENDIX 6

My Universalism and World State (Two Extracts from Presentation to World Philosophical Forum in Athens)

APPENDIX 1

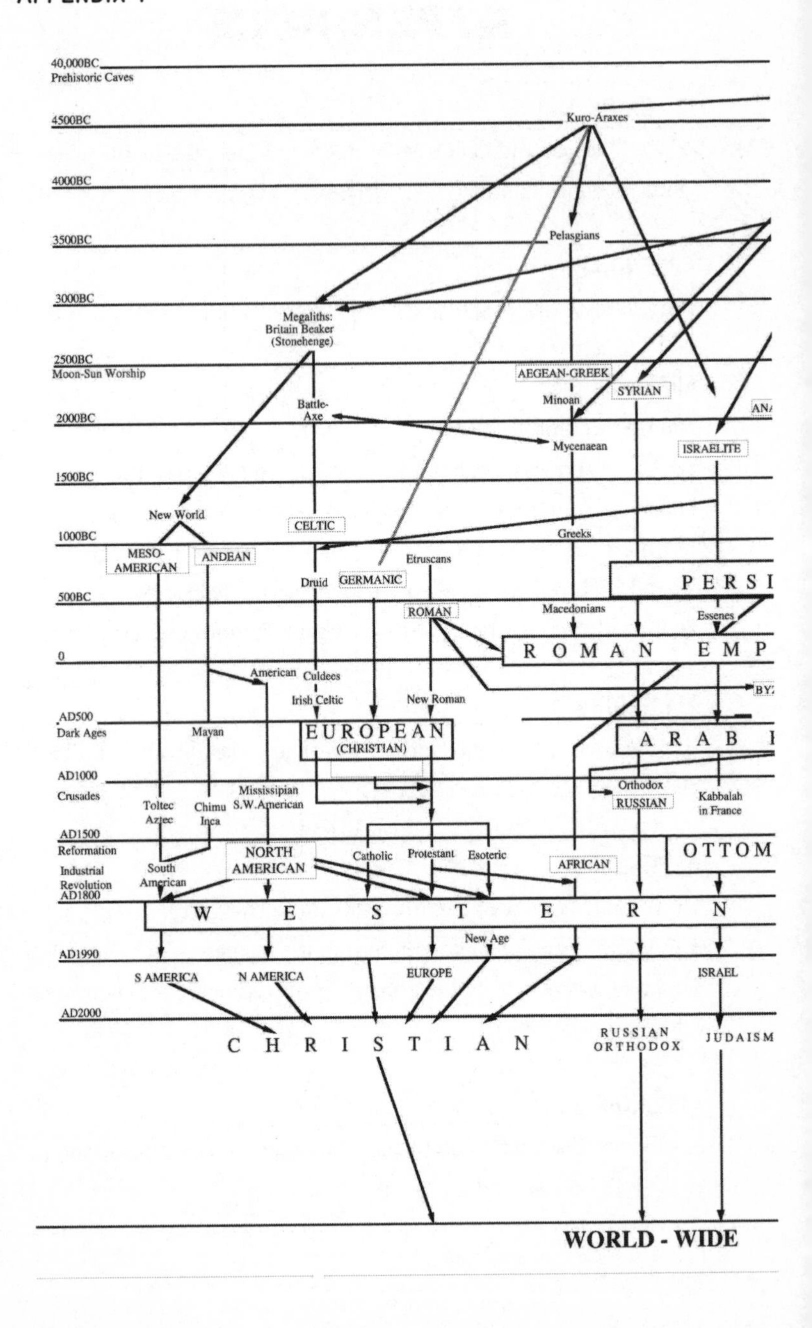
40,000BC
Prehistoric Caves
4500BC
Kuro-Araxes
4000BC
3500BC
Pelasgians
3000BC
Megaliths:
Britain Beaker
(Stonehenge)
2500BC
Moon-Sun Worship
AEGEAN-GREEK
SYRIAN
Minoan
Battle-
Axe
2000BC
Mycenaean
ISRAELITE
1500BC
New World
CELTIC
1000BC
Greeks
MESO-
AMERICAN
ANDEAN
Etruscans
Druid
GERMANIC
P E R S I
500BC
ROMAN
Macedonians
Essenes
0
R O M A N E M P
American
Culdees
Irish Celtic
New Roman
AD500
Dark Ages
Mayan
E U R O P E A N
(CHRISTIAN)
A R A B
AD1000
Crusades
Orthodox
RUSSIAN
Kabbalah
in France
Mississipian
S.W.American
Toltec
Aztec
Chimu
Inca
AD1500
Reformation
O T T O M
Industrial
Revolution
AD1800
South
American
NORTH
AMERICAN
Catholic
Protestant
Esoteric
AFRICAN
W E S T E R N
New Age
AD1990
S AMERICA
N AMERICA
EUROPE
ISRAEL
AD2000
C H R I S T I A N
RUSSIAN
ORTHODOX
JUDAISM
WORLD - WIDE

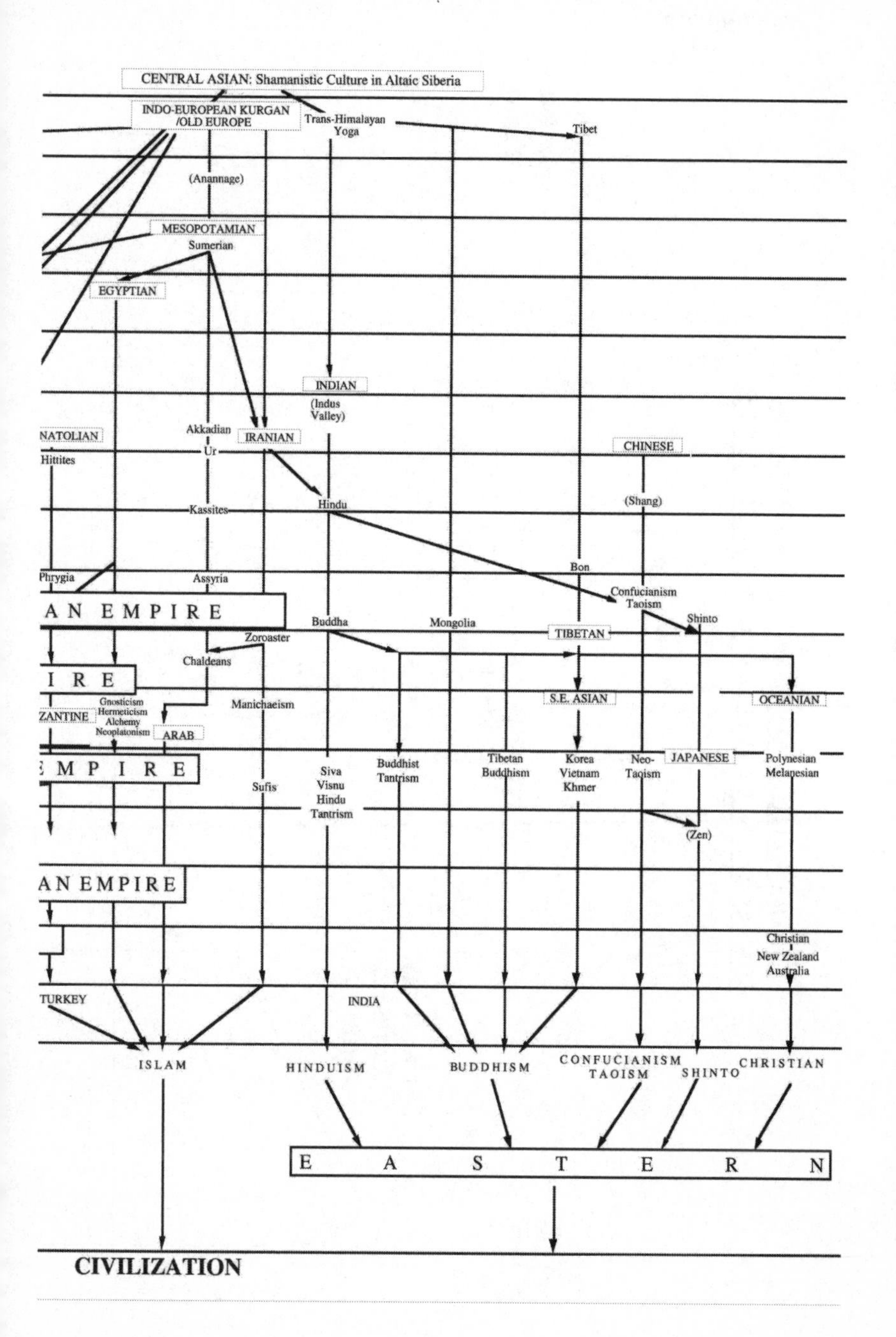

CENTRAL ASIAN: Shamanistic Culture in Altaic Siberia
INDO-EUROPEAN KURGAN /OLD EUROPE
Trans-Himalayan Yoga
Tibet
(Anannage)
MESOPOTAMIAN
Sumerian
EGYPTIAN
INDIAN
(Indus Valley)
NATOLIAN
Hittites
Akkadian
Ur
IRANIAN
CHINESE
Kassites
Hindu
(Shang)
Bon
Phrygia
Assyria
Confucianism Taoism
AN EMPIRE
Buddha
Mongolia
Shinto
TIBETAN
Zoroaster
Chaldeans
IRE
Manichaeism
S.E. ASIAN
OCEANIAN
ZANTINE
Gnosticism Hermeticism Alchemy Neoplatonism
ARAB
MPIRE
Sufis
Siva Visnu Hindu Tantrism
Buddhist Tantrism
Tibetan Buddhism
Korea Vietnam Khmer
Neo-Taoism
JAPANESE
Polynesian Melanesian
(Zen)
AN EMPIRE
Christian New Zealand Australia
TURKEY
INDIA
ISLAM
HINDUISM
BUDDHISM
CONFUCIANISM TAOISM
SHINTO
CHRISTIAN
E A S T E R N
CIVILIZATION

APPENDIX 2

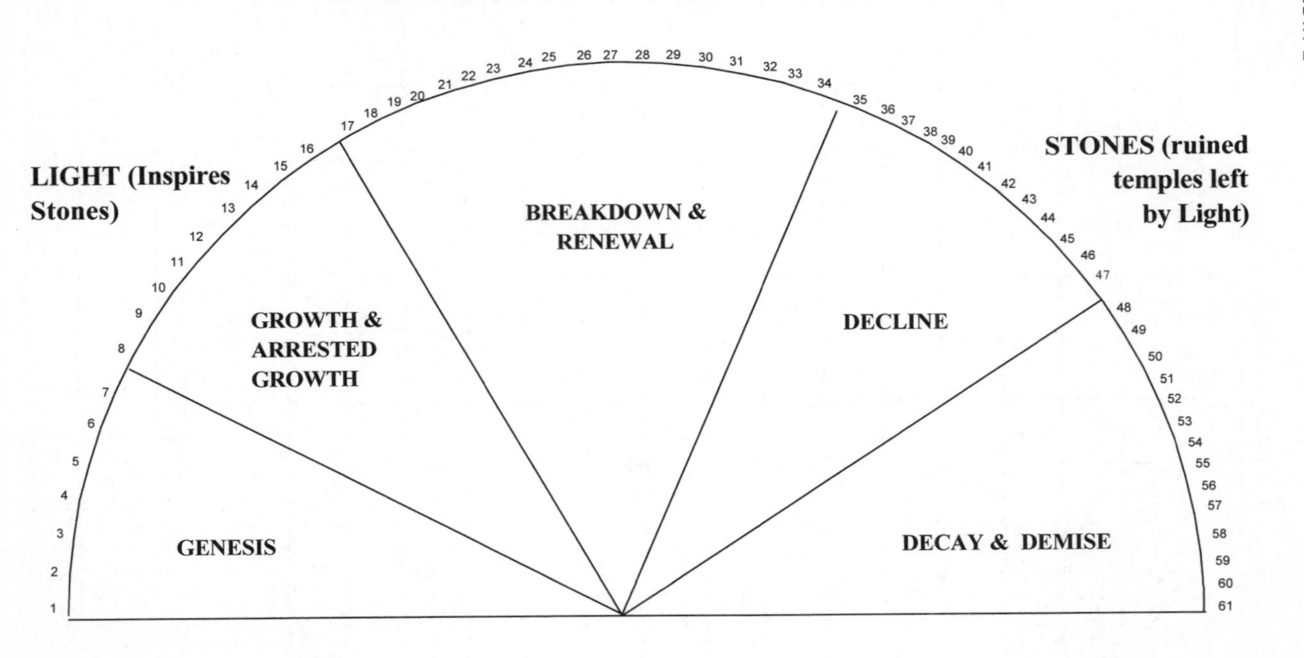
CHART 1; THE RAINBOW-LIKE PARABOLA
61 STAGES IN A CIVILIZATION'S LIFE CYCLE
LIGHT (Inspires Stones)
STONES (ruined temples left by Light)
GENESIS
GROWTH & ARRESTED GROWTH
BREAKDOWN & RENEWAL
DECLINE
DECAY & DEMISE
1 2 3 4 5 6 7 8 9 10 11 12 13 14 15 16 17 18 19 20 21 22 23 24 25 26 27 28 29 30 31 32 33 34 35 36 37 38 39 40 41 42 43 44 45 46 47 48 49 50 51 52 53 54 55 56 57 58 59 60 61

1 Light originates in earlier civilization
2 Light migrates to new culture
3 Light absorbs new culture
4 Light creates new religion through religious unification
5 Light precedes genesis
6 Light creates Central Idea amid 16 alternatives
7 Light attracts, converts & unifies peoples round Central Idea
8 Light strong during growth
9 Light inspires stones
10 Doctrinal controversy round Light
11 Political unification
12 Schism between supporters of rival gods
13 Foreign military blow
14 Arrest in growth of secularized civilization (50 years)
15 Counterthrust: expansion into Empire, Light-led renewal of growth
16 Heroic epic literature with god of Light-led growth
17 Creation of Light-based heretical sect
18 Persecution of heretical sect
19 Decline of religion as a result of heretical sect & foreign influence
20 Mystics resist decline
21 Foreign military blow
22 Breakdown of civilization (100 years)
23 Secularization in response to foreign threat
24 Revival of past culture of another civilization
25 Civil War: Rulers v heretical New People
26 New People in limelight
27 Heresy grafted on to Central Idea as new religious focus
28 New people's heretical renewal of Light and Central Idea
29 Geographical expansion of New People
30 Secession from New People's God
31 New People persecute seceders and become New Orthodoxy
32 Scientific materialism weakens religion
33 Artistic reaction
34 Further expansion into Empire over-extends civilization
35 Light weakens as energy is dispersed abroad
36 Light disappears from official religion
37 Breakdown of certainties after military event
38 Central Idea/Religion weaken, Arts become secular
39 Rationalism & scepticism weaken religion
40 Industrial decline as civilization over-extends itself
41 Colonial conflict ending in decolonization & occupation
42 Proletarianization & egalitarianism
43 Loss of national sovereignty to secularizing conglomerate
44 Syncretism & Universalism round Light
45 Revival of lost past of civilization
46 Counterthrust under foreign federal influence
47 Economic decline & inflation, class conflict
48 Light ceases to be publicly recognized by religion
49 Invaders undermine Lightless religion
50 Foreign invaders destroy Stones
51 Loss of Central Idea as peoples secede to foreign invaders' culture
52 Final independent phase
53 Further occupation by foreign power
54 Contemplative mystics turn from decaying religion to foreign cults
55 Civilization resists occupier
56 Occupier persecutes defectors from its cults
57 Coteries continue Light & Central Idea in mysteries
58 Further occupation
59 Occupier's religion suppresses & kills Lightless religion
60 Sudden final conquest or religionless civilization
61 Demise of civilization which now passes into a successor civilization

APPENDIX 3

A selection of smaller numbers is given below in words, figures and power-of-ten notation.

One	1	10^0
Ten	10	10^1
Hundred	100	10^2
Thousand	1,000	10^3
ten thousand	10,000	10^4
hundred thousand	100,000	10^5
Million	1,000,000	10^6
ten million	10,000,000	10^7
hundred million	100,000,000	10^8
Billion	1,000,000,000	10^9
ten billion	10,000,000,000	10^{10}
hundred billion	100,000,000,000	10^{11}
Trillion	1,000,000,000,000	10^{12}
ten trillion	10,000,000,000,000	10^{13}
hundred trillion	100,000,000,000,000	10^{14}

And:

one-tenth	1/10	10^{-1}
one-hundredth	1/100	10^{-2}
one-thousandth	1/1,000	10^{-3}
one-ten-thousandth	1/10,000	10^{-4}
one-hundred-thousandth	1/100,000	10^{-5}
one-millionth	1/1,000,000	10^{-6}
one-ten-millionth	1/10,000,000	10^{-7}
one-hundred-millionth	1/100,000,000	10^{-8}
one-billionth	1/1,000,000,000	10^{-9}
one-ten-billionth	1/10,000,000,000	10^{-10}
one-hundred-billionth	1/100,000,000,000	10^{-11}
one trillionth	1/1,000,000,000,000	10^{-12}
one-ten-trillionth	1/10,000,000,000,000	10^{-13}
one-hundred-trillionth	1/100,000,000,000,000	10^{-14}

1/10 can be written as 0.1, 1/100 as 0.01 and so on.

Larger Numbers in Powers of Ten

Larger numbers follow the same principles as smaller numbers. A selection of larger numbers is given below in words, figures and power-of-ten notation.

quadrillion or
1,000,000,000,000,000 10^{15}
quintillion or
1,000,000,000,000,000,000 10^{18}
sextillion or
1,000,000,000,000,000,000,000 10^{21}
septillion or
1,000,000,000,000,000,000,000,000 10^{24}
octillion or
1,000,000,000,000,000,000,000,000,000 10^{27}
nonillion or
1,000,000,000,000,000,000,000,000,000,000 10^{30}
decillion or
1,000,000,000,000,000,000,000,000,000,000,000 10^{33}
undecillion or
1,000,000,000,000,000,000,000,000,000,000,000,000 10^{36}
duodecillion or
1,000,000,000,000,000,000,000,000,000,000,000,000,000 10^{39}

And:

one-quadrillionth or
1/1,000,000,000,000,000 10^{-15}
one-quintillionth or
1/1,000,000,000,000,000,000 10^{-18}
one-sextillionth or
1/1,000,000,000,000,000,000,000 10^{-21}
one-septillionth or
1/1,000,000,000,000,000,000,000,000 10^{-24}
one-octillionth or
1/1,000,000,000,000,000,000,000,000,000 10^{-27}

one-nonillionth or
1/1,000,000,000,000,000,000,000,000,000,000 10^{-30}
one-decillionth or
1/1,000,000,000,000,000,000,000,000,000,000,000 10^{-33}
one-undecillionth or
1/1,000,000,000,000,000,000,000,000,000,000,000,000 10^{-36}
one-duodecillionth or
1/1,000,000,000,000,000,000,000,000,000,000,000,000,000 10^{-39}

The above figures assume the short-scale (eg 1 billion = 1,000 million) as opposed to the long-scale (eg 1 billion = 1 million million) convention.

The image of the astronaut-surfer who breasts the infinite on the top edge of our expanding universe (see facing page). For more on the surfer see pp 46, 47, 150, 159, 172, 284–5.

This graphic shows how the universe began from a 'point', the shuttlecock-like shape of the universe, and the surfer.

APPENDIX 5

Universalism's View of the Structure of the Universe

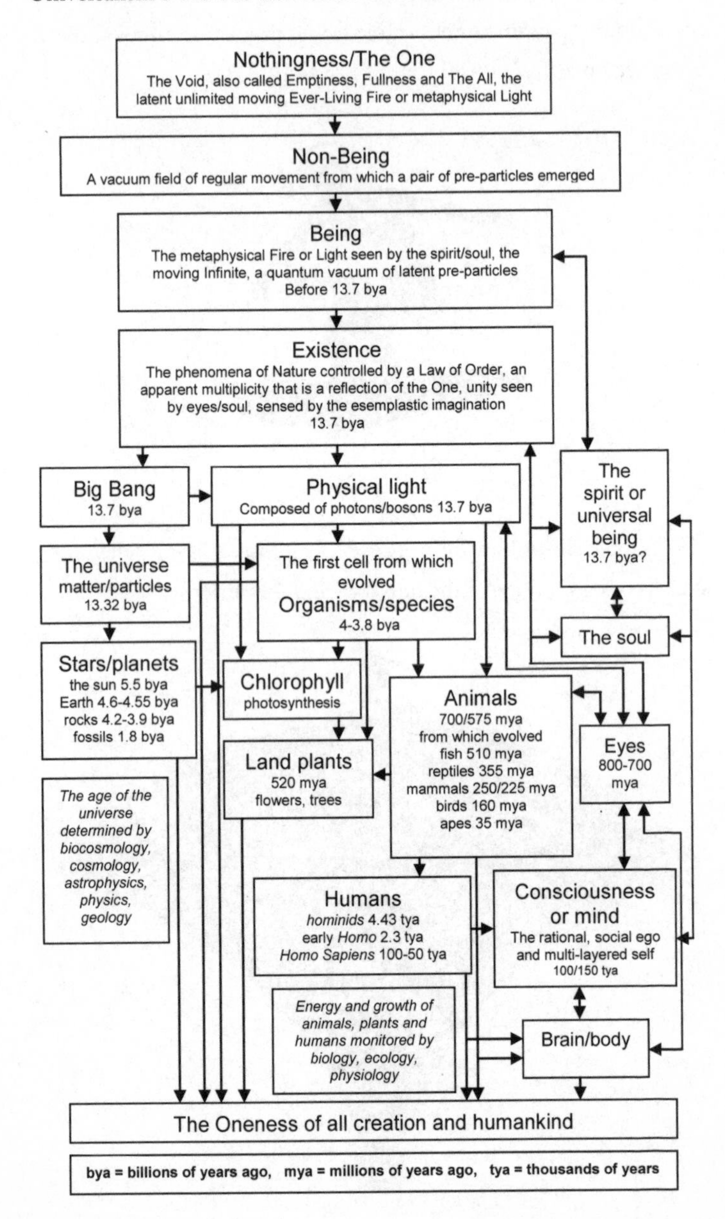

APPENDIX 6

Two extracts from a paper presented by Nicholas Hagger to the World Philosophical Forum at their symposium in Athens, 4–9 October 2015, are reproduced here for the light they throw on the emergence of his Universalism, on his vision of unity, on his dialectical method and on the influence of Plato's *Republic* on his statecraft and view of a World State.

FIRST EXTRACT

> 'I never stopped thinking how things might be improved and the constitution reformed .... Finally I came to the conclusion that all existing states were badly governed, and that their constitutions were incapable of reform without drastic treatment and a great deal of good luck. I was forced, in fact, to the belief that the only hope of finding justice for society or for the individual lay in true philosophy, and that mankind will have no respite from trouble until either real philosophers gain political power or politicians become by some miracle true philosophers.'
>
> Plato, letter VII, stating the theme of *The Republic*, c353/2 BCE

It's a pleasure to be addressing fellow Universalists in the cradle of Greek democracy, which was founded during the reforms of Solon in c594/3 BCE and established by Cleisthenes in c508/7 BCE. We are in the heart of the Athenian political empire of Themistocles and Pericles, and near the prison where Socrates was put to death in 399 BCE and near Plato's Academy, the school for statesmen Plato founded in 386 BCE. Plato's philosophical dialogues established Socrates's dialectical thinking, and his *Republic* associated philosophers with an ideal political state and the practice of statecraft. Plato's pupil Aristotle set out the constitution of the Athenians, the political system of ancient Athens, in *Athenaion Politeia*, c329/8 BCE, a further example of a philosopher practising statecraft.

Ancient Greek political philosophy and statecraft devised a new system of universal government by free citizens for Athens, and now we modern political philosophers and practisers of statecraft are following in the footsteps of Plato and Aristotle as we devise a new system of universal government by free citizens for the world, which I call Universalism.

HOW I CAME TO UNIVERSALISM

I'd like to tell you how I came to Universalism. In the early 1960s I was a British Council-sponsored lecturer at the University of Baghdad in Iraq and I then spent four years as Visiting Professor at three universities in Tokyo, where I also wrote speeches on world banking for the Governor of the Bank of Japan and tutored Emperor Hirohito's second son in world history. I was asked to teach a postgraduate course at one of my universities on 'The Decline of the West', which I based on Gibbon, Spengler and Toynbee, and while doing this I saw a fourth way of understanding history, which led to my study of 25 rising and falling civilizations, *The Fire and the Stones* (1991). In that work of historical Universalism, which sees all world history as an indivisible unity, I saw civilizations as rising following a mystic's vision of metaphysical Fire or Light that passed into their religions.

I titled the Preface 'Introduction to the New Universalism' and in January 1991, nearly 25 years ago, wrote that 'an Age of Universalism is ahead'. I developed the philosophical implications of Universalism in *The Universe and the Light* (1993), which contained three essays. In the middle one, titled 'What is Universalism?', I pointed out that the word 'Universalism' incorporates the words 'universe', 'universal' and 'universality'. Universalism sees each discipline from the perspective of the whole of humankind. A Universalist sees the universe as a unity – sees the oneness of the universe, of humankind and of all world history.

I led a group of a dozen British Universalist philosophers in London from 1993 to 1994. Like the Existentialists who had different shades of Existentialism, we all had different shades of Universalism but were able to call ourselves Universalists. I went on to have 43 books published in seven disciplines, all from a Universalist perspective. I reflected the oneness of the universe in my philosophical work, *The One and the Many* (1999). I set out philosophical Universalism in *The New Philosophy of Universalism* (2009), which sees the philosophical universe as an indivisible unity and the traditions of philosophy within a whole; and literary Universalism in *A New Philosophy of Literature* (2012), which presents the fundamental theme of world literature. I've described all this in two autobiographical works published earlier in 2015, *My Double Life 1: This Dark Wood* and *My Double Life 2: A Rainbow over the Hills*, which was subtitled 'The Vision of Unity'.

MY VISION OF UNITY

I arrived at my vision of unity in Japan. I visited Zen Buddhist temples and meditated, and found myself on a Mystic Way outside denominational religion: I underwent an awakening, then purgation, then illumination (which I experienced in Japan and more profoundly in London) and eventually, after ordeals, a centre-shift that left me permanently perceiving unity. I came to see the world and the universe as a unity *instinctively*. I reflected the vision of unity in my literary work: in over 1,500 poems, more than 300 classical odes, two epic poems, five verse plays, a masque and over 1,000 short stories.

I don't exclude the rational approach but I'm aware that the reason, the rational faculty I used in my university teaching, analyses and makes distinctions and seeks differences within separate disciplines, and fragments. I discovered from my experience that there is also an intuitive faculty that perceives unity, that pieces together the fragmented disciplines and restores their wholeness and unity. My Universalist approach to the world's problems combines these two faculties. The vision of unity draws strength from science's rational recognition of the order in the universe and from the intuitive perception of the oneness of the universe and of humankind.

PHILOSOPHICAL UNIVERSALISM AND THE METAPHYSICAL PERSPECTIVE

My philosophical Universalism sees the universe and humankind as a whole. It reflects the oneness of the universe and includes the metaphysical view of manifestation: the universe manifests from Nothingness to Non-Being, to Being and (with the Big Bang) Existence – through four levels or tiers of metaphysical Reality. My philosophical Universalism restores the metaphysical perspective of the universe which in the 1920s and 1930s was stripped aside by the sceptical, secular Vienna Circle, who were more interested in logic and language than in the universe.

I have set out the metaphysical philosophical tradition in my books – for example, in chapters 1 and 2 of *The New Philosophy of Universalism* ('The Origins of Western Philosophy' and 'The Decline of Western Philosophy and the Way Forward'). I have also set out the scientific, more empirical tradition which co-existed with it. The two traditions arguably began with Plato and Aristotle and co-existed at the Academy not far from here.

My philosophical Universalism reconciles the two traditions. The universe manifested before the Big Bang from the infinite, which the pre-Socratic Anaximander of Miletus called 'the boundless' (*to apeiron*), an eternally moving Reality, c570 BCE. The universe has been expanding since the first whoosh of inflation in the first second, and is now shaped like a shuttlecock (the 'ball' with a ring of feathers batted in badminton) and surrounded by the infinite from which it manifested. I have a picture of a surfer on the front cover of *The*

New Philosophy of Universalism. His feet are in space-time on the edge of the expanding universe, but his head, arms and body are in the infinite, the 'boundless'. The surfer is a symbol of Universalism's reconciliation of the metaphysical and scientific/social perspectives and traditions.

MY DIALECTICAL THINKING: +A + –A = 0

Dialectical thinking can be found in all my books. Junzaburo Nishiwaki, Japan's T S Eliot, introduced me to it in 1965, 50 years ago. In a restaurant with sawdust on the floor, just him and me drinking *saké*, I asked him, 'What is the wisdom of the East?' He wrote down: '+A + –A = 0.' Above 0 he wrote 'Great Nothing'. I immediately grasped what he meant. All the opposites – day and night, life and death, time and eternity, finite and infinite, every thesis and antithesis – are reconciled within a synthesis, an underlying unity. This synthesis is the Universalist reconciliation. He said, 'The Absolute is where there is no difference.' Metaphysics + the scientific, social perspective = underlying order within the universe, on which the philosophy of Universalism is based.

This dialectical thinking goes back to the symposia ('drinkings together') in the elegies of the Greek lyric poet Theognis of Megara (6th century BCE) and in the Socratic dialogues of Plato's *The Symposium* (c385–370 BCE) and Xenophon's *The Symposium* (late 360s BCE). 'Dialectic' was explained by Plato in *The Republic*, book 7 (c380 BCE), as a method which challenges its own assumptions, and dialectical thinking may look back beyond Plato's Socratic dialogues to Heraclitus. The dialectic of Marxism, taken from Hegel, is well known: +A (thesis, workers) + –A (antithesis, employers) = 0 (synthesis, the Communist State which allegedly kept them in balance). I arrived at my dialectic not through social thinking but, as I have said, through the ultimate vision of unity of mysticism and metaphysics. My dialectic now includes social thinking: +A (the metaphysical perspective) + –A (the secular, social perspective) = 0, the Universalist vision of unity and its expression in statecraft.

MY UNIVERSALISM – AND SEVEN DISCIPLINES

My Universalism, which is similar to secular Transuniversalism in some respects, has applications in a number of disciplines. In *My Double Life 2: A Rainbow over the Hills* I set out seven disciplines and describe them as bands in a rainbow. Universalism has applications in mysticism, literature, philosophy and science, history, comparative religion, international politics and statecraft, and world culture. (It also has applications on the environment, but we'll leave that aside, as environmental Universalism is an aspect of scientific Universalism.) My works reflect all these disciplines and have Universalism at their core. It can be said that there are seven Universalisms like bands of a rainbow: mystical Universalism; literary Universalism; philosophical and scientific Universalism (I treat these as one, as I see the two as enmeshed, even though scientists such as Hawking have claimed, wrongly, that science has replaced philosophy); historical Universalism; religious Universalism; political Universalism; and cultural Universalism. But there is, in actual fact, just one Universalism which, like an overarching rainbow, includes these seven bands.

My Universalism sees each discipline as a unified whole – thus my work on literary Universalism, *A New Philosophy of Literature*, sees all world literature as a whole and presents the fundamental theme of world literature – and sees all disciplines as a unified whole. In my works Universalism reconciles all opposites, including classical and Romantic styles in literature, rational and intuitional approaches in philosophy, metaphysical and secular perspectives in the seven disciplines – and nation-states and federalism in international politics.

HISTORICAL UNIVERSALISM AND MY WORLD STATE

I now want to dwell on historical Universalism, which sees world history as a whole. I have said that, according to my study of civilizations in *The Fire and the Stones* (revised and brought up to date in *The Light of Civilization* and *The Rise and Fall of Civilizations*), each of 25 civilizations rose following a metaphysical vision which passed into its religion, and declined when it turned secular and lost contact with that vision. After passing through 61 similar stages, each civilization passes into another civilization (just as the Egyptian and Mesopotamian civilizations passed into the Arab civilization in 642 and their own gods were abandoned for Allah).

The goal of historical Universalism is to create a partial World State within this pattern, a partly federal supranational state that would abolish war, nuclear weapons, famine, disease and poverty and run the world for humanity on the principle of universality. If such a World State comes into being within the rising-and-falling pattern, it will last for a while like the Roman Empire, not forever. Eventually the rising-and-falling pattern of civilizations will resume, but the world will have benefited from the abolition of war, nuclear weapons, famine, disease and poverty while the World State lasts.

SECOND EXTRACT

Not far from here Plato, practising statecraft for his school for statesmen, devised his ideal republic in *The Republic*, in book 6 of which he showed Socrates associating the philosopher with practical government through his conception of the 'philosopher-king' or 'philosopher-ruler'. We modern practisers of philosophical statecraft who are creating a World State look back to Plato's ideal society in which it is essential (Plato says in letter VII) that 'real philosophers gain political power or politicians become by some miracle true philosophers', and to Socrates's association of philosophers with practical government.

NOTES AND SOURCES

Author's Note/Acknowledgements

1 Nicholas Hagger, *My Double Life 2: A Rainbow over the Hill*, p 873.

Prologue: The Universalist Vision

1 Hagger, *The Secret American Dream*, p 229.
2 Emma Lazarus, 'The New Colossus', a sonnet written in 1883 and engraved on a bronze plaque and mounted on the inside of the pedestal of the Statue of Liberty in 1903.
3 See Pew Research Center's 2012 survey, http://www.washingtontimes.com/blog/watercooler/2012/dec/23/84-percent-world-population-has-faith-third-are-ch/.
4 Hagger, *My Double Life 2: A Rainbow over the Hills*, p 873.
5 C P Snow, *The Two Cultures: and A Second Look*.
6 Hagger, *The Rise and Fall of Civilizations*, pp 112, 116–17.
7 *Ibid.*, pp 131–2.
8 Hagger, *My Double Life 1: This Dark Wood*, pp 372–5.
9 Pascal's 'Fire' parchment: facsimile in Abbé Bremond's *Sentiment Religieux en France*, iv, 368; quoted in Dom Cuthbert Butler, *Western Mysticism*, p 74.

PART ONE

Conflict in World Culture

Chapter 1 **Conflicting Approaches in Seven Disciplines**

1 Hagger, *The Secret American Dream*, pp 224–5.
2 See WIN Gallup International survey, April 2015; http://www.patheos.com/blogs/friendlyatheist/2015/04/12/global-survey-finds-63-of-worlds-population-is-religious-while-11-are-convinced-atheists/.
3 Adherents.com survey, 2012; see http://www.adherents.com/.

See also details of Adherents.com's survey in https://en.wikipedia.org/wiki/List_of_religious_populations.

4 See Pew Research Center survey, December 2012, http://www.pewforum.org/2012/12/18/global-religious-landscape-exec/.

5 Hagger, *The Fire and the Stones*, pp 378–414; *The Rise and Fall of Civilizations*, pp 11–64.

6 T S Eliot, *Notes Towards the Definition of Culture*, p 26; Hagger, *The One and the Many*, p 105.

7 W B Yeats, *The Autobiography of William Butler Yeats*, p 128.

8 Hagger, *The Rise and Fall of Civilizations*, pp 244–90.

9 *Ibid.*, p 274.

10 *Ibid.*, pp 188–278.

11 *Ibid.*, p 285, predicted a 48-state Europe. See Hagger, *The Dream of Europa*, which predicts a 50-state Europe.

12 Pew Research Center 2013 found 37 per cent; Gallup 2013 found 39 per cent.

13 See http://ec.europa.eu/public_opinion/archives/ebs/ebs_341_en.pdf.

14 Hagger, *The Secret American Dream*, p 221.

15 Hagger, *The Rise and Fall of Civilizations*, pp 116–17.

16 *Ibid.*, pp 510–12. For Nicholas Hagger's articles in *The Times* on the World Council of Churches' funding of the African liberation movements, 'The war against racialism', 3 October 1970, see *My Double Life 1: This Dark Wood*, pp 522–7.

17 Evelyn Underhill, *Mysticism*, pp 75–82.

18 *Ibid.*, p 169.

19 See Hagger, *My Double Life 1: This Dark Wood*; pp 372–80.

20 Hagger, *The Light of Civilization*, pp 29–355, which cite all sources reflected in this section.

21 *Ibid.*, pp 113–227, which cite all sources reflected in this section.

22 *Ibid.*, pp 228–34.

23 *Ibid.*, pp 359–494, which cite all sources reflected in this section.

24 Hagger, *The Universe and the Light*, p 8; *The Light of the Civilization*, pp 498–9, which cite all sources reflected in this section.
25 Hagger, *The Light of Civilization*, pp 7–10.
26 St Augustine, *Confessions*, 7.10.
27 Hildegarde von Bingen quoted in John Ferguson, *An Illustrated Encyclopaedia of Mysticism and the Mystery Religions*, p 77.
28 Hagger, *My Double Life 1: This Dark Wood*, pp 53, 60–61, 92–3 and 110–11.
29 William Wordsworth, 'Lines composed a few miles above Tintern Abbey', lines 100–02.
30 Hagger, *A New Philosophy of Literature*, pp 5–6. Further details and sources for these and the next set of bullet points are available in the Notes and References of *A New Philosophy of Literature*.
31 Hagger, *My Double Life 1: This Dark Wood*, p 166; Hagger: 'The Contemporary Literary Scene in England, The Missing Dimension', *The Rising Generation*, 1 July 1964.
32 Hagger, *My Double Life 2: A Rainbow over the Hills*, p 330.
33 *Selected Poems* draws on my *Collected Poems*, *Classical Odes*, my two poetic epics *Armageddon* and *Overlord*, and *Collected Verse Plays*; and *Selected Stories* draws on the 1,001 short stories of my *Collected Stories*.
34 Hagger, *The New Philosophy of Universalism*, pp 11–22, 23–54, which cite all sources reflected in this section.
35 Aristotle, *Metaphysics IV*, 1–2/1003a.
36 Hagger, *The Universe and the Light*, pp 95–120.
37 Hagger, *The Fire and the Stones*, pp 350–53; *The Light of Civilization*, pp 502–6.
38 For details see *Ibid.*, pp 525–9, 'Toynbee's Choice of Civilizations'.
39 Hagger, *The Rise and Fall of Civilizations*, pp 11–56.

40 Hagger, *The Light of Civilization*, p 506.
41 Hagger, *The Universe and the Light*, pp 139–61; *The Rise and Fall of Civilizations*, pp 11–34.
42 Hagger, *The Universe and the Light*, pp 140–61.
43 *Ibid.*, p.140.
44 Hagger, *The Light of Civilization*, pp 523–5.
45 Hagger, *The Fire and the Stones*, pp 317–24; *The Light of Civilization*, pp 216–18.
46 Hagger, *The Fire and the Stones*, pp 743–53; *The Rise and Fall of Civilizations*, pp 412–28.
47 *Ibid.*, pp 274–7.
48 Hagger, *The Libyan Revolution* and *The Last Tourist in Iran.*
49 Hagger, *The Secret American Dream*, pp 129–30.
50 Hagger, *The World Government*, pp 110, 278, note 37, see http://bushstole04.com/monetarysystem/rothschild_bank.htm; Hagger, *The Secret American Dream*, pp 144, 151, 185.
51 Hagger, *The World Government*, pp 18–20.
52 *Ibid.*, p 21.
53 *Ibid.*, pp 28–35. Also see p v.
54 *Ibid.*, pp 122–58.
55 Hagger, *The Light of Civilization*, pp 534–5.
56 Hagger, *The New Philosophy of Universalism*, pp 339–40.
57 David Hackett Fischer, *Albion's Seed: Four British Folkways in America*. See also Hagger, *The Secret Founding of America*, chs 1 and 2.
58 Colin Woodard, *American Nations.*
59 Hagger, *The One and the Many*, pp 105–36.

***Chapter 2* Order and Accident in the Scientific Universe**

1 Hagger, *The New Philosophy of Universalism*, chs 3 and 5.
2 *Ibid.*, pp 56–78, which cite all sources reflected in this section.
3 Stephen Hawking, *A Brief History of Time*, pp 140–41.

4 J R Gott III *et al.*, 'A Map of the Universe' (2005), *Astrophysical Journal* (2), pp 463–84.

5 John D Barrow, *The Infinite Book, A Short Guide to the Boundless, Timeless and Endless*, p 96; Hagger, *The New Philosophy of Universalism*, pp xvii, 69, 72, 97–8, 112, 121, 262, 286.

6 Hagger, *The New Philosophy of Universalism*, pp 80–95, which cite all sources reflected in this section.

7 *The Born-Einstein Letters*, trans. Irene Born, p 91.

8 David Bohm, *Wholeness and the Implicate Order*.

9 *The Daily Telegraph*, 26 February 2008, p 27.

10 Hagger, *The New Philosophy of Universalism*, p 90.

11 *Ibid.*, pp 99–101.

12 Hagger, *The New Philosophy of Universalism*, pp 102–22, which cite all sources reflected in this section.

13 *Ibid.*, pp 372–87, 394–5.

14 *Ibid.*, pp 127–33.

15 *Ibid.*, pp149–55.

16 Bryan Sykes, *The Seven Daughters of Eve*, ch 1 and p 277.

17 Hagger, *The New Philosophy of Universalism*, p 164.

18 Hagger, *My Double Life 2: A Rainbow over the Hills*, pp 751–6.

19 For 2 million, see http://hypertextbook.com/facts/2003/FelixNisimov.shtml. For 2–30 million, see Jonathan Weiner, *The Beak of the Finch*, p.134. For 10–100 million, see http://www.iucn.org/en/news/archive/2007/11/12_pr/bear.htm.

20 Hagger, *The New Philosophy of Universalism*, pp 193–7.

21 *Ibid.*, pp 198–9.

22 *Ibid.*, pp 200–05.

23 *Ibid.*, pp 206–09.

24 *Ibid.*, pp 209–11.

25 *Ibid.*, pp 211–16.

26 Fred Adams, *Origins of Existence*, pp 189, 202.

27 Hagger, *The New Philosophy of Universalism*, p 219.

28 *Ibid.*, pp 221–9.
29 *Ibid.*, pp 238–40.
30 *Ibid.*, pp 241–3.
31 *Ibid.*, p 244.
32 *Ibid.*, pp 250–51.
33 William A Dembski, *The Design Revolution*, p 85: 'Computer scientist Seth Lloyd sets 10^{120} as the maximum number of bit-operations that the universe could have formed throughout its entire history (*Physical Review Letters*, 10 June 2002). That number corresponds to a universal probability bound of 1 in 10^{120}. Stuart Kaufman in his most recent book, *Investigations* (2000), comes up with similar numbers.' Also: Paul Davies, *The Goldilocks Enigma*, pp 270–71, which reflect the bit-operations calculation. See Seth Lloyd, 'Computational capacity of the universe', *Physical Review Letters*, vol. 88, 2002, p 237901, and his book *The Computational Universe.*
34 *Darwinism, Design and Public Education*, pp 241–2.

PART TWO

Towards a Reunification: The Hidden Order of the Universe and its Opponents, the Tussle between the Metaphysical and Social Approaches

Chapter 3 The Metaphysical Tradition, and Order

1 See J J Williamson, *The Structure of ALL*, lectures delivered at the RAF College, Cranwell, Lincolnshire, UK, which defines metaphysics as 'the science of ALL'.
2 Hagger, *The New Philosophy of Universalism*, p 265.
3 *Ibid.*, p 282.
4 *Ibid.*, p 283.
5 *Ibid.*, p 299.
6 *Ibid.*, pp 300–01.

7 *Ibid.*, p 320.
8 Hagger, *My Double Life 1: This Dark Wood*, pp xxvi–xxxi.
9 Albert Einstein, *Letters to Solovine*, p 131; see http://hyper physics.phy-astr.gsu.edu/nave-html/faithpathh/einstein.html
10 Albert Einstein, *Letters to Solovine*, pp 114–15.
11 Hagger, *The New Philosophy of Universalism*, pp 227–8.
12 Aristotle, *Metaphysics*, p xxviii.
13 Renée Weber, *Dialogues with Scientists and Sages: The Search for Unity*, p.48. For matter as frozen light, see p 45.
14 Hagger, *The Universe and the Light*, pp 162–6; *The New Philosophy of Universalism*, pp 269–73, which cite all sources reflected in this section.
15 Hagger, *My Double Life 2: A Rainbow over the Hills*, pp 413–17.
16 Aristotle, *Physics*, 8.6; 260a.
17 Hagger, *The New Philosophy of Universalism*, pp 270–73.

***Chapter 4* The Social and Reductionist Denial of the Metaphysical, and Accident**

1 Plato, *The Collected Dialogues, Laws*, 10.885b, 887c, 888a; 12.948c.
2 Thomas Altizer and William Hamilton, 'Radical Theology and the Death of God'; see http://media.sabda.org/alkitab-2/Religion-Online.org%20Books/Altizer,%20Thomas%20%26%20Hamilton,%20William%20-%20Radical%20Theology%20and%20t.pdf, which refers to Bonhoeffer's letter of 16 July 1944.
3 Hagger, *The Light of Civilization*, p 74.
4 Richard Dawkins, *The God Delusion*, p 11.
5 Christopher Ricks, *Essays in Appreciation*, pp 311–12, 'Literary principles as against theory'.
6 Hagger, *The New Philosophy of Universalism*, pp 44–7.
7 Hagger, *My Double Life 2: A Rainbow over the Hills*, pp 409–13.

8 See www.thehindu.com/new/65-terror-group-active.
9 Hagger, *The Syndicate*, pp 287–8.
10 Stephen Hawking, *A Brief History of Time*, p 8.
11 Brian Cox and Andrew Cohen, *The Human Universe*, p 176.
12 Eric R Kandel, *In Search of Memory*, p 384. For the paper Crick wrote with Koch, 'What is the function of the claustrum?', see Eric R Kandel, *In Search of Memory*, p 384. Also: http://publishing.royalsociety.org/media/philtrans_b/crick.pdf.
13 W N Cottingham and D A Greenwood, 'An Introduction to the Standard Model of Particle Physics', formula extracted by J A Shifflett and updated from Particle Data Group tables at pdg.1b1.gov, 2 February 2015; see http://einstein-schrodinger.com/Standard_Model.pdf.
14 Cox and Cohen, *op. cit.*, pp 179–83.
15 *Ibid.*, pp 186–8.

PART THREE

The Universalist Synthesis: The Reunification of World Culture

Chapter 5 Universalism's Reconciliation

1 Hagger, *My Double Life 1: This Dark Wood*, p xxiii.
2 *Ibid.*, pp 372–80.
3 Hagger, *A New Philosophy of Literature*, pp 329–30.
4 *Ibid.*, p 347.
5 *Ibid.*, p 351.
6 *Ibid.*, pp 325–7.
7 *Ibid.*, pp 262–3.
8 Arnold Toynbee, *A Study of History*, one-volume edition, p 97. Quoted in Hagger, *The Light of Civilization*, pp 525–7.
9 Hagger, *The Rise and Fall of Civilizations, passim.*
10 Hagger, *The Fire and the Stones*, *The Light of Civilization*, *The Rise and Fall of Civilizations*.

11 Hagger, *The New Philosophy of Universalism*, pp.334–7.
12 *Ibid.*, pp 357–60.
13 *Ibid.*, pp 355–7.
14 *Ibid.*, pp 347–55.
15 Edward Burnett Tylor, *Primitive Culture*, p 1; see https://books.google.co.uk/books?id=AucLAAAAIAAJ&redir_esc=y.
16 Hagger, *The Light of Civilization*, p 510.
17 Hagger, *The New Philosophy of Universalism*, pp 337–44.
18 Hagger, *The One and the Many*, pp.132–4; *The New Philosophy of Universalism*, pp 340–43.
19 Letter from Vincent van Gogh to Theo van Gogh, 11 August 1888.
20 Hagger, *The One and the Many*, pp 134–5; *The New Philosophy of Universalism*, p 343.
21 See Willis W Harman, *A Re-examination of the Metaphysical Foundations of Modern Science*; and *New Metaphysical Foundations of Modern Science*, ed. Willis Harman with Jane Clark.
22 Hagger, *The Universe and the Light*, pp 111–12; *The New Philosophy of Universalism*, pp 328–9.
23 David Bohm, *Wholeness and the Implicate Order*, pp 185, 186, 190–93.
24 Alfred North Whitehead, *An Introduction to Mathematics*, pp 41–2.

Chapter 6 Prospects for World Unity

1 Hagger, *The Secret American Dream*, p 223.
2 *Ibid.*, pp ix, 272: 'The traditional seven seas are the Mediterranean Sea (including the Tyrrhenian and Aegean), the Adriatic Sea, the Black Sea, the Red Sea, the Arabian Sea, the Persian Gulf, and the Caspian Sea. The seven continents are Asia, Africa, North America, South America, Antarctica, Europe, and Australia.'
3 Carl Van Doren, *Benjamin Franklin*, pp 777–8, quoted in James Srodes, Franklin: *The Essential Founding Father*, pp 386–7.

Quoted in Hagger, *The Secret Founding of America*, pp 115–16.

4 Paul F Boller, Jr, *Washington and Religion*, p 92. Quoted in Hagger, *The Secret Founding of America*, p 119.

5 Boller, *op. cit.*, pp 8–11, 14–18, 93–4. Quoted in Hagger, *The Secret Founding of America*, pp 119–20.

6 Trevor B McCrisken, 'Exceptionalism: Manifest Destiny,' in *Encyclopaedia of American Foreign Policy*, vol 2, p 68. Quoted in Hagger, *The Secret American Dream*, p 70.

7 Samuel P Huntington, *The Clash of Civilizations and the Remaking of World Order*, p 310. Quoted in Hagger, *The Secret American Dream*, p 160.

8 Hagger, *The Secret American Dream*, p xi.

9 Hagger, *The World Government*, chs 8 and 9

10 Hagger, *The Secret American Dream*, chs 10 and 11.

11 *Ibid.*, pp 205–09.

12 Hagger, *The Secret American Dream*, p 210.

13 Hagger, *The Fire and the Stones*, pp 463–70; *The Rise and Fall of Civilizations*, pp 127–37.

14 Hagger, *The One and the Many*, pp 40–69, 'A New Mystic and Philosophical Universalism: a Spiritual Vision for all Humankind'; and pp 96–105, 'The Fire or Light as Common Ground for a Universal or Worldwide Civilization and Religion'.

15 Hagger, *The Rise and Fall of Civilizations*, pp 532–51.

16 Hagger, *The Syndicate*, p 261.

17 Hagger, *The Secret American Dream*, pp 186–90.

18 *Ibid.*, pp 189–90.

19 *Ibid.*, pp 254–5.

20 See http://www.businessinsider.com/the-15-oil-and-gas-pipelines-changing-the-worlds-strategic-map-2010-3?op=1&IR=T.

21 See obituary of the Estonian physicist Endel Lippmaa in *The Telegraph*, 16 August 2015, http://www.telegraph.co.uk/news/obituaries/11801251/Endel-Lippmaa-physicist-obituary.html.

22 See Hagger, *My Double Life 2: A Rainbow over the Hills*, pp 143, 154 and 935–7 on FREE and pp 246–7 for Nicholas Hagger's challenging of the 1943 Tehran Agreement on 4 November 1986.
23 See http://www.unhcr.org/pages/49c3646c23.html.
24 See http://www.theguardian.com/global-development/2015/jul/09/syria-refugees-4-million-people-flee-crisis-deepens.
25 See http://www.mercycorps.org/articles/turkey-iraq-jordan-lebanon-syria/quick-facts-what-you-need-know-about-syria-crisis.
26 See http://www.mercycorps.org/articles/turkey-iraq-jordan-lebanon-syria/quick-facts-what-you-need-know-about-syria-crisis.
27 See http://www.theguardian.com/world/2015/jun/16/syria-assad-regime-is-weaponising-chlorine-us-congress-to-hear.
28 *The Daily Telegraph*, 12 September 2015, 'They're Using Mustard: US Says Isil Has Let Loose Chemical Weapons at Least Four Times'; see also http://www.theguardian.com/world/2015/aug/26/mustard-gas-likely-used-in-suspected-islamic-state-attack-in-syria.
29 See http://www.telegraph.co.uk/news/worldnews/islamic-state/11819472/Islamic-State-accused-of-using-mustard-gas-in-the-battle-around-Aleppo-in-Syria.html.
30 See http://www.unhcr.org/pages/49c3646c23.html.
31 *The Washington Post*, see http://www.washingtonpost.com/blogs/the-fix/wp/2014/07/23/the-most-important-sentence-president-obama-uttered-on-tuesday/.

PART FOUR

Order and America's Destiny

***Chapter 7* Restoring the Metaphysical Vision of Order in World Culture**

1 Hagger, *The New Philosophy of Universalism*, p 194.
2 *Ibid.*, pp 196–7.
3 *Ibid.*, p 199.

Chapter 8 America's World View and World Unity

1 Hagger, *The Secret American Dream*, p 215.

2 Hagger, *The Rise and Fall of Civilizations*, 'Living Civilizations' Coming Stages', pp 444–9; and 'More Detailed Predictions for Surviving Civilizations', pp 470–85.

3 Hagger, *The Secret American Dream*, pp 181–3.

4 *Ibid.*, p 191.

5 *Ibid.*, pp 193–6.

6 For the 2012 figure, see Stockholm International Peace Research Institute figures, http://www.stripes.com/news/despite-cuts-nato-still-accounts-for-most-of-world-s-military-spending-1.269882.

7 See http://www.stripes.com/news/despite-cuts-nato-still-accounts-for-most-of-world-s-military-spending-1.269882.

8 Hagger, *The Secret American Dream*, pp 203–04.

9 See Hagger, *The Dream of Europa*.

10 Hagger, *The Secret American Dream*, p 87, see also http://www.guardian.co.uk/news/datablog/2009/sep/06/nuclearweapons-world-us-north-korea-russia-iran.

11 See http://www.ploughshares.org/world-nuclear-stockpile-report?gclid=CMKfl-Ca4sYCFeoJwwodqO8OTg.

12 See http://www.icanw.org/the-facts/nuclear-arsenals/.

13 See https://www.populationinstitute.org/resources/populationonline/issue/18/110/.

14 See https://www.populationinstitute.org/resources/populationonline/issue/18/110/.

15 See http://www.sciencedaily.com/releases/2015/08/150810110634.htm and http://motherboard.vice.com/read/new-un-estimates-predict-a-global-population-of-11-billion-in-2100.

16 See http://wpf-unesco.org/.

BIBLIOGRAPHY

Adams, Fred, *Origins of Existence*, The Free Press, Cambridge, UK, 2002

Aristotle, *Metaphysics*, books I–IX, trans. Hugh Tredennick, Harvard University Press, Cambridge, Massachusetts, 1933/2003

Augustine, St, *Confessions*, trans. R S Pine-Coffin, Penguin, London, 1961

Barrow, John D, *The Infinite Book, A Short Guide to the Boundless, Timeless and Endless*, Jonathan Cape, London, 2005

Bohm, David, *Wholeness and the Implicate Order*, Routledge & Kegan Paul, London, 1980

Boller, Jr, Paul F, *Washington and Religion*, S M U Press, Texas, 1963

Born-Einstein Letters, The, trans. Irene Born, Macmillan, London, 1972

Butler, Dom Cuthbert, *Western Mysticism*, Arrow Books, London, 1922 and 1960

Cottingham, W N, and Greenwood, D A, 'An Introduction to the Standard Model of Particle Physics', 2nd edn, Cambridge University Press, Cambridge, UK, 2007

Cox, Brian, and Cohen, Andrew, *The Human Universe*, William Collins, London, 2014

Cox, Michael, *A Handbook of Christian Mysticism*, Crucible, New York, 1986

Darwinism, Design and Public Education, ed. John Angus Cappell and Stephen C Mayer, Michigan State University Press, Michigan, 2003

Davies, Paul, *The Goldilocks Enigma*, Allen Lane, London, 2006

Dawkins, Richard, *The God Delusion*, Bantam, London, 2006

Dembski, William A, *The Design Revolution*, InterVarsity Press, Illinois, 2004

Einstein, Albert, *Letters to Solovine*, Citadel Press, New York, 1993

Eliot, T S, *Notes towards the Definition of Culture*, Faber, London, 1962
– , *The Man of Letters and the Future of Europe*, Horizon, London, 1944
Ferguson, John, *An Illustrated Encyclopaedia of Mysticism and the Mystery Religions*, Thames & Hudson, London, 1976
Fischer, David Hackett, *Albion's Seed: Four British Folkways in America*, Oxford University Press, Oxford, 1989
Hagger, Nicholas, *A New Philosophy of Literature*, O Books, Alresford, 2011
– , *Armageddon*, O Books, Alresford, 2010
– , *Collected Poems, 1958–2005*, O Books, Alresford, 2006
– , *Collected Stories*, O Books, Alresford, 2007
– , *Collected Verse Plays*, O Books, Alresford, 2007
– , *My Double Life 1: This Dark Wood*, O Books, Alresford, 2015
– , *My Double Life 2: A Rainbow over the Hills*, O Books, Alresford, 2015
– , *Overlord*, O Books, Alresford, 2006
– , *Selected Poems, A Metaphysical's Way of Fire*, Element Books, Shaftesbury, 1991
– , *The Dream of Europa*, O Books, Alresford, 2015
– , *The Fire and the Stones*, Element Books, Shaftesbury, 1991
– , *The Last Tourist in Iran*, O Books, Alresford, 2008
– , *The Libyan Revolution*, O Books, Alresford, 2009
– , *The Light of Civilization*, O Books, Alresford, 2006
– , *The New Philosophy of Universalism*, O Books, Alresford, 2009
– , *The One and the Many*, Element Books, Shaftesbury, 1999
– , *The Rise and Fall of Civilizations*, O Books, Alresford, 2008
– , *The Secret American Dream*, Watkins, London, 2011
– , *The Secret Founding of America*, Watkins, London, 2007
– , *The Secret History of the West*, O Books, Alresford, 2005
– , *The Syndicate*, O Books, Alresford, 2004

– , *The Universe and the Light*, Element Books, Shaftesbury, 1993

– , *The World Government: A Blueprint for a Universal World State*, O Books, Alresford, 2010

Happold, F C, *Mysticism*, Penguin, London, 1963

Harman, Willis W, *A Re-examination of the Metaphysical Foundations of Modern Science*, Institute of Noetic Sciences, Sausalito, California, 1991

Harman, Willis with Jane Clark, ed., *New Metaphysical Foundations of Modern Science*, Institute of Noetic Sciences, Sausalito, California, 1994

Hawking, Stephen W, *A Brief History of Time from the Big Bang to Black Holes*, Bantam Press/Transworld, London, 1988

Huntington, Samuel P, *The Clash of Civilizations and the Remaking of World Order*, Simon & Schuster, New York, 1996

Kandel, Eric R, *In Search of Memory*, W W Norton, London, 2006.

Plato, *The Collected Dialogues including the Letters*, ed. Edith Hamilton and Huntington Cairns, Princeton University Press, Princeton, New Jersey, 1961

Ricks, Christopher, *Essays in Appreciation*, Oxford University Press, Oxford, 1996

Snow, C P, *The Two Cultures: and A Second Look,* Cambridge University Press, Cambridge, UK, 1959

Srodes, James, *Franklin: The Essential Founding Father*, Regnery Publishing, Washington, DC, 2002

Stace, Walter T, *The Teachings of the Mystics*, New American Library Mentor Books, New York, 1960

Sykes, Bryan, *The Seven Daughters of Eve*, Bantam Press, London, 2001

Tylor, Edward Burnett, *Primitive Culture*, John Murray, London, 1871

Toynbee, Arnold, *A Study of History*, revised one-volume edition, OUP/Thames and Hudson, London, 1972

Underhill, Evelyn, *Mysticism*, Methuen, London, 1911, 1960

Van Doren, Carl, *Benjamin Franklin*, Viking Press, New York, 1938; reprinted Penguin Books, London, 1991

Van Over, Raymond, *Eastern Mysticism*, New American Library Mentor Books, New Jersey, 1977

Warnke, Frank, *European Metaphysical Poetry*, Yale University Press, New Haven, 1961

Weber, Renée, *Dialogues with Scientists and Sages: The Search for Unity*, Routledge & Kegan Paul, London, 1986

Weiner, Jonathan, *The Beak of the Finch*, Vintage Books, London, 1995

Whitehead, Alfred North, *An Introduction to Mathematics*, Oxford University Press, Oxford, 1958

Williamson, J J, *The Structure of All*, The Society of Metaphysicians, Hastings, UK, 1986

Woodard, Colin, *American Nations*, Penguin, London, 2011

Yeats, W B, *The Autobiography of William Butler Yeats*, Collier Books, New York, 1965

INDEX